Refiguring

ENGLISH STUDIES

Refiguring English S
scholarship on Englis.
fession, and a vocation. ᴛᴏ ᴛnat end, the series publishes historical work that considers the ways in which English studies has constructed itself and its objects of study; investigations of the relationships among its constituent parts as conceived in both disciplinary and institutional terms; and examinations of the role the discipline has played or should play in the larger society and public policy. In addition, the series seeks to feature studies that, by their form or focus, challenge our notions about how the written "work" of English can or should be done and to feature writings that represent the professional lives of the discipline's members in both traditional and nontraditional settings. The series also includes scholarship that considers the discipline's possible futures or that draws upon work in other disciplines to shed light on developments in English studies.

Volumes in the Series

Stephen M. North, with Barbara A. Chepaitis, David Coogan, Lâle Davidson, Ron MacLean, Cindy L. Parrish, Jonathan Post, and Beth Weatherby, *Refiguring the Ph.D. in English Studies: Writing, Doctoral Education, and the Fusion-Based Curriculum* (2000)

Bruce Horner and Min-Zhan Lu, *Representing the "Other": Basic Writers and the Teaching of Basic Writing* (1999)

Michael Blitz and C. Mark Hurlbert, *Letters for the Living: Teaching Writing in a Violent Age* (1998)

Jane Maher, *Mina P. Shaughnessy: Her Life and Work* (1997)

Robin Varnum, *Fencing with Words: A History of Writing Instruction at Amherst College during the Era of Theodore Baird, 1938–1966* (1996)

James A. Berlin, *Rhetorics, Poetics, and Cultures: Refiguring College English Studies* (1996)

Jed Rasula, *The American Poetry Wax Museum: Reality Effects, 1940–1990* (1995)

David B. Downing, editor, *Changing Classroom Practices: Resources for Literary and Cultural Studies* (1994)

English Studies

An Introduction to the Discipline(s)

Edited by

BRUCE McCOMISKEY
University of Alabama at Birmingham

National Council of Teachers of English
1111 W. Kenyon Road, Urbana, Illinois 61801-1096

Staff Editor: Bonny Graham
Manuscript Editor: L. L. Erwin
Interior Design: Jenny Jensen Greenleaf
Cover Design: Frank P. Cucciarre, Blink Concept & Design, Inc.

NCTE Stock Number: 15442

ISSN 1073-9637

It is the policy of NCTE in its journals and other publications to provide a forum for the open discussion of ideas concerning the content and the teaching of English and the language arts. Publicity accorded to any particular point of view does not imply endorsement by the Executive Committee, the Board of Directors, or the membership at large, except in announcements of policy, where such endorsement is clearly specified.

Every effort has been made to provide current URLs and e-mail addresses, but because of the rapidly changing nature of the Web, some sites and addresses may no longer be accessible.

Library of Congress Cataloging-in-Publication Data

English studies : an introduction to the discipline(s) / edited by Bruce McComiskey.
    p. cm. — (Refiguring English studies)
  Includes bibliographical references and index.
  ISBN-13: 978-0-8141-1544-2 (pbk.)
  1. English language. I. McComiskey, Bruce, 1963–
PE1072.E57 2006
420—dc22
                                                              2006021078

For Lena

Steady drops hollow the stone.

THEODOR ADORNO

CONTENTS

INTRODUCTION

BRUCE MCCOMISKEY
University of Alabama at Birmingham

A speaker rises and moves to the podium at the front of a large auditorium. As a hush falls over the audience, the speaker addresses three panelists seated at the table next to her: "You're taking a trip, a cruise in the South Pacific, and, to the passengers' dismay, the ship begins to tilt leeward. You aid in the escape. Lifeboats fill quickly and leave for the relative safety of open waters, where cargo ships will rescue those adrift at sea. Soon, however, you find yourself one of three remaining passengers standing on the sinking hull. There is only one vessel left, an inflatable raft that can support the weight of a single person; to attempt to fit more than one passenger into the raft would ensure the demise of all three."

The speaker turns to the audience: "The three remaining passengers happen to be professors at the University of Alabama at Birmingham." The audience erupts in laughter.

The speaker continues, "Let me introduce this year's participants in the Raft, a debate in which three UAB scholars must convince a crowd of colleagues and students that their academic discipline makes them, by association, worthy of being the sole survivor. Our panelists may praise their own disciplines, of course, but they may also criticize the others as well. Following the debate, the audience will determine each professor's fate with applause. The professor who garners the loudest applause wins the raft and floats to safety. The two who garner less applause go down with the ship."

In 1999, I was only the second English professor at UAB to compete in the Raft, which, by the way, I lost to a professor of public health. I remember saying that we didn't need hygiene police nagging us to brush our teeth three times a day while we bobbed up and down on the waves; and I remember the public health professor saying that we didn't need grammar police correcting our screams for help. It was, of course, all in good fun. But it was also quite serious. Our students (English majors, public health majors) and our colleagues from all across the university were there, cheering or jeering us.

Participating in the Raft forced me to promote and defend English studies (to a hilariously hostile audience) in ways that I had never done before, and this experience (coupled with the fact that I *lost*) initiated a long process for me, a process of considering and attempting to articulate, in more and more concrete terms, the value of English studies within the context of a changing university and a changing world. The fact is, as John L. Kijinski points out, English studies "is not simply a 'natural' subject for university study that any humane person would endorse; it is, instead, a discipline that must work to define its aims clearly" (44). And we cannot argue for the value and aims of an academic enterprise if we are unable to articulate what that enterprise entails.[1]

Yet one of the primary obstacles facing twenty-first-century English studies, in both academic and public contexts, is its disciplinary opacity, its murky content, and its uncertain boundaries, which defy definition. In fact, since the day I lost the Raft, one question has continued to haunt me: *What exactly is English studies?* As I began to read different accounts of the rise (and sometimes fall) of English, I discovered, to my surprise, that adequate answers to this seemingly simple question are not only elusive but also fraught with conflict. In fact, many historians of English studies answer the question with a resounding, "I have no idea."

For some scholars, the disciplinary opacity, murkiness, and indefinable quality of English studies cause no discomfort at all. In fact, curricular incoherence is at times even heralded as one of English studies' strengths, or at least as something that should not concern us very much. In 1990 Peter Elbow, reflecting on his participation in the 1987 English Coalition Conference, was struck, above all, by the fact that English "cannot define what it is" (v). Yet Elbow suggests that this disciplinary uncertainty "is probably a good thing" (v). In a similar vein, Gerald Graff declares, "It seems doubtful to me that English is now, ever has been, or ever will be a coherently defined 'discipline,' but I do not find this troubling in the least" ("Is There" 11). These scholars view the very term *discipline* negatively, as a force that limits academic freedom, squelches scholarly creativity, and confines inquiry to a particular subject. And as a limiting and confining force, disciplinary status is something to be energetically avoided.

For other scholars, the disciplinary incoherence of English studies constitutes nothing less than a crisis, and these apocalyptic accounts of troubled times often take on a certain Chicken Little tone. James Berlin tells us, "English studies is in crisis. Indeed, virtually no feature of the discipline can be considered beyond dispute" (xi). To Berlin's drama, Terry Eagleton adds a touch of humor but makes a similar point: "[I]n a post-imperial, postmodernist culture, 'English,' which for some time now has been living on like a headless chicken, has proved to be an increasingly unworkable discourse" ("End" 8). Finally, Ian Small and Josephine Guy explain that "English departments have always contained within them the potential for crisis simply because there has always been dissent over the nature of the subject" (191); and Small and Guy give practitioners of English studies an ultimatum: "[E]ither English as a discipline will continue to exist in a state of crisis, *or* a dominant epistemology and therefore a dominant intellectual authority will begin to re-emerge" (194).[2]

My own position is a negotiation of crisis rhetoric and nonchalance. With Berlin and Eagleton, I am concerned about the way that disciplinary incoherence affects the entire project of English studies, both inside and outside the academy. However, it is also true that specialization, and its constant companion, incoherence, have been endemic to modern universities since their emergence in the late nineteenth century, and the push toward further specialization will surely not abate anytime soon. With Elbow and Graff, I do not see any good reason to declare that the sky is falling or that English studies is in crisis. For one thing, I believe that the problems English studies faces at the moment are, in fact, thoroughly solvable; and, in any case, if we want to fix an academic problem in a discipline that we care about, the very worst thing we can do is declare that discipline to be in crisis.[3]

One way to begin answering our seemingly simple question (What is English studies?) is to look at the historical development of English as a field and the intersections among the disciplines that it comprises: linguistics and discourse analysis, rhetoric and composition, creative writing, literature and literary criticism, critical theory and cultural studies, and English education. Kijinski points out that "a better understanding of the controversial beginnings of our own profession should give us an enlightened historical perspective on the current debate over the scope and aims of English studies which attracts so much attention today" (38). Historical perspective is a precious commodity, and, as Phyllis Franklin points out, English studies has only recently tried to find some.[4] I argue that we must know where we've been in order to understand where we are and to plan for a better future.

English Studies in Historical Context

The first schools in the West took shape in the fertile Athenian democracies of the fifth, fourth, and third centuries BCE. Plato's Academy and Aristotle's Lyceum, in particular, served as models of higher education for centuries to follow. In the Academy and the Lyceum, and in subsequent schools shaped after their example, knowledge was treated as an integrated system, and academic inquiry drew from whatever arts and sciences were most useful in solving the problem at hand (Charlton). Medieval education, based on the ancient model, was mainly tutorial in structure. The curriculum consisted of initial studies in the *trivium* (rhetoric, grammar, logic) and the *quadrivium* (arithmetic, astronomy, geometry, music), followed by more advanced studies in law, medicine, or religion (Moran 3–5). Students proceeded through the same curriculum, with each "class" taking all of their subjects together as a coherent group. These subjects were soon called "disciplines" because of their integration of academic and moral studies; the word *discipline*, then, had ethical overtones in its earliest academic uses.

Toward the end of the Middle Ages, certain subjects were extracted from the whole system of integrated knowledge, and some of the teachers (*magistri*) at these "ancient" universities began to concentrate their academic efforts more and more on specific disciplines. In this context, the study and practice of rhetoric held a privileged position over other disciplines, since knowledge is useless unless it can be communicated effectively, and literary and historical discourse served as examples for analysis and imitation. Rhetoric was the foundation of a liberal education.[5]

With the rise of Enlightenment rationalism during the seventeenth and eighteenth centuries, a dramatic shift occurred in the academic values and curricular structures associated with European higher education, and a result of this shift was the proliferation of new "modern" universities where knowledge was treated as thoroughly specialized and discipline-specific, not integrated.[6] Proponents of Enlightenment rationalism considered each discipline to have its own exclusive methods and objects of inquiry, and new disciplines were constantly emerging as new methodologies were developed in the various arts and sciences (Moran 6). Interestingly, the very first division of knowledge (or what the Germans called *Wissenschaft*) separated the natural sciences (*Naturwissenschaft*) from the arts and humanities (*Geisteswissenschaft*), relieving the sciences of moral and cultural responsibilities.

Administrators at these new modern universities established specialized academic "departments" that would produce new knowledge (rather than reproduce traditional knowledge) within the scope of their assigned methods and objects of inquiry, and with the explosion of disciplinary knowledge and the division of traditional disciplines into sub- and sub-subdisciplines, each with its own exclusive department, the curriculum turned from an integrated whole into a fragmented mess. With the proliferation of new disciplines specializing in narrow fields of inquiry, integrated knowledge and coherent curricula were quickly becoming archaic notions. As Robert J. Connors points out, the coherent curriculum of the ancient universities was converted into a system of requirements-plus-electives, with the number of requirements constantly falling in concert with the number of new disciplines that were exploding on the academic scene ("Overwork" 185–86). Each discipline in this new elective-based curriculum could divide its courses into even more specialized subdisciplines, and each course could be split further into sections, keeping enrollments low and workloads reasonable, and preserving time for research, or the pursuit of new and original knowledge. Among European nations, Germany was leading the way in establishing these modern universities, where academic inquiry was specialized, original research was privileged, and overlap among disciplines was viewed as inefficient and a direct deterrent to intellectual progress.

Throughout the eighteenth and early nineteenth centuries, American higher education was modeled largely after the "ancient" universities of Medieval Europe, offering an integrated liberal arts curriculum designed to prepare elite (and usually wealthy) students for community leadership roles. During the mid-nineteenth century, however, the U.S. government perceived a problem in higher education. The small liberal arts colleges that dotted the landscape did not consider the practical sciences and technology to be worthy subjects for a humanistic education, yet these were exactly the areas of knowledge and skill that the states needed to foster among their citizens in order to function as relatively independent units of a larger republic. This infrastructural need led the U.S. Congress to pass the Morrill Act of 1862, which established in every state one or more land-grant universities designed to train a new citizenry, tuition-free, for careers in agriculture, mining, and mechanical engineering. At these new "state" universities, the liberal arts were relegated to general education requirements, preprofessional preparation for more specialized, advanced, and technical curricula. By the 1880s, most European universities and the American universities established by the Morrill Act based their structures and values on the model of the German research university, where objective inquiry and scientific methods guided the establishment of distinctly nonhumanistic criteria for determining the worth of academic scholarship and teaching.

It is in this context of the new "modern" university in Europe and America that English studies emerged as a discipline. In *Professing Literature*, Graff explains that "Strictly speaking, there were no 'academic literary studies' in America or anywhere else until the formation of language and literature departments in the last quarter of the nineteenth century" (1). While there must have been an air of tremendous excitement over the rapid intellectual progress that was being made before the turn of the century, this was also, to be sure, a time of instability in academic inquiry as a whole. Small and Guy explain that "when English was constituted as an academic discipline in English universities in the late nineteenth century, there was a general crisis of intellectual authority in a large number of disciplines of knowledge, for the first time finding themselves in competition with each other as explanations of human affairs" (192). For many of these disciplines, debates eventually settled into coherent practices, but this was not to be the case for English studies.

In its earliest manifestations, attempting in part to distinguish itself from other more established disciplines like classics, "English" meant a mixture of things: the practice of oratory, the study of rhetoric and grammar, the composition of poetry, and the appreciation of literature, not just in the English language, but written in England by English authors. (American literature was a twentieth-century addition to the English studies curriculum.) W. Jackson Bate points out that "English departments, for good or ill, took into receivership a variety of subjects that other departments, becoming concerned more with methodology, began to neglect" (196). And Graff adds, "with [. . .] size and power came diversification. The colonizing of composition was just one instance of how the territorial ambitions that led English departments to widen their range of interests made it difficult to maintain a unitary definition of the discipline. English departments seem to be forever stretching their boundaries to absorb new functions and then wondering why their boundaries are so unclear ("Is There" 16). In the context of the new modern university, where disciplines were defined by clear methodological boundaries and exclusive objects of study, English studies' mixture of functions was not respected.

English studies had other problems as well. The first university-level departments of English lacked rigorous courses—they are described more as casual chat sessions than meaningful learning experiences—and the teachers who staffed them often wrote uneven scholarship using vague methodologies based on undefined aesthetic values. English was an undisciplined discipline, and its reputation among the scientific departments that dominated the emerging modern universities was slipping fast. Interestingly, the humanistic impulse that gave rise to English studies did not hold sway for long.

During the nineteenth century, philology emerged out of the German research universities, and, in an effort to become a legitimate academic discipline, joined forces with English studies. Philology included, among other things, according to Geoffrey Sampson, "the investigation of the history of languages, the uncovering of their relationships, and the reconstruction of the lost 'proto-languages' from which families of extant languages descend" (13). Philology was, in part, the distinctly historical or diachronic study of language as it changed over time (an aspect of philology that, following WWI, became known as comparative linguistics), but it also had a clearly cultural dimension. Julie Tetel Andresen says that philology also "viewed language as a means to study the literature and culture of a people" (134). Modern languages evolved differently out of the first protolanguages, and philologists believed that national cultures accounted for many of the linguistic divergences that led eventually to distinct modern languages. In American philology, Andresen tells us, "there was an inalienable association of language and nation" (32). Within English studies in the late nineteenth century, literary texts were viewed by philologists as examples of historically evolving languages in specific cultural contexts; Andresen describes this interest as "the literary orientation of traditional philology" (40). Literature worked very well as an object of analysis for philologists.

The first philologists, trained in German research universities and embarrassed by their "undisciplined" colleagues, turned English broadly speaking into the *science* of language and literary studies, bringing historical fact finding, empirical linguistic methodologies, and Enlightenment rational inquiry to bear on imaginative texts. It became the "mission" of these early philologists, in both Europe and the United States, Graff tells us, "to turn English and other modern languages into a rigorous academic subject" ("Is There" 15). Further, it was the philologists who defined the structure of English studies: their interest in national languages and literatures accounts for the emphasis in twenty-first-century English departments on the separation of British and American literature, and their interest in historical language shifts accounts for the classification of these national literatures into distinct periods.

Yet even as the philologists came to dominate early departments of English, the humanists, or "literary critics" (as opposed to "language scientists"), who had been largely responsible for initiating English studies in the modern university, refused to fade into the background. As Graff explains, there remained a group of "generalists" in English studies who were committed to "the old college ideal of liberal or general culture against that of narrowly specialized research," and this group "defended appreciation over investigation and values over facts" (*Professing* 55). It was among this group of generalists (and in opposition to technical philology) that creative writing first emerged as a way to link literary appreciation with literary production, enhancing students' overall experience with imaginative texts. Graff points out that "[t]he union of Arnoldian humanism and scientific research which gave birth to academic literary studies was never free from strain" (*Professing* 3), and that, because of this constant conflict (which, by the way, persists in many universities even today), "early efforts to unify English as a discipline were frustrated" ("Is There" 16).

The split between the humanist critics and the language scientists was not the only one that created tensions in these early English departments. Graff writes, "Another rift opened when English departments by the turn of the century became responsible in most universities for freshman writing courses" ("Is There" 16). Connors points out in "Overwork/Underpay" that during the last quarter of the nineteenth century, a "literacy crisis" (caused by loose admissions policies resulting from the Morrill Act) led to the *requirement* of first-year composition (183). Rhetoric, no longer viewed among students as the foundation of integrated knowledge, quickly became little more than an obstacle they would have to negotiate before moving on to more interesting electives and more relevant courses in their major departments.

Further, while other disciplines were dividing their courses into subspecialties and multiple sections, required first-year composition was still taught to an entire entering class—*en masse*

(Connors, "Overwork" 185–88). With the shift in interest from oral to written media, and a corresponding shift from group to individual attention to students, rhetoric professors, once the most respected members of the academic community, became over-worked and underappreciated, reading hundreds, sometimes thousands, of student essays every term—to the envy of absolutely no one (181–85). The image of the rhetoric professor hunched over a stack of student essays was hardly appealing to the youngest intelligentsia in English studies, who, seeking careers in the discipline, would do anything to avoid that fate, focusing instead on literary studies where the class sizes were comparatively small (188–92). Required composition was, by the turn of the century, so dreaded that it was relegated almost entirely to the ranks of graduate teaching assistants and part-time non-tenure-track instructors (192–95), further damaging the subject's academic reputation and creating a marginalized workforce that remains in place today. Once regarded as a central discipline in liberal education, rhetoric soon became a shallow collection of exercises and assignments with little concern for or reflection upon what unifies those assignments and what makes those exercises worthwhile; the once-respected discipline of rhetoric had become un-disciplined.

The two simultaneous processes of expansion and specialization had unfortunate consequences. As Maureen Daly Goggin explains, "In claiming separate intellectual and material spaces via constructing distinct and competing identities, the early threads connecting the various factions [making up English studies]—literary studies, speech communication, linguistics, rhetoric/composition, and creative writing—were severed" (65). But while English studies appeared on the surface to be a mixture of unrelated interests and enterprises, it was, nevertheless, philology that held institutional power, legitimated as the science of language in a university system that valued science more than anything else. Early in the new century, in fact, English studies, in both Europe and America, was almost exclusively equated with philology.

If literary studies, by way of philology, had—for the most part, at least—become a science, and the other enterprises housed in English departments were not scientific, then what *were* those other enterprises? Two journals, *English Studies* (published in the Netherlands since 1919) and *Review of English Studies* (published in England since 1925), continue to this day to publish scholarship based in the science of philology, and, in their early years, they clearly distinguished between "scientific" disciplines and "practical" disciplines. In "A Guide to English Studies," published in Volume 7 (1925) of *English Studies,* the journal's coeditor, E. Kruisinga, wrote that the field of English studies is best described as philology, and "philology suggests the study of language on its *scientific* or at least *non-practical* side" (1, my emphasis). Thus, even in the very first journals to publish (and thereby legitimate) research in the emerging discipline of English studies, theory was privileged over practice, knowledge over application, and mind over body. So much for *using* what you know; so much for oratory, literary criticism, composition, and creative writing (cultural studies didn't exist at the time, but it wouldn't have made the cut either).

Particularly in American higher education, as philology-based literary studies increased in prestige with the other sciences, what were perceived as "practical" and therefore (by definition) less rigorous academic endeavors received less attention and less funding from university administrators, ultimately forcing these endeavors to either secede and form separate departments (oratory seceded from English and became communication studies) or remain under the umbrella of scientific literary studies and accept marginal status (composition, for example).

John Dewey, turn-of-the-century philosopher and educator, deplored these oppositions that favored the life of the mind over life in the world. In his 1901 treatise *The Educational Situation,* Dewey writes,

> He who upholds the banner of discipline in classics or mathematics, when it comes to the training of a man for the profession of a teacher or investigator, will often be found to condemn a school of commerce, or technology, or even of medicine, in the university on the ground that it is too professional in character—that it smacks of the utilitarian and commercial. The kind of discipline which enables a man to pursue one vocation is lauded; the kind of training that fits him for another is condemned. Why this invidious distinction? (308)

Although Dewey still saw a clear *separation* between theory and practice in American universities at the turn of the century, he nevertheless believed that, by 1901, the debates surrounding theory/practice had lost their vitriolic tone. There were no longer heated arguments about value; the two interests simply ignored each other. Indeed, according to Dewey, maintaining the theory/practice distinction as an antagonism was tantamount to maintaining old-school elitism, which was simply no longer possible in the turn-of-the-century American democratic milieu (309).[7]

For Dewey, the political structure of American democracy itself was motivation enough to destroy the oppositions that divided people into intellectual versus working classes, and the institution that was poised and ready to enact this destruction (if it chose to take on the task) was, of course, the newly formed modern university. Dewey writes,

> All this, I say frankly and emphatically, I regard as a survival from a dualistic past—from a society which was dualistic politically, drawing fixed lines between classes, and dualistic intellectually, with its rigid separation between the things of matter and of mind—between the affairs of the world and of the spirit. Social democracy means an abandonment of this dualism. It means a common heritage, a common work, a common destiny. It is flat hostility to the ethics of modern life to suppose that there are two different aims of life located on different planes; that the few who are educated are to live on a plane of exclusive and isolated culture, while the many toil below on the level of practical endeavor directed at material commodity. The problem of our modern life is precisely to do away with all the barriers that keep up this division. If the university cannot accommodate itself to this movement, so much the worse for it. Nay, more; it is doomed to helpless failure unless it does more than accommodate itself; unless it becomes one of the chief agencies for bridging the gap, and bringing about an effective interaction of all callings in society [. . .]. To decline to recognize this intimate connection of professions in modern life with the discipline and culture that come from the pursuit of truth for its own sake, is to be at least one century behind the times. (310)

Now, over a century on from Dewey's 1901 *The Educational Situation*, those who continue to cling to the old theory/practice, mind/body, and education/training dichotomies are at least two centuries behind the times. Theory and practice are interdependent, Dewey argued: knowledge that is not reinforced by experience is empty, and experience that is not reinforced by critical reflection is blind.

One reason Dewey was so concerned with destroying these insidious oppositions is that he believed "pedagogy," or the art and science of teaching, should be a university course. But pedagogy was viewed as pragmatic, and was thus firmly marginalized in the value structure of the turn-of-the-century research university. In "Pedagogy as a University Discipline," originally published in 1898, Dewey makes a convincing argument (perhaps the first of its kind) for offering education as an academic subject at the university level. Dewey explains that the normal schools, where the bulk of teacher training took place, rarely prepared students in the rigors of subject knowledge; and those students who graduated from universities and decided to teach were well versed in subject knowledge, but had no skills in or knowledge of the craft of teaching. If universities could take responsibility for teaching pedagogy as an academic subject, the quality of education at all levels would dramatically improve. The success of Dewey's argument, he believed, ultimately rested on the dissolution of the distinction between knowledge and praxis.

So convinced was Dewey of the insidiousness of the theory/practice dichotomy that he ends *The Educational Situation* with a confident claim and an unwavering prediction: "The fact is sure," Dewey writes, "that the intellectual and moral lines which divide the university courses in science and letters from those of professional schools are gradually getting obscure and are bound finally to fade away" (311). Yet, despite Dewey's confident tone, his prediction did not play out. In certain disciplines, English not the least among them, the "intellectual and moral lines"—between theory and practice, education and training, and mind and body—intensified unabated throughout the first half of the twentieth century, even when the class-based assumptions that served as their foundation had been forgotten, or at least suppressed. The vitriolic tone of the debates had returned with a vengeance, especially in English studies, with conflicts among literature and composition and English education, linguistics and literary criticism, critical theory and creative writing occurring with too much regularity. Dewey's dream of interdependence had, in English studies at least, turned into a nightmare of divisiveness. With this divisiveness came an equal interest in disciplinary secession from English.

The first battle in English studies, between literary criticism and language science, had already been fought and won by the philologists. And while there was continued tension between these groups throughout the late nineteenth century, philology's most vexing rival around 1900 turned out to be its own disciplinary sibling, linguistics. Linguistics emerged in Europe as the ahistorical (or synchronic) study of language as a coherently structured system, and the object of inquiry for linguistics was naturally occurring spoken language. Sampson describes "synchronic linguistics" as "the analysis of languages as communicative systems as they exist at a given point in time (often the present), ignoring (as their speakers ignore) the route by which they arrived at their present form" (13). While the early philologists were clearly interested in written (especially literary) texts, the new linguists argued that speech is prior to writing and is also, therefore, primary in importance. Since literature is not spoken and does not represent a person's natural capacity to produce intelligible language (and thus cannot represent the system of rules for constructing that language), linguists did not turn to imaginary texts as objects of analysis. If they did, it was in the very limited capacity of data gathering and stylistics. Roger Fowler admits that although linguistics "may be a means of assuring a sound factual basis for many sorts of critical judgment," it does not "provide ways of unfolding and discussing precise textual effects" (28); and G. N. Leech confesses, "the most interesting and illuminating aspect of communication in literature is beyond the scope of linguistics" (155–56).

Not only did "synchronic" linguists study oral language instead of written language, but some of them also began to take a rather negative view of written *literary* language, perhaps in direct response to the common attitude among their colleagues that "modern linguistic theory [is] a contributory discipline to literary criticism" (Freeman 3). Fowler points out that the valorization of speech over writing contributes to linguistics' incompatibility with literary studies: "[T]his attitude leads to an implied denigration of written language, to a view of particular literary forms as modifications of 'normal usage'" (4), and, accordingly, Leech (a linguist) defines literature as "the use of unorthodox or deviant forms of language" (135).

In a strange twist of fate, it was actually philology (literary history and culture), not linguistics (language structure and grammar), that seceded from English departments during the first half of the twentieth century. Andresen explains that the founding in 1902 of the American Anthropological Association began a steady process by which philologists recognized more affinities with the empirical and cultural work of anthropology than with the literary criticism and universal values expounded by their colleagues in English.[8]

Soon another event would complicate the evolving tension between philology and the rest of English studies. As the United States and England entered World War I, they found themselves fighting the very nation that had brought scientific methodologies to literary studies: Germany. Eagleton writes, "One of the most strenuous antagonists of English—philology—was closely bound up with Germanic influence; and since England [and the United States] happened to be passing through a major war with Germany, it was possible to smear classical philology as a form of ponderous Teutonic nonsense" (*Literary* 26). Andresen agrees, arguing that "World War I (1914–1918) could justifiably be identified as a turning point. American reaction against Germany during the war freed American linguists to work on non-Indo-European languages" (207), resulting in a "slightly pugnacious attitude of post–World War I American linguists toward their European counterparts" (208).

Although linguistics had, for the most part, come to dominate philology by the first quarter of the twentieth century, the secession of philology to anthropology left structural linguists (who did not secede, at least not yet) in an uncomfortable alliance that was clearly more a matter of convenience than common interest; these linguists were the lone language scientists in a department whose humanists seemed to be gaining strength. Many of the philologists who remained in English departments after the general split became viewed as arcane historians, turning once dominant faculty members into a merely tolerated old guard.[9] In

1924, the Linguistics Society of America was established in order to give linguistics credibility as a discipline in its own right. Some synchronic linguists formed their own departments as well, leaving a number of English departments across the country with no linguists at all.

With the fall (and secession) of philology came renewed interest in literary criticism and composition, and creative writing played a role (albeit a failed one) in this renewal. First, creative writing emerged during the decades after the turn of the century, according to D. G. Myers, "as a means for unifying the two main functions of English departments—the teaching of writing and the teaching of literature." As Myers points out, however, "creative writing failed to achieve its goals," and English departments continued their divisive ways (xiv). Second, literary critics, enjoying their newfound freedom from the domination of philology, used creative writing as a way to "reform and redefine the academic study of literature, establishing a means for approaching it 'creatively'; that is, by some other means than it had been approached before that time, which was historically and linguistically." Creative writing, then, became an "institutional arrangement for treating literature as if it were a continuous experience and not a mere corpus of knowledge" (4); and it was a way for literary studies to provide students with a total experience of the intersection of literary analysis and production (4–5). As we will see, creative writing also did not achieve this second goal.

While the philologists, linguists, and literary critics (with the help of creative writing) were vying for dominance, yet another tension had been emerging in English studies. Speech communication, which was once combined with composition in a powerful alliance, no longer desired to be associated with this service discipline. Further, linguists, the only other members of English departments who were interested in oral communication, considered themselves to be scientists; but speech communication was an art, not a science. In 1914, the National Association of Academic Teachers of Public Speaking was formed and those interested in the pragmatic art of oral communication broke from English to establish departments of speech communication, leaving structuralist linguists with few colleagues interested in oral language and leaving beleaguered composition specialists with few colleagues interested in the rhetorical tradition.[10]

The split between speech communication and English was a rich context for, but not a direct cause of, literary criticism's rise to power. In fact, World War I had a much more direct effect on this transition. I have already mentioned that World War I created a distaste among British and American scholars for anything German, including philology. But in addition to this directly anti-German sentiment, the devastation that the war caused in England dramatically increased feelings of patriotism and created a "spiritual hungering" to which, Eagleton suggests, "poetry seemed to provide an answer" (*Literary* 26). Although there was no material devastation in the United States, Americans also, nevertheless, experienced an increased sense of national pride, which accounted for the legitimation of American literature as an academic subject. It was largely, then, the *social* influence of World War I that caused a welling-up of national pride, and this burgeoning patriotism created a new desire among students to read the literature that represented their nation's values and greatness. University administrators and literary critics were quick to capitalize on the newfound cachet of imaginative literature. But, while English departments had a new interest (literature itself, rather than the scientific method of analyzing it) as their central concern, the discontentment and frustrations among English studies' other disciplines (linguistics, composition, creative writing, and the emerging discipline of English education) were reaching their zenith.

The divisiveness that characterized "factions" within English departments as midcentury approached was not to be soothed by historical developments to come. Quite the opposite. Not only were some of the disciplines within English already marginalized (at least partly) for their inherently "pragmatic" orientation, literary studies itself, while on the privileged side of the theory/practice dichotomy still being maintained at most universities, at least until the 1940s, was to face new challenges. In the aftermath of World War II, the U.S. government turned its interests (and financial support) squarely in the direction of national defense, which required an equal shift in education toward science and technology. During this time, government grants encouraged research in the disciplines that could produce advanced weapons and develop a space program, and the Soviet launch of Sputnik in 1957 only accelerated these changes in higher education. Further, the universities where this research was being conducted often had to match federal funds or construct new facilities and hire additional personnel for these scientific endeavors. Thus, not only were the humanities and English not able to access large federal grants (slated, as they were, for science and technology), but many of these grants also drained university funds that would have otherwise gone to humanities disciplines (ACLS 6). The 1950s and 1960s, then, saw a more radical devaluation of English studies than any other age in American history, and this devaluation was a direct result of government intervention.

With humanities education rapidly declining in importance (again), and with the disciplines associated with science and technology reaching nearly superhero status in the academy, it was no longer sufficient to declare that English (or at least its dominant discipline, literature) was theoretical, not practical, that it was instruction in the best that has been thought and said, not training in workaday technology. The values associated with these oppositions (theory/practice, education/training, mind/body) had flipped on their heads. Graham Hough, writing in 1964, offers a sarcastic summary of the problem: "[T]he humanities do not make anything explode or travel faster, and the powers that be at present are not much interested in anything else" (96).[11] English could no longer rest on its laurels, assured that the humanities would always hold a privileged position in the modern university and that the practical disciplines, in the event of a real crisis, would be the first to go. Still, no one could have imagined that, in time, the humanities as a whole would come under fire.

What kept English going during these lean years? Not a resurgence of interest in literature; not a new way of reading old texts. Instead, it was English studies' old "sore subject" (Ohmann, *English* 132), required first-year composition. Most historians of English studies, in fact, acknowledge that without composition the study of literature as we know it simply would not exist (Applebee; Berlin; Graff, *Professing*; Parker). Graff writes, "Without that enterprise [i.e., composition] the teaching of literature could never have achieved its central status" (*Professing* 2), and "though the grading of freshman themes was often scorned as an activity beneath the dignity of an English professor, it was the English department's control over required composition courses that enabled it to grow into the largest and most powerful department in the humanities" ("Is There" 16). Required first-year composition courses paid the bills because most universities distribute at least part of their budgets according to credit-hour production. Since these composition courses were general education requirements, since most of the courses were taught by part-time non-tenure-track instructors, and since the full-fledged discipline that we know today as rhetoric and composition studies did not yet exist, English departments, wealthy among humanities disciplines, could run low-enrollment literature courses without the administrative threat of cutting back or eliminating low-productivity literature programs. This windfall for literary studies would end (or should have ended) during the late twentieth century with the evolving professionalization of composition studies and its emergence as a full academic discipline in its own right.

With the general shift in education from theory to practice, linguistics, composition, creative writing, and English education had an opportunity to (re)assert themselves as pragmatic arts, as means to communicate effectively in a troubled social context. But no such (re)assertion emerged, partly because English studies was so strongly associated then with literature, because the humanities in general were being devalued, and because science ruled with an iron fist.

English education, in particular, was hit hard by the pervasive influence of scientific paradigms that were infiltrating every nook and cranny of university life. Dewey had gotten his wish; education was, by early- to midcentury, an academic discipline in its own right at most universities. But if English is one discipline and education is another, what did that make English education? Early English education was, in the words of George H. Henry, "an 'odd' discipline," a "hybrid—one very large area called 'education' apparently to be 'grafted' upon another even larger one called 'English'" (4). This "odd" discipline would, however, experience a period of rejuvenation during the 1960s, when teachers and administrators alike were enthusiastic about expanding the curriculum in new and interesting directions and developing pedagogical methods that were specific to English and not necessarily relevant to the entire scope of education. At this time, what English education lacked in theoretical coherence it certainly made up for in energy.

But the energy and enthusiasm of the 1960s would be crushed during the 1970s. Advancement in science and technology required a literate workforce, and English education was in the business of literacy. There was, however, a simultaneous push toward "accountability," the "scientific" demonstration through statistical measures of the success of education generally. Observable behavioral objectives became the criteria by which educators would determine the success or failure of their students as well as of their own teaching methods (Henry 7–11). By 1973, Ben Nelms explains,

> our professional landscape had changed drastically. *Accountability* was the new watchword. The back-to-the-basics movement was in full swing. Budgets were cut; federal dollars for English practically disappeared [. . .]; public criticism of our profession became more shrill [. . .]; and our professional posture became more and more defensive [. . .]. This sensed loss of professional autonomy and the tension between public mandates and the shared professional vision that had emerged in the late 1960s became acute in the mid 1970s. (185)

The 1970s was the era of national and state-mandated competency testing, and the schools that tested low were threatened with government takeover. English education was deeply implicated, since the teachers of the 1960s could not "demonstrate" statistically their students' newfound sense of self-worth and sensitivity toward others. Nelms writes, "the minimum-competency movement would foster the teaching of isolated skills rather than conceptual wholes, teaching for the test rather than for growth, and an emphasis on actuality rather than possibility" (190). Further, state-mandated curricula, Gordon M. Pradl explains, left "far too many teachers and learners [. . .] trapped in conditions that seek to *control* their lives through external management rather than *transform* them through collaborative partnership" (217).

During these troubled times, every humanities discipline, including literary studies, would have to adapt to its new context. For a few decades, literary scholars had been developing and practicing what we now know as the New Criticism, a kind of literary scholarship that abandoned subjective humanism (particularly Romanticism) in favor of more objective and disinterested critical values. Although New Critics turned their attention mostly to poetic language as a reaction against what they perceived as the mechanistic language of scientific positivism, it remains true that objective and disinterested methods of inquiry (in direct contradistinction to Romantic subjectivist methods) were simultaneously being promoted in science and technology. But New Criticism, or the objective and disinterested practice of examining tropes and figures, ironic paradoxes, and tripartite structures (among other things) through close readings of poetic texts, could not save English studies from imminent decline. New Criticism was certainly useful in the years following the 1944 GI Bill, which entitled throngs of new students, who previously would not have attended college, to cheap student loans and a full undergraduate education. New Criticism could be learned and practiced by almost anyone: possession of elitist values and a detailed understanding of European history were no longer prerequisites to the meaningful study of literature. In fact, because it is so amenable to pedagogical adaptation, New Criticism is still prevalent in many English classrooms across the country.

Following World War II, while the New Critics and other literary scholars turned toward objective and disinterested values, a rift opened between literary critics and creative writers. Whereas early creative writing classes were taught by literary critics whose primary goal was to enhance students' total literary experience, the new creative writing classes were increasingly being taught by actual writers, not critics. Creative *writers,* not interested in "close reading," which they believed destroyed the aesthetic experience, maintained ties to romantic notions of creativity and emotion, opening a seemingly unbridgeable gulf between critics and writers. Differences soon turned to politics. Myers writes, "In the hallways of the English department, exchanges between poets and scholars are marked by mutual hostility. The poets complain that literary study has 'no point of contact with the concerns of most working poets'; the scholars dismiss creative writing as 'pseudo-literature'" (4–5; also see Scholes 5–7).

But, objective and disinterested though it may have appeared, the fact is that New Criticism detached itself from any relevance outside of the academy by locating meaning entirely within the confines of the text: rigorous, perhaps, but socially and politically irrelevant. Literary criticism, by the end of the 1950s, had transformed itself right into a tight corner. Mimicking the sciences, which were already well established and basking in prestige, English had become overly unified, dominated by a single discipline and a single approach, and this approach took no account of the trouble that was brewing outside the hallowed halls of the ivory tower.[12] The social revolutions of the 1960s were affecting every facet of life in America, and the academy seemed to be blindsided by the social transformations that were breaching its unstable ramparts.

With the demise of New Criticism and the impending transformations that would come during the 1960s, English studies had another prime chance to redeem itself from many of its past failures. Disciplines associated with the sciences and technology had been one up on New Criticism because they were directly concerned with developments outside of academia—they were "relevant." This extra-academic concern on the part of science and technology was viewed positively until the 1960s; but now students and citizens alike began to realize that if the world ends it will be at the hands of scientists and technicians. Nuclear physics, for example, once heralded as offering a potential solution to the American energy crisis, was now deplored as the potential destruction of the human race.

During the especially formative later years of the 1960s, the so-called literary canon (a term with Biblical overtones) was called into question, filled, as it was, with "dead white males," and the greatest challenges to this tradition grew out of theoretical approaches that took root in the early women's rights movement, adult education, the civil rights movement, and a general distaste for authority. Many of these theories (feminism, cultural studies, multiculturalism, and deconstruction, among others) that were now being applied to literary texts had developed and matured in the grassroots efforts of social activists, outside the context of literary criticism. English was rapidly expanding its methodological scope in certain much-needed directions.

What came out of this critical period, however, was a frustrating mixture of successes and failures. While it is true that English studies was beginning to abandon the methodologies that did not take account of the world outside of academia, it is also true that English studies did not apply its newly developed "social" methodologies to texts beyond imaginative literature. Thus, although certain methodological problems had been remedied, the application exclusively to literature of these more socially relevant critical methodologies retained for English studies a kind of elitism that would, again, hardly endear the discipline to students, administrators, and citizens outside of the academy. We were ridiculed in the popular press (at times justifiably) for our elitist discourses, and with no application to texts or contexts outside of the academy, these discourses did in fact develop in some extreme directions. Continuing the legacy of senseless specialization, there came a point in the 1980s where critics of different orientations were no longer able to converse easily, and some, deploring this new incoherence in literary studies, declared another crisis—a crisis in criticism (Cain; Levin).

While the so-called crisis in criticism was declared mostly on the grounds of literary theory's incoherence, this new problem also offered easily gathered kindling for conservative flames. Roger Kimball, for example, argues that the radical students who had challenged the most virtuous ideals of higher education during the 1960s had become "tenured radicals," and Stanley Aronowitz and Henry Giroux admit that "the attack on the liberal arts gained momentum in part because its various fields had become havens for a new radical professoriate" (175). Allan Bloom and Dinesh D'Souza have been outspoken critics of contemporary literary theory, arguing that the relativism inherent in multiculturalism, with its attending assault on truth, has destroyed American culture and education. Echoing Bloom and D'Souza, Lynne Cheney, who has a PhD in English and served as chair of the National Endowment for the Humanities from 1986 through 1992, argues in *Telling the Truth* that academic scholarship in the humanities and English studies has lost its foundation in truth, the pursuit of universal knowledge and transcendent values; and scholarship has lost this foundation because academics have become interested in pursuing radical political projects that benefit particular groups rather than pursuing objective knowledge that benefits humankind. Some of the culprits Cheney cites (and critiques) include feminism, cultural studies, Afrocentrism, deconstruction, multiculturalism, psychoanalysis, Marxism, discourse theory, postmodernism, media studies, poststructuralism, critical pedagogy, social constructionism, critical legal studies, relativism, political correctness—and wicca.

Adding to the problem of hyperspecialization in literary studies was the rapid emergence of disciplines that had once been suppressed in the administrative structure of most English departments. Throughout the 1950s, 1960s, and 1970s, a new generation of American scholars emerged; this group, disillusioned by the failure of humanistic values to save the world (and one war after another seemed to be a constant reminder of this failure), became interested in educating emerging middle-class students in the long-marginalized practical arts of linguistics, composition, English education, and creative writing. Connors explains that the rapid emergence of these disciplines grew "out of a great change in the American professoriate, especially in English, after World War II" ("Writing" 205). Connors continues,

> Before that time, college had tended to be for an elite social class and the professors there had been an elect group. After the war, however, the GI Bill made education loans easy for servicemen to get, and a great rush of veterans into colleges and universities resulted. [. . .] And from this mass of GI Bill students came a generation of graduate students and young faculty members who changed the face of English. These younger men [and women], who were from all American social classes, brought fresh ideas with them, many of which democratized the staid old English field. In literature they championed American literature and the New Criticism; their teaching changed textual analyses from something only a trained philologist could do to something any earnest student was capable of. In composition their populist influence was even more powerful. Young professors had always been forced to teach composition, and most of them had gritted their teeth, served their time, and escaped to literature as soon as possible. A notable group within this post–World War II genera-

tion, however, determined to study composition, analyze it, and
try to do it as best it could be done. (205)

This new generation of composition professors began the difficult and invigorating work of reconnecting writing studies with
its original disciplinary foundation—rhetoric—a foundation that
had been missing from composition studies since the secession of
speech communication in 1914. As Janice Lauer points out, a
renewed attention to rhetoric meant a renewed attention to important topics like invention, audience, structure, style, voice,
and discourse; and throughout the late 1960s and 1970s, these
issues permeated scholarship in rhetoric and composition's leading journals, including *College Composition and Communication* and the *Rhetoric Society Newsletter* (later renamed the
Rhetoric Society Quarterly). With rhetoric as its renewed foundation, composition studies quickly emerged as a credible academic subject in its own right, and English studies began to create
institutional space for it. By the end of the 1970s, no fewer than
fifteen new PhD programs in rhetoric and composition had
emerged, and their graduates were devoted almost exclusively to
teaching the composing process, administering writing programs,
studying the history and theory of rhetoric, and exploring
rhetoric's contemporary applications (Lauer).

Further, during the late 1970s and 1980s, the new populist
and democratic impulses that had taken hold of rhetoric and
composition had also begun to emerge more vigorously in literary studies, where many of those who were newly versed in the
discourses of critical theory and cultural studies adopted the stance
toward students and teaching known as critical pedagogy. Critical pedagogy, in its heyday during the 1980s and 1990s, seemed
to be a common language that many in English studies wanted to
speak, despite whatever disputes there were among its constituent disciplines. Thus, in its most useful manifestations, critical
pedagogy drew actively upon the strengths of linguistics and discourse analysis, rhetoric and composition, creative writing, literature and literary criticism, critical theory and cultural studies,
and English education to accomplish a unified purpose, to teach
working-class students how to critique the dominant power formations (institutions like school and work, for example) that were

the source of their oppression. After a long and fruitful court-
ship, the love affair between English and critical pedagogy began
to fade at the turn of the twenty-first century. Critical pedagogy
was ultimately too limited in scope, and its political project was
not always shared by everyone, including some progressive practitioners of the discipline. Feminists, for example, were at times
put off by critical pedagogy's Marxist influence, which, they argued, reduced all social conflict to issues of class and ignored
important issues that were actually more specific to gender.

Nevertheless, this new generation of American scholars, still
delighted by the energetic eclecticism that was emerging in their
departments and in the discipline, encouraged a shift in terminology from "English" to "English *studies*" (the plural stud*ies*
modifying the singular English of previous decades), thus representing in name the plurality of the discipline at the end of the
twentieth century.[13] One of the primary goals of *English Studies:
An Introduction to the Discipline(s)* is to seek and describe a
language (more *common* than the discourse of critical pedagogy)
through which all of the disciplines comprised by English studies
can speak to one another with less descent into divisiveness and
greater reference to common purpose.

The Problem of Specialization

The history of English studies is a history of academic specialization. It is important to recognize, however, that the process of
specialization was, from the very inception of the discipline, not
only endemic to institutions of higher learning; it was a fact of
life in culture generally. John Higham explains, "Initially, disciplinary specialization ran counter to American ideals; there was
no place for a Renaissance man or woman in the newly de(com)-
partmentalized university. Soon after the turn of the century, however, specialization became more and more accepted as a way to
advance knowledge beyond a kind of general application" (4).
Even Dewey, writing in the thick of things at the turn of the century, recognized that specialization was not just an academic
phenomenon:

> The problem of the multiplication of studies, of the consequent congestion of the curriculum, and the conflict of various studies for a recognized place in the curriculum; the fact that one cannot get in without crowding something else out; the effort to arrange a compromise in various courses of study by throwing the entire burden of election upon the student so that he shall make out his own course of study—this problem is only a reflex of the lack of unity in the social activities themselves, and of the necessity of reaching more harmony, more system in our scheme of life. This multiplication of study is not primarily a product of the schools. The last hundred years has created a new world, has revealed a new universe, material and social. The educational problem is not a result of anything within our own conscious wish or intention, but of the conditions in the contemporary world. (*Educational* 303)

The shift from preindustrial to industrial economies, and the specialization that came with industrialization, created a parallel shift in academic culture. Joe Moran points out that the late nineteenth and early twentieth centuries were marked by the emergence of a "new society" in which "the division of labor within an increasingly professionalized bureaucracy" created specialized corporate positions that, in turn, required more and more specialized treatment in academic institutions (13). Specialization, as a general cultural phenomenon, not *just* an academic one, was inevitable, and it has had a number of consequences, many of them negative.[14]

In "The Division, Integration, and Transfer of Knowledge," David Easton argues, "With increasing acceleration in the twentieth century, the social sciences and the humanities began to specialize with a vengeance so that today the basic disciplines have not only clearly identified themselves, but have subdivided internally into many subfields; and often, even within these, specialization continues apace" (11). This statement is more accurate in relation to English studies than it is to any other discipline in the humanities and social sciences.[15] In order to illustrate the difficulties that specialization has caused certain academic disciplines, Easton describes what he calls "the Humpty Dumpty problem":

> To understand the world it has seemed necessary to analyze it by breaking it into many pieces—the disciplines and their own divi-

sions—in much the way that Humpty Dumpty, now the egg of knowledge, fragmented when he fell off the wall. But to act in the world, to try to address the issues for which the understanding of highly specialized knowledge was presumably sought, we need somehow to reassemble all the pieces. Here is the rub. Try as we may, we have been no more able than all of the king's horses and all of the king's men to put our knowledge together again for coping with the whole real problems of the world. (12–13)

Perhaps it is not a coincidence that the poem about Humpty Dumpty first appeared during the 1880s, the same period in which specialization and fragmentation were transforming public and academic culture irretrievably. But Easton's fairy tale is not as grim as the nineteenth-century version. He continues,

Recognition of the Humpty Dumpty problem created by the high degree of specialization does not, of course, deny the importance of disciplinary knowledge. The disciplines are invaluable, and undoubtedly inescapable, in that they develop precise skills, concepts, and theories that improve our understanding of various aspects of the world. They provide a solid departure point for linkages to other areas of inquiry. But for the most part they do not do a good job of preparing the way for the application of this knowledge. (22)

While specialization has advanced our knowledge in all of the disciplines that make up English studies, the fact is that specialization has also caused several interrelated problems.

The first problem is related to the English studies curriculum. Most English departments structure their course offerings and major requirements according to the "coverage model," which has been with English studies since its inception in the late nineteenth century. The coverage model suggests that students, in order to be fully educated, need to demonstrate familiarity with the whole spectrum of literature, from the major periods to the three genres to certain influential authors.[16]

Once the curriculum was divided up into periods, genres, and authors, and these divisions became part of the literary subconscious (institutionalized realities that are beyond question, as they have become today), the need arose to house experts for each specialized area in which courses were offered. Each of these specialties in English studies has, during the past century, come to conceive of itself as a *discipline* in its own right, with a mutually exclusive scope and unique methods of inquiry. "Thus," Bate explains, "in literature, you confine your area, to begin with, to one author, a group of authors, or one aspect or genre of a period of a half century. And you ask *only* certain kinds of questions—those you have been hearing about or those most capable of systematization, leaving aside the larger difficulties and uncertainties of the subject" (201). What disciplinary status means is that specialists in a certain period, genre, or author, for example, *practice their discipline differently* from other specialists, even within literary studies. Thus, not only do the different specialists study different literary texts (appropriate to their period, genre, or author), but the very means of *producing* knowledge are different among specialists as well—they ask different questions, use different critical methodologies, and publish their research in different specialized forums, among other things.[17] Easton contends that as of the late twentieth century, "there is little place [in humanities education] for the generalist" (23), and this is especially true for English studies, the most specialized of all humanities disciplines. When a department loses a Victorian prose specialist or a Miltonist, that vacancy must be filled with another Victorian prose specialist or Miltonist, since shifting periods or genres means more (under the present system of disciplinarity) than just shifting objects of study.

In my own department, out of twenty-three tenured or tenure-line faculty members, nineteen wrote PhD dissertations in literature (either British or American), two wrote dissertations in rhetoric and composition, one wrote a dissertation in linguistics, and one wrote a creative thesis for an MFA. To say the least, this unbalanced structure causes logistical problems, as in cases of tenure and promotion. For example, scholarship in English education and rhetoric and composition is often "pedagogical." While pedagogical scholarship is highly valued in the disciplinary structures of English education and rhetoric and composition, in the context of tenure criteria based on literary studies, it is worth less than theoretical criticism. Critical theory and cultural studies evolved mostly external to its application to literary texts, and those scholars who consider themselves to be cultural theorists are sometimes criticized for "avoiding" literature. And even the best creative writers in the country are often admonished if they only write fiction or poetry or drama and do not write critical essays about literature or the craft of creative writing.[18] In English studies, disciplinary imbalance persists in the most problematic ways, since, to adapt a phrase from Dewey (already quoted above), "one [discipline] cannot get in without crowding something else out" (*Educational* 303), and no discipline, no matter how narrowly conceived, wants to be crowded out.

Although I do not argue for a nostalgic return to the bygone days of literary generalists, I do think that a certain amount of institutional power is lost when common purpose dissolves. For with radical specialization, as English studies has experienced in the last half century, we are no longer able to represent ourselves to university administrations or public audiences as having coherent goals (other than the material fact that we work side by side). Although I cited Graff earlier as being relatively unconcerned about the disciplinary status of English studies, his position is actually more complex than that. Graff argues that "we *do* have good reason to be disturbed [. . .] if students and other nonprofessionals find the diverse activities of the English department mysterious and unintelligible" ("Is There" 11; my emphasis). Graff explains that academic departments represent themselves to students and nonacademics through their curricula, and if these curricula appear to be disconnected, with little logic to their overall structure, then "not only is the curriculum damaged [. . .] but the university's intelligibility in the eyes of its constituencies also suffers" (20).

If a department that houses disciplines as diverse as linguistics and discourse analysis, rhetoric and composition, creative writing, literature and literary criticism, critical theory and cultural studies, and English education defines for itself a limited function and scope—the criticism (method) of literature (object)—then many vital functions of that department will not fit into its expressed or implied scope, making the work of the department as a whole appear incoherent and completely unexplainable. Nancy A. Gutierrez writes, "While diversity is a strength, it can also be perceived as a weakness, especially if a particular entity believes it is homogeneous when it is heterogeneous."

Further, because of disciplinary hyperspecialization, English departments, as administrative structures based largely on the coverage model, are unable to represent in their curricula transformations in the field of English studies generally. For example, as the study of African American literature gains credibility in the field of English studies, and its specialists increasingly and rightfully demand representation in the formal curriculum of the English major, one of three things must happen in the context of the coverage model: African American literature courses are offered as electives, African American literature courses replace other American literature requirements, or the number of credit hours needed for an English major is increased to accommodate the new required courses. And what of Native American literature, Southern literature, Caribbean and other postcolonial literature, Latina literature, Asian American literature, and gay and lesbian literature, to name just a few?

To compound the problem (though I will argue later that this problem is also the beginning of a solution), since about the 1970s and 1980s English studies has experienced a surge of renewed interest in disciplines that were once overshadowed by the dominance of philology and New Criticism. Linguistics and discourse analysis gained a broader audience through attention to sociopolitical aspects of language use, as in systemic-functional linguistics and critical discourse analysis. Rhetoric and composition was revitalized by its turn from realist to social-constructionist, epistemic, and classical rhetorics. Creative writing was increasingly legitimated by its burgeoning professional workshops and conferences. Literature and literary criticism broadened their scope through renewed interest in public and popular (not just literary) texts. Critical theory and cultural studies gained broader acceptance among activist critics through their push toward participating in civic life and gaining what Michael Bérubé calls "public access." And English education was revitalized by the turn to pedagogy as a legitimate object of scholarly inquiry. With so many interesting disciplines laying rightful claim to curricular territory and financial resources, the period-based coverage model does not represent the verve and energy that define the field of English studies in the twenty-first century.

Another problem that specialization has created for English studies has to do with the narrow and insular kind of scholarship that is produced within the confines of our mutually exclusive disciplines. The more specialized our scholarship is the more divorced it becomes from the nonacademic world. While the best (i.e., most specialized) academic problems are narrow and focused, "real-world" problems are complicated mixtures of forces that all combine to create dissonance. As Easton puts it, "[T]he fact is that society confronts us with problems that are, for example, definable as neither political, philosophical, linguistic, economic, nor cultural alone. They may be all of these and more" (12). No single methodology from linguistics or discourse analysis or creative writing or rhetoric or composition or literature or literary criticism or critical theory or cultural studies or English education—no single methodology (or set of specialized methodologies) can solve a complex social problem. But if these disciplines comprised in English studies join forces, not merging their methods into a coherent supermethod, but maintaining their differences and directing their particular methods toward different parts of the problem, then power is gained, not lost. If English studies is to become "relevant" in the new century, it must turn its critical and productive lenses not only toward academic problems, which remain important, but also toward nonacademic ones, which must be viewed as equally important (Cushman). As Gunther Kress puts it, "[T]here is no aspect of practice in the English classroom that is not laden with social significance" (*Writing* 6).

A final problem that specialization creates for English studies is the devaluation of lower-division courses and the privileging of upper-division ones. Specialized course content is viewed as more "advanced" than courses covering broad subject matters, which also means, in the context of the coverage model, that specialized courses are offered less frequently than others. Thus, the Victorian prose specialist lives for the annual Victorian prose seminar in which all of her or his research can be put to good use. Within this value system, all other courses are treated as little more than professional duty, service to the department and university. With less specialization and more common purpose, I argue, will come a natural interest in revitalizing lower-division courses, which may also help to ease some of the labor problems that have plagued English departments from the very beginning.[19]

A number of scholars have responded to the problems of specialization in English studies with specific proposals for curricular reform. Stephen North describes three such proposals: secession, corporate compromise, and fusion. Later, I will propose a fourth model, *integration*.

When specialization becomes so advanced that we cannot have meaningful conversations with our colleagues or convince the keepers of the coverage model that there are important aspects of English studies not represented by it, some overlooked disciplines abandon Humpty Dumpty and go find their own wall to sit on.

Secession from English is by no means an uncommon or new occurrence. It happened in the early twentieth century when philology seceded to anthropology and oratory formed its own departments of speech communication; and throughout the twentieth century, viewing their methodologies to be more relevant to the social sciences than to literary studies, some linguistics faculty gradually broke away from English and formed separate departments. Some rhetoric and composition programs, too, perceiving the ideological gulf between humanistic literary studies and pragmatic writing studies to be too great to bridge, have seceded, creating departments of rhetoric and writing separate from departments of English.[20] Creative writers, caught up in the battle between literature and composition, have often been forced to make a difficult choice (to borrow words from the Clash): Should I stay or should I go? Some scholars, trained in literature and literary criticism, became, during the 1960s and 1970, more interested in applying their critical methodologies to popular culture than to literary texts, and many of these scholars seceded from English to form their own departments of American studies or popular culture. Scholars in critical theory and cultural studies, also not interested in literary texts as the paradigmatic object of analysis, broke away from English, establishing separate departments of cultural studies or film studies or women's studies or African American studies, and so on. Finally, some English education programs were developed in departments or schools of education, but others that began in English have shifted over to education because education, quite simply, seemed more accommodating.

Is secession good for English studies? It depends. If English departments continue to describe their scope as literary texts and their function as, in the words of Richard Ohmann, "the fostering of literary culture and literary consciousness" (*English* 13), then there is only one logical course of action for linguistics and discourse analysis, rhetoric and composition, creative writing, critical theory and cultural studies, and English education. Secede. A truly democratic English department (one that exercises the power of each of its composite disciplines equally in the service of a larger goal) can, quite simply, never evolve out of a discipline that defines its scope and function purely in terms of literature.

A paradigmatic example of the conception of English studies that leads to secession is described by Ohmann (quoted above) in *English in America,* which was first published in 1976. I take Ohmann's 1976 edition of *English in America* to represent the kind of class warfare that was common in English departments after World War II and that, although the situation is, fortunately, changing, still remains entrenched in some departments across the country. The problem begins with Ohmann's description of the mission or function of an English department:

> I shall assume that we believe the study of literature to be the most central of our concerns—that, in fact, there would not *be* a field of English if literature did not exist. Our other concerns would then be distributed among linguists, communications experts, teachers of writing, and so on. Literature is what holds our interests together in a loose confederation, and I think it a safe guess that literature is what brought nearly all of us into the profession. Literature is our subject matter, and, this being so, an inquiry into the state of the profession must ask how we stand vis-à-vis literature: what are our responsibilities toward it, and how well are we executing them? (5–6)

Following this inauspicious introduction to "English," Ohmann then spends some time illustrating the failure of linguistics to illuminate more than the bare structural facts of literary language, and he devotes at least two chapters to critiquing composition's interest in praxis and its lack of concern with the highest literary values.[21] "Freshman English is our sore subject," Ohmann writes, and "our inability to make sense of freshman English for ourselves and our colleagues has made hard times even harder" (132). Ohmann cannot make sense of composition, of course, because it does not fit into his narrow definition of English *as literature*. Further, Ohmann ignores creative writing completely, and he seems strangely unaware of certain critical trends that had been current before he wrote *English in America*.

Stanley Fish, writing sometime after *English in America*, takes up (in some frustrating ways) the banner that Ohmann had hoisted. To begin with, Fish argues that academic disciplines are defined equally according to what they do and what they do not do. English studies endangers itself, its very academic survival is at stake, when it calls itself amorphous. English studies "must conceive of itself and be conceived by others as doing a specific, particular job. As doing this and not that, and surely not as doing everything, which is in effect to do nothing" (161–62). The discipline of English studies must be "defined by our being able to have a share of a franchise to which no one else can lay a plausible claim"; English studies must, in other words, be "distinctive" (162). Fair enough.

But this leads to Fish's claim that English studies needs to get back to *literature* and abandon historicism, political criticism, and interdisciplinarity, all of which infect English studies with external, extradisciplinary (i.e., extra*literary*) interests (164–72). The plea to return to literature, however, is especially problematic because, as historians of English studies repeatedly point out, "literature" simply cannot be defined ontologically, as a category of texts with "literary attributes" that no other texts possess (Brantlinger 15; Eagleton, *Literary* 1–14; Pratt, *Toward* xii). Eagleton writes,

One can think of literature less as some inherent quality or set of qualities displayed by certain kinds of writing all the way from Beowulf to Virginia Woolf, than as a number of ways in which people relate themselves to writing. It would not be easy to isolate, from all that has variously been called "literature," some constant set of inherent features [. . .]. There is no "essence" of literature whatsoever. Any bit of writing may be read "non-pragmatically," if that is what reading a text as literature means, just as any writing may be read "poetically." (*Literary* 8)

Fortunately for English studies, as Graff puts it, "the return to literature declared by Fish and others seems about as likely as a return to manual typewriters" ("Is There" 14). Ohmann's and Fish's own values blind them to the fact that they are citizens in a broader community, a community whose primary goal is not to "foster literary culture and literary consciousness" but to analyze, critique, and produce discourse in social context. One crucial aspect of the discourses to be analyzed and critiqued is *literature,* to be sure, but there are other texts, not called literature, that are equally important and must fall under the purview of English studies in order for the discipline to be demonstrably coherent in the eyes of students, administrators, nonacademic audiences, and even many of its own practitioners.[22]

Exclusionary values such as those described by Ohmann and Fish are, of course, the same values that foster a desire for secession among some English studies disciplines. However, secession leads to further specialization, and in time it is conceivable that there may be separate departments housing professional writing, classical rhetoric, screenwriting, poetry writing, generative grammar, discourse linguistics, young adult literature, whole language, critical theory, media studies, and literacy studies. Secession, in other words, may alleviate some immediate problems relating to curriculum and budget, but it does not solve these problems in the long run; given time, they will recur, along with the divisiveness that comes with constant specialization. Further, the kind of specialization that both leads to and follows secession actually reduces the institutional power of *all* disciplines involved. As David B. Downing points out, "The aesthetic and the political, the literary and the rhetorical, the textual and the extratextual are deeply intertwined, and their disciplinary separation has been costly. Administrators out to cut budgets are the only ones to gain from the internecine warfare among competing subdivisions. In the end, disciplinary isolation makes any small unit or program more vulnerable to administrative surveillance" (31). Better to integrate than to separate.

A second response to specialization in English studies is, as North suggests, "corporate compromise." North describes corporate compromise as the designation of a "synthesizing term" that will hold "the conflicted enterprise [of English] together" while "finding some way to present and preserve all of its competing interests" (71). Corporate compromise usually involves one discipline in English studies taking managerial responsibility for the others, ideally (but certainly not always) in a democratic fashion. Although it has been the most common strategy to unify the various disciplines that constitute English studies, corporate compromise has not been without its own problems.[23]

Recognizing the failure of literary studies to govern democratically, some scholars, including Patrick Brantlinger and Eagleton, have argued that cultural studies should take over the helm. Cultural studies recognizes all texts (all discourses) as falling within its scope, and its methods of analysis are better suited to making the knowledge produced in the discipline (and the other disciplines that make up English studies) useful to a larger public. Alternatively, Berlin argues that (social-epistemic) rhetoric should manage the disciplines that comprise English studies because it is the study of signifying practices, and all disciplines (even those outside of English studies itself) are defined by the signifying practices they use to produce and convey knowledge. But cultural studies and rhetoric are coherent and active disciplines within English studies, and, as such, would risk promoting their own values over those of other disciplines.

One of the most interesting attempts at corporate compromise is the reference to literacy as the managing term. Literacy itself is not a discipline in English studies, and so it would not, it seems at first, favor any over others. Tilly Warnock explains,

> English departments teach reading and writing; all members of the department are engaged in literacy work of various kinds, from functional literacy to highly theoretical literacy work. De-

spite differences in teaching, research, and service, we are all committed to teaching language and literature as strategies for coping and as equipment for living [. . .]. I advocate that we present
ourselves as literacy workers of various kinds, degrees, and purposes, understanding that our decisions are ethical and that our
work as teachers of reading and writing consists of strategic responses to specific, stylized questions. (148)

Warnock concludes with what she calls a "decree":

> We in English departments are all already engaged in literacy
> education of various kinds, and presenting ourselves as united in
> teaching reading and writing is the most persuasive rhetoric we
> can use in certain contexts with our colleagues across the univer-
> sity and with the citizens of our local communities and states
> [. . .]. This is how we are known and understood by people within
> the university, and this is how we are known and respected by
> people outside the university. Although we have spent years dis-
> tinguishing ourselves from each other, within the department, to
> outsiders we are more alike than we are different. (151–52)

The problem here, of course, is that *literacy*, particularly as Warnock (a rhetoric and composition scholar) describes it, is amenable to linguistics and discourse analysis, rhetoric and
composition, and English education, but it would simply not be
accepted as the scope of English studies by creative writing, literature and literary criticism, or critical theory and cultural studies. It is, in the end, not as inclusive as it first appears to be.

Opponents of corporate compromise argue that these equally
specialized managerial disciplines—whether cultural studies,
rhetoric, or literacy—do not in any way represent the interests of
all the other disciplines that make up English studies, and the
move is little more than a political attempt to colonize and
marginalize important scholarly enterprises. If it is our purpose
(and it *is*) to illustrate the equally crucial roles that linguistics
and discourse analysis, rhetoric and composition, creative writing, literature and literary criticism, critical theory and cultural
studies, and English education all play in accomplishing the mission of English studies generally, then corporate compromise is
the wrong model for reforming the discipline.

The third response to specialization in English studies that North describes is called "fusion," a seldom practiced variety of curriculum reform that took hold of the SUNY Albany PhD program during the 1990s. North writes,

> [. . .] fusion, it might be called; bringing disparate elements together under sufficient pressure and with sufficient energy to transform them into a single new entity, one quite distinct from any of the original components. Or, to put it in terms specific to English Studies: rather than ending the field's divisions by breaking it up along the lines of conflict (dissolution), or packaging those conflicts for the purposes of curricular delivery (corporate compromise), the object would be to harness the energy generated by the conflicts in order to forge some new disciplinary enterprise altogether. (73)

North proposes that a fusion-based curriculum would incorporate elements of every discipline (he only lists three: literature, rhetoric and composition, and creative writing) in each course; thus, a course primarily in Victorian literature would also include studies in Victorian rhetoric as well as response poems or dramatic performances, etc.

While fusion is certainly one of the most promising models for curricular reform in English studies, I do have objections to North's description of it. First, while I like the *idea* of fusion, I am uncomfortable that, if each course includes content from all of the disciplines, the curriculum might never extend beyond a basic level. Further, the American professoriate is thoroughly specialized, and entrusting the integrity of every discipline to every professor is not a desirable scenario to my mind. Besides, if any curriculum should be fused it is the *undergraduate* curriculum, not the graduate curriculum.

If specialization defines English studies, and has been its constant companion since the inception of the discipline, and if secession, corporate compromise, and fusion are not adequate models for a renewed English studies, is there *any* hope for coherence, or are we doomed to a life of talking to ourselves? James C. Raymond believes that we should not hold our breath:

> Of course there is no discipline in the English department. It is a collection of disparate activities with multiple objects of inquiry, vaguely articulated methodologies, and diverse notions of proof. Whatever arrangement exists among its competing scholarly, artistic, and pedagogical interests is a marriage of inconvenience, grounded not on any passion or admiration that would justify the union but on habit, historical accident, economic dependency, and perhaps anxiety about what people would think if we went our separate ways and whether we would actually survive. ("Play's" 1)

But Graff thinks "there is potential coherence in English studies." He is careful, however, to warn us that "it is a coherence that cannot be reduced to the kind of consensus on fundamentals that has traditionally constituted our idea of a discipline. For me [i.e., Graff], the source of this potential coherence lies precisely in the conversations between different and conflicting languages of justification and practices, conversations that will likely remain unresolved and whose outcome is not predictable" ("Is There" 12). But unresolved and unpredictable outcomes should not deter the effort. Graff concludes, "Today, English seems further than ever from defining a common disciplinary project, [. . .] yet the failure to confront the conflicts that result from the increased diversity creates the fragmentation that leaves students and other onlookers confused" (20). I believe the answer lies in a democratic (though certainly not radical) conception of English studies as the disciplinary *integration* of linguistics and discourse analysis, rhetoric and composition, creative writing, literature and literary criticism, critical theory and cultural studies, and English education.

The New English Studies

If conversation among the disciplines constituting English studies is, as Graff suggests, one way to begin healing the wounds caused by hyperspecialization, how can we begin the communication process? Benedict Anderson might say that each discipline in English studies has imagined itself as a sovereign community, independent and self-enclosed, and the difficult work of disciplinary integration requires us to *re*imagine ourselves as members of a larger community, a community of English studies disciplines committed to the analysis, critique, and production of discourse in social context. I believe that two models for integration, Kenneth Burke's notion of *identification* and Stuart Hall's theory of *articulation,* lead us productively in the direction of reimagining English studies as a coherent community of disciplines.

In *A Rhetoric of Motives,* Burke describes *identification* as a process whereby two or more entities (or disciplines, in our case) perceive a union of interests despite their unique qualities. Burke writes,

> A is not identical with his colleague, B. But insofar as their interests are joined, A is *identified* with B. Or he may *identify himself* with B even when their interests are not joined, if he assumes that they are, or is persuaded to believe so [. . .]. In being identified with B, A is "substantially one" with a person other than himself. Yet at the same time he remains unique, an individual locus of motives. Thus he is both joined and separate, at once a distinct substance and consubstantial with another [. . .]. A doctrine of *consubstantiality,* either explicit or implicit, may be necessary to any way of life. For substance, in the old philosophies, was an *act;* and a way of life is an *acting-together;* and in acting together, men have common sensations, concepts, images, ideas, attitudes that make them *consubstantial.* (20–21).

And later, Burke continues, "Any specialized activity participates in a larger unit of action. 'Identification' is a word for the autonomous activity's place in this wider context" (27). In English studies, then, the disciplines that constitute the field are not identical—they do not examine the same objects or use the same methods—but their *interests* are joined in that they identify themselves with the larger project of English studies. They are substantially one yet sovereign enough to pursue unique subgoals and satisfy individual motives. They are both joined and separate; they are consubstantial.

In "On Postmodernism and Articulation," Stuart Hall describes *articulation* as a method for understanding and changing power structures in particular communities. Hall writes,

> In England, the term [articulation] has a nice double meaning
> because "articulate" means to utter, to speak forth, to be articu-
> late. It carries that sense of language-ing, of expressing, etc. But
> we also speak of an "articulated" lorry (truck): a lorry where the
> front (cab) and back (trailer) can, but need not necessarily, be
> connected to one another. The two parts are connected to each
> other, but through a specific linkage that can be broken. An ar-
> ticulation is thus the form of the connection that *can* make a
> unity of two different elements under certain conditions. It is a
> linkage that is not necessary, determined, absolute and essential
> for all time. You have to ask, under what circumstances *can* a
> connection be forged or made? So the so-called "unity" of a dis-
> course is really the articulation of different, distinct elements which
> can be re-articulated in different ways because they have no nec-
> essary "belongingness." (141)

English studies, within this framework, has historically been articulated in an unfortunate way, with literary studies as the per-
petual cab and the "other" disciplines as trailers. But the linkages
that constitute any articulation of discourses can be broken and
rearranged to form a new unity, a new English studies. Herein
lies the central problem with defining English as literary studies
(or cultural studies or rhetoric or literacy, for that matter): when
social problems, nonacademic problems, problems in the so-called
real world emerge, and these problems are related to discourse,
to communication, to representation, then English studies is diminished if the linkages that define its articulation are perceived
as inalterable, determined, inevitable.

In order for English studies to approach nonacademic problems (and it must do this in order to retrieve its sense of worth in
the larger social community), that lorry must be able to be
*re*articulated in different ways depending on the needs of the situation. If Birmingham, Alabama (or any other city or town, for
that matter), experiences a decline in public literacy, it would be
remarkable if the representatives of English studies said, "Sorry,
we just do literature." English studies should be—*must be*—the
leader in solving this problem, perhaps by starting a literacy center funded by the university and the community.

English studies can move from being a set of unrelated subdisciplines to a powerful collection of *integrated* (structurally
separate but functionally interrelated) disciplines with a coher-

ent and collective goal that does not compromise each discipline's unique integrity. I propose that the goal of this integrated English studies should be the analysis, critique, and production of discourse in social context. And all of the various disciplines that make up English studies—linguistics and discourse analysis, rhetoric and composition, creative writing, literature and literary criticism, critical theory and cultural studies, and English education—contribute equally important functions toward accomplishing this goal. But there must be constant dialectical contact between the specialized disciplines and the larger project of English studies in order to curb further separation and divisiveness.

The three activities that I call "analysis, critique, and production" need, first, to be rearticulated as functionally complementary, not ideologically opposed. They are different, yes, but interrelated and interdependent as well. The long-standing debate between linguists and literary critics is an ideological one in which the values associated with objective analysis (for linguists) and subjective critique (for literary scholars) conflict in destructive ways (Hayes). In fact, analysis can never be fully objective, since the selection of texts and the selection of analytical methodologies are intentional, subjective, and political in nature; and critique without analysis is equivalent to an academic knee-jerk reaction. Analysis is the foundation of critique (even for the literary critic), and critique is integral to the analytical process (even for the linguist).

Literary studies is often ideologically opposed to disciplines that foreground the production of language, such as creative writing, rhetoric and composition, and even cultural studies, with its recent interest in the production of public discourse. Robert Scholes points out that, from a traditional literary perspective, creative writing results in the production of "pseudo-literature and composition results in the production of pseudo-non-literature" (5–7). But if, as I will argue, curricula need to take account of the world for which their students (subjects) are being prepared, then critique simply is not enough. In *Writing the Future*, Kress argues, "[T]he traditional role of the academic [has been] to offer critique of actions set in train by others. My view is that our own present is a time when critique is no longer enough, and in fact it is no longer the real issue; the real issue is that of the proposal of alternative visions; reviving that unfashionable genre of the utopia, and acting strongly in contesting, in public life, alternatives that do not offer the values that I, you, we believe should shape our tomorrow" (xi). Analysis, critique, and production are distinct skills and processes, but all three are necessary and crucial aspects of a complete education in English studies.

The next keyword in the proposed functional definition of English studies is *discourse*. There is a well-known passage in Burke's *The Philosophy of Literary Form* that describes discourse as a conversation or, better yet, an argument. Burke writes,

> Imagine that you enter a parlor. You come late. When you arrive, others have long preceded you, and they are engaged in a heated discussion, a discussion too heated for them to pause and tell you exactly what it is about. In fact, the discussion had already begun long before any of them got there, so that no one present is qualified to retrace for you all the steps that had gone before. You listen for a while, until you decide that you have caught the tenor of the argument; then you put in your oar. Someone answers; you answer him; another comes to your defense; another aligns himself against you, to either the embarrassment or gratification of your opponent, depending upon the quality of your ally's assistance. However, the discussion is interminable. The hour grows late, you must depart. And you do depart with the discussion still vigorously in progress. (110–11)

This notion of discourse, then, implies that language is never static; it is always part of a larger process or set of processes. While it is possible to study language as a product (i.e., synchronically), we must always keep in mind the dynamic nature of language and discourse.

The last keyword, *social context*, is crucial to a full and productive understanding of English studies that has the potential for relevance outside of academia. In 1923, C. K. Ogden and I. A. Richards published *The Meaning of Meaning,* a landmark volume on language, thought, and symbolism that was popular among literary critics before World War II. This book contained a "supplementary essay" by renowned anthropologist Bronislaw Malinowski. In this essay, titled "The Problem of Meaning in Primitive Languages," Malinowski explains that the languages of primitive cultures are comprehensible only in social context;

thus, the anthropologist must not only provide literal translations of primitive language, but also "free" translations that provide the English "sense" of the language, and also (most important) a description of the social activities that surround the language and give it meaning. Just over a decade later, Malinowski would admit that context infuses language with meaning in all cultures, not just primitive ones (Halliday and Hasan 7–8). Similarly, in "Context and Thought," Dewey claims that philosophy has lost its meaning and significance because it ignores the social context in which thought takes place and to which it applies. Any utterance is meaningless outside the constraining purview of a specific context; context imbues utterances with meaning. I believe that literary studies, as the sole representative of English, ignores the broader context of English studies, and thus lacks the significant meaning imbued by that broader context.

The dual processes of specialization and expansion have transformed English studies into a "contact zone" of epic proportions. A contact zone is a space of conflict in which different groups come into contact, usually under conditions of inequality and coercion (Pratt, "Arts" 34). For over a century now, English departments have been a space of conflict within which ideological and material struggles among the disciplines comprised by English studies have been marked by inequality and coercion. And the English studies curriculum has been the most contested space within the administrative structure of English departments. We may speak all we want about fusion and integration, but until the actual curriculum changes—until the path through which English studies students pass is made representative of the discipline as a whole—English studies will remain mired in colonializing discourses that suppress and marginalize crucial enterprises. How can this new definition of English studies translate into curriculum? This is a question that must not be overlooked for some very important reasons.

Graff highlights the politics of curriculum design: "[T]he curriculum is the major form of representation through which academic departments identify themselves to the world (or fail to do so)" ("Is There" 12). And Kress points out the ethics of curriculum:

> A curriculum is a design for a future social subject, and via that envisioned subject a design for a future society. That is, the curriculum puts forward knowledges, skills, meanings, values in the present which will be telling in the lives of those who experience the curriculum, ten or twenty years later. Forms of pedagogy experienced by children now in school suggest to them forms of social relations which they are encouraged to adopt, adapt, modify and treat as models. The curriculum, and its associated pedagogy, puts forward a set of cultural, linguistic and social resources which students have available as resources for their own transformation, in relation to which (among others) students constantly construct, reconstruct and transform their subjectivity. ("Representational" 16)

If it is the goal of the new English studies to prepare students for a full and meaningful existence both inside and outside of the classroom, and if we envision a world where literature is one of many important kinds of texts with which our students will have to contend, then some curricular reform is necessary, and I believe that integration is the best model for that reform.

But what about the English departments that have already experienced secession, that, for example, have no composition, linguistics, or English education courses or programs?[24] These departments must undergo a process of *re*integration. Yet it is simply not realistic (or even wise) to expect stand-alone composition or linguistics or English education programs to insert themselves back into the dominant administrative structure of literature-based English departments. There are at least three conditions that must be met for reintegration to succeed.

First, reintegration after secession must begin with a strong desire to join forces. If any party involved is apathetic about reintegration, then no significant bonds will (or should) be formed. The desire to reintegrate comes from what Burke calls identification, or the recognition that all of the disciplines making up English studies share in a greater context, some larger substance—they are consubstantial. When departments of literature (even when they call themselves departments of English) view their objects of study, their critical methodologies, and their social mission as indissolubly rooted in poetics alone (i.e., when literature faculty view themselves as sovereign heirs to the departmental throne), then, for the sake of all other disciplines in English studies, reintegration must not occur. But where identification is present and there is a desire to reintegrate, then reintegration leads to greater disciplinary coherence.

Second, reintegration must be based on the pursuit of a common goal, the analysis, critique, and production of discourse in social context. Competing goals, or a dominant goal defined by a single object of analysis, literature, will only result in the kind of divisiveness that leads to secession in the first place. Coexistence without any sense of common purpose breeds infighting that weakens English studies as a whole project, not just the individual departments where the battles are most severe. As we have seen in recent years, English programs that generate intense internal strife (SUNY Albany, for example) are easy fodder for conservative media that revel in making the discipline of English seem petty and narcissistic. Reintegration must be accompanied with a transcending sense of common purpose, a shared *telos* or goal, if it is to succeed without senseless marginalization or a damaging descent into trifling spats.

Third, reintegrated disciplines must create institutionally recognized bonds that are functional. Functional relationships emerge most productively from external, not internal, exigencies and motivations. Internal exigencies, such as the need for increased funding, lead to self-serving motives, for example regaining control over required first-year composition courses in order to increase a literature department's credit-hour production and fatten its purse. But functional relationships based on external exigencies require cooperation without the administrative connections that can enable domination. For example, a stand-alone writing program may join forces with English education to establish a National Writing Project site in response to a felt need to improve writing instruction at all levels of the local curriculum. A literacy crisis in a city or town might motivate linguists to join forces with critical theorists, seeking funding for a literacy center to teach the power of language to those who need it most. Literary critics might join forces with creative writers to establish a young authors' conference promoting literary culture and values throughout the state. Functional relationships like these lead to the cooperative search for new resources, not the self-interested allocation of existing funds that have led many disciplines to leave

English departments in search of more equitable administrative homes. National Writing Project sites, literacy centers, and young authors' conferences—just a few among dozens of possibilities—require a fundamental change in the ways the disciplines that constitute English studies are conceived, or, as Hall might say, "articulated."

But teachers and administrators are only a portion of our full audience. In order for *students* to rearticulate the "lorry" of English studies according to the demands of any given situation, they need instruction in all of the disciplines that it comprises. Functional relationships among these disciplines will lead to productive pedagogical relationships, and when these functional relationships are explored in different academic and public contexts, themes may emerge as a basis for a new English studies: pedagogy or public discourse, for example. Linguistics and discourse analysis, rhetoric and composition, creative writing, literature and literary criticism, critical theory and cultural studies, and English education will each, in its own way, contribute to the development of these themes, equipping students with tools they will need to be productive citizens of their own academic, professional, personal, and public communities.

English Studies: An Introduction to the Discipline(s) is our response to these felt needs. Throughout the remaining pages, readers will discover the important qualities and functions of English studies' constituent disciplines and explore the productive differences and similarities among them that make English studies worth learning about. Although the chapters in this book are arranged in a certain order, readers may approach the book as a kind of textbook or as a resource. Since each chapter is written mainly for nonspecialists, readers might begin with the chapters on disciplines they know the least about and progress toward other, more familiar chapters. Other readers, less familiar with English studies as a whole, might read the chapters in their present order. However readers choose to approach *English Studies: An Introduction to the Discipline(s)*, its editor and authors have three main goals in mind for the book.

Our first goal is the most crucial, yet also the most modest: to educate English studies practitioners (students, teachers, and administrators) about the intricacies of the composite disciplines that make up English studies. Students who understand the full scope of English studies and its disciplines will be better equipped to make informed choices about their plans for advanced studies or career options. Teachers who specialize in one English studies discipline will serve their students more effectively if they can make connections among the other disciplines. Administrators who are responsible for evaluating and rewarding diverse faculties will serve their departments more fairly if they are able to assess the work of every faculty member with real knowledge and without disciplinary bias.

The second goal of this book is to open up the possibility for identification among English studies practitioners. Few functional relationships can be formed if specialists do not inquire into (let alone respect) the other disciplines that make up English studies. Effective National Writing Project sites, interdisciplinary literacy centers, and young authors' conferences will not emerge unless every discipline in English studies comes to respect the creative energy, academic values, and public commitments of every other discipline in English studies. If English studies practitioners see in each chapter of this book a glimmer of common purpose among the constituent disciplines that make up the field (a glimmer not perceived before), then our second goal will have been achieved.

This book's third goal cannot be achieved within the confines of these pages, so we leave its fate in the hands of our readers. The third goal is to create a new attitude toward English studies, one that leads to the equal use of strengths from all of its composite disciplines to solve problems that are not only restricted to rooms with desks and chalkboards (or computers and whiteboards). English is useful. *English* is *use*ful. And we must learn to *use* it more fully to solve important problems. When we scan our dusty bookshelves, we do not see the material representations of our disciplines. Our books are not us. Disciplines are constituted in the ways that knowledge is generated, developed, used, and integrated—by people—into a larger system of knowledge whose concerns press beyond the narrow disciplinary scopes of linguistics or discourse analysis or rhetoric or composition or creative writing or literature or literary criticism or critical theory or cultural studies or English education. But, as I have argued, the first step in this difficult process is to understand each of the composite disciplines comprised by English studies, to respect their differences, and to strive for identification.

In Chapter 1, Ellen Barton describes the uneasy relationship between linguistics, or the scientific study of language, and the rest of the English studies disciplines, which are usually conceived as arts (not sciences). However, Barton finds common ground in discourse analysis, which examines the organization and implications of language use beyond the sentence level. In her own study of medical discourse, for example, Barton finds problematic differences between physicians' uses of "back-stage" discourse (honest and blunt) in diagnosis discussions with other physicians and "front-stage" discourse (vague and circuitous) in treatment consultations with their cancer patients. Some physicians, according to Barton, find it difficult to merge these different discourses, desiring not to destroy hope in seriously ill patients. As Barton points out, such studies, drawing on linguistics, rhetoric, cultural studies, and other disciplines, can have a significant influence on the understanding of the discourse of medicine and the ways in which physicians are trained to interact with patients.

Chapter 2 describes the formation of rhetoric and composition as a disciplinary force within English studies. Janice M. Lauer explains that while rhetoric was the cornerstone of education from antiquity through much of the nineteenth century, composition studies did not exist as a full discipline until its emergence in the 1960s. What fueled this emergence was composition's rediscovery of its old kin, rhetoric. With rhetoric as its new (or renewed) foundation, composition grew in scope and significance. Now, with dozens of journals, annual conferences, and abundant PhD programs in the field, rhetoric and composition is recognized as a critical enterprise in the whole project of English studies. No discipline can progress without practitioners who write clearly and argue forcefully for their view of the universe of English (or any other universe, for that matter).

Katharine Haake, in Chapter 3, takes us on two intertwining journeys, first, through her own experience as a struggling creative writer, and second, though the experience of creative writing as a struggling discipline in the context of English studies. Through its close relationship to literary studies and composition, and also with the establishment of respected workshops and seminars, creative writing has become a crucial discipline that highlights aesthetic production, enhancing students' experiences with literature and making them effective communicators.

In Chapter 4, Richard C. Taylor examines the history of literature and literary criticism in the context of the institutions that foster its development. Here Taylor takes on difficult issues, such as the literary canon and who belongs in it, periodicity and the politics of historical division, and the nature and function of literature itself.

Chapter 5, on critical theory and cultural studies, describes the development of certain critical methodologies, such as Marxism, new historicism, psychoanalysis, feminism, and multiculturalism, in the grassroots efforts of political activists. Amy J. Elias explains that these methods serve the interests of English studies practitioners generally, as new approaches to interpretation, and they also extend the scope of English studies beyond the literary canon and beyond the university.

Finally, Robert P. Yagelski describes in Chapter 5 the competing interests of English education, first, as a pragmatic discipline that trains teachers to maintain the social status quo in secondary education, and second, as a theoretical discipline that generates knowledge on the socially transformative possibilities of education generally. For Yagelski, education (at whatever level) produces social citizens, and in order for education to be a viable social institution, it must produce citizens who contribute to a sustainable future. English education is a more naturally integrated discipline than others in English studies, and, that being the case, this chapter serves as a fitting conclusion.

Each chapter of this book, then, is an argument for the value—the right to equal status—of each individual discipline among all English studies disciplines, yet it is also an argument for disciplinary integration. Although disciplinary sovereignty is cherished, no chapter argues in favor of total secession; although disciplinary knowledge is valued, no chapter argues for managerial control over all of English studies; although disciplinary integration is proposed, no chapter argues for a (re)turn to English generalists who teach anything and everything under the sun. If, through this book, readers who specialize (or want to specialize) in one discipline in English studies learn something about the intellectual value of, or find some common purpose with, other disciplines in English studies, then our first two goals will have been achieved. The third goal, however, remains (as I have said) in the hands of our readers.

Notes

1. In "An Identity Crisis?" Nancy A. Gutierrez writes, "we are at a disadvantage in lobbying for public resources if we cannot explain what we are, for it is clear that the larger public and even some of our own colleagues across our campuses have defined 'English departments' in ways that hurt us—either as narrowly ideological sites; as sites at which only rarefied, rather silly discussions occur; or as sites in which only such skills as writing and document production are taught, with no realization that those skills are grounded in theoretical constructs."

2. Less dramatic (though no less serious) declarations of crisis in English studies are also made by W. Jackson Bate, Peter Brooker, Graham Hough, Jonathan Brody Kramnick, Gunther Kress (*Writing*), Alan Sinfield, and Peter Widdowson. Richard Ohmann, interestingly, situates "English and the Humanities within the long, historical crisis of capitalism" (*Politics* 6).

3. In 1966, when the "relevance" of nearly every social institution in Europe and America was being called into question, Frank Kermode explained that "crisis is a way of thinking about one's moment, and not inherent in the moment itself" (345). Indeed, when we idealize the past and imagine a utopian future, how can the present be anything but a crisis? Kermode explains,

> When you read, as you must almost every passing day, that ours is the great age of crisis—technological, military, cultural—you may well simply nod and proceed calmly to your business; for this assertion, upon which a multitude of important books is founded, is nowadays no more surprising than the opinion that the earth is round. There seems to me to be some danger in this situation, if

only because such a myth, uncritically accepted, tends like prophesy to shape a future to confirm it. Nevertheless crisis, however facile the conception, is inescapably a central element in our endeavors toward making sense of our world. (339)

In the age of academic accountability, declaring a discipline to be in crisis is far more likely to result in radical budget cuts than radical intellectual change.

4. In "Theses on the Philosophy of History," Walter Benjamin describes an image that highlights the crucial intersection of history and progress:

A Klee painting named "Angelus Novus" shows an angel looking as though he is about to move away from something he is fixedly contemplating. His eyes are staring, his mouth is open, his wings are spread. This is how one pictures the angel of history. His face is turned to the past. Where we perceive a chain of events, he sees one single catastrophe which keeps piling wreckage upon wreckage and hurls it in front of his feet. The angel would like to stay, awaken the dead, and make whole what has been smashed. But a storm is blowing from Paradise; it has got caught in his wings with such violence that the angel can no longer close them. This storm irresistibly propels him into the future to which his back is turned, while the pile of debris before him grows skyward. This storm is what we call progress. (257–58)

5. In *What Is English?* Elbow writes, "it's only a recent development for English departments to define themselves as departments of literature. We descend from departments of rhetoric" (95). And in "Overwork/Underpay," Robert Connors explains that "Rhetoric as a college-level discipline entered the nineteenth century as one of the most respected fields in higher education" (181).

6. For a detailed history of the development of English studies before the rise of the modern university, see Thomas P. Miller's *The Formation of College English.*

7. Dewey writes, "Like the similar conception of a fixed and obvious gulf between the elect and the unregenerated, it cannot stand the pressure of the free communication and interaction of modern life. It is no longer possible to hug complacently the ideal that the academic teacher is perforce devoted to high spiritual ideals, while the doctor, lawyer, and man of business are engaged in the mercenary pursuit of vulgar utilities" (*Educational* 309).

8. Andresen writes,

> The development and codification of American anthropology clearly
> plays a role in the history of American linguistics in that, with the
> separation of the arcs of development, a field known as "linguistic
> anthropology" must be carved out as something distinct from "lin-
> guistics" with no qualifying adjective. With the progressive disman-
> tling of the political conception of language, which had built in the
> language-nation intersection, and with the concomitant rise of the
> mechanical conception of language, which became coextensive with
> the field of "linguistics," the concept of "nation" shifted disciplin-
> ary ground from language studies to anthropology. (170)

9. "By the end of the century," Sampson writes, "the data for historical
linguistics came to seem a mere assembly of sound-shifts which had
occurred for no good reason and which tended in no particular direction [. . .]. Now it really did begin to seem fair to regard these scholars
as mere antiquarians studying individual quirks of particular languages
for their own sake, rather than as serious scientists" (33).

10. Connors points out that speech communication maintained its ties
to the rhetorical tradition, which composition did not, and this simple
historical fact had a lot to do with speech communication's subsequent
success and composition's continued marginalization:

> Rhetorical history never died, but the bulk of the work done there
> from the 1920s through the 1940s was the effort of scholars in the
> relatively new field of speech communication. Unlike composi-
> tionists, speech rhetoricians had never severed their ties to the his-
> tory of rhetoric, and they were thus able to grid historical
> methodologies onto their work in ways immediately recognizable
> as scholarly. As a result, speech departments had established the
> legitimacy of their discipline and were granting their own doctor-
> ates a scant decade after declaring the secession of speech teachers
> from the National Council of Teachers of English in 1914. They
> were speaking a language the rest of the academy could understand
> and accredit. ("Composition" 407)

11. Writing a few years after Hough, and clearly echoing his indignant
tone, Douglas Bush writes,

> Displaying our usual emotional instability, we had an immediate
> wave of zeal for the despised egghead, for "crash programs" in
> science. It would all be rather comic if it were not tragic. The first
> large specific consequence was the government's program for fi-

nancial aid for scientific education. This was not based on any concern for science but only on fear of Russia; astrology or alchemy would have got the same support if they could have helped in the arms race. So, in the middle of the twentieth century, the chief end of American education is the training of military engineers, and our nearest approach to the angels is by way of missiles and spaceships. (182)

12. Patrick Brantlinger writes, "no text contains meanings the way an apple contains seeds; meanings are generated in communicative relations; the understanding of a text always relies on what lies beyond it, on contexts, including 'the reader'" (22).

13. It is important to note that in late-nineteenth-century Europe, the word *studies* had been added to *English* by philologists in order to *restrict* this unwieldy and haphazard subject into a more specific and credible one (the scientific *study*, as opposed to the aesthetic *appreciation*, of language and literature). In America, however, the word *studies* was added to *English* much later, following the social revolutions of the 1960s, to represent an *expanding* notion of what it means to study English.

14. Bush writes, "it was no doubt inevitable that the immense growth of modern knowledge should lead to subdivision and specialization, but it was no less inevitable that such specialization should be in many ways disastrous" (173).

15. In their introduction to *Redrawing the Boundaries*, Stephen Greenblatt and Giles Gunn attribute specialization in English studies to "changes in the underlying organization of knowledge that defines the discipline" (2). Greenblatt and Gunn write,

> As the parameters of individual historical fields have been redrawn and new theoretical and methodological orientations have been devised, the possibility of a unifying, totalizing grasp of our own subject has, for all but the very few, receded [. . .]. In the face of new pressures of professionalization, the global generalities and disciplinary distinctions that once held departments together are coming to seem less meaningful. We are fast becoming a profession of specialties and subspecialties whose rapid formation and re-formation prevent many members from keeping abreast of significant developments even in their own areas of expertise. (2–3)

16. Most of us will recognize the following dates as periodic divisions for British literature:

Unknown–428, the Celtic and Roman period, which ends when the Germanic tribes invade Celtic Britain;

428–1100, the Old English period, which ends with the conclusion of the First Crusade and the beginning of the reign of Henry I;

1100–1350, the Anglo-Norman period, which ends during the early part of the Hundred Years' War and with the waning of the Black Plague;

1350–1500, the Middle English period, which ends during the reign of Henry VII, the first Tudor king, and with the publication of *Everyman;*

1500–1660, the Renaissance period, which ends near the completion of Shakespeare's Globe theater;

1660–1798, the Neoclassical period, which ends with the "Triumph of Romanticism";

1798–1870, the Romantic period, which ends a year before the publication of Darwin's *Descent of Man;*

1870–1914, the Realistic period, which ends with the beginning of World War I;

1914–1965, the Modernist period, which ends with the social revolutions of the 1960s;

1965–present, the postmodernist period, is still with us.

These dates and period titles are taken from the "Outline of Literary History" in C. Hugh Holman's *Handbook to Literature*, fourth edition, which I purchased during the early 1980s while an undergraduate English education major at Illinois State University. Although there may be some discussion about the beginning and ending dates of certain periods, and other periods may be further divided, there is rarely any discussion about the institutional *practice* (let alone the politics) of periodizing literature.

The practice of periodizing literature began in the late nineteenth century. As all of the disciplines in the new modern universities were dividing into more and more specialized subdisciplines, the philologists, who dominated English departments at the time, followed suit. It is crucial to remember that these philologists were not interested in literature *per se,* or in the aesthetic experience of reading it; they were scientists interested in the intricacies of language change over time, and literature was their object of analysis because it had been consistently recorded and, more than any other texts, had survived the ravages of

time. The first and third periods in British literary history, then, were established and named, not because of any unique *literary* qualities of the writing produced during that time, but because the *language* of the literature was dominated by different national influences: Celtic and Roman influences in the first period and Anglo-Norman influences in the third. The dates of the Old English period were established because of the Germanic *linguistic* influences on the language of the time, not because the *literary* qualities of the language shifted. And the Middle English period is different from the Old English period, again, because the languages (not necessarily the literatures) are significantly different:
    Old English, from *The Vercelli Book* ("The Dream of the Rood"):

> Hwæt, ič swefna cyst secgan wille
> Behold, I desire to tell the best of dreams

Middle English, from *The South English Legendary* (Prologue) (pronounce þ as *th*):

> Nou blouweþ þe niwe frut þat late bygan to springe
> Now bloweth the new fruit that late began to spring

Once divided, the periods stuck, though the ways in which the periods were explained soon shifted. As the philologists seceded to anthropology departments and literary critics again rose to power in English, these critics maintained the early philological period dates but began to explain them as shifts in *literary* and *aesthetic* (no longer linguistic) qualities.

17. David B. Downing argues,

> While the strict processes of disciplining have become the quintessential measure of academic value, the institutionalized protocols for disciplinary practices often exclude or delimit a significant range of socially valuable intellectual labor. This is especially the case for certain activities many English practitioners perform: research or teaching that focuses on ameliorating the local needs of specific groups of people, process-oriented work, research that does not narrowly define objects of investigation, work that engages rhetorical modes other than expository argumentation, or writing for broad audiences through publication in nonacademic magazines and books. (26)

18. Downing points out that

> Within English departments, one of the key points of contact for the exercise of disciplinary power takes place through evaluation

and hiring committees and the particular criteria they deploy to make crucial personnel decisions. Disciplinary evaluation criteria become measures of competitive individualism as colleagues strive to acquire symbolic capital primarily through their publications and other forms of acceptable labor. Without significant alteration, disciplinarity both discourages and devalues the kind of collaboration necessary for many of the diverse forms of rhetorical, political, and intellectual work that English professors actually perform. Without considerable study of how to alter our evaluation practices, disciplinary criteria reign in powerful de facto ways. (32)

19. For critiques of problems relating to incoherent intellectual labor and the oppressive contingent labor force in English studies, particularly in literature and composition, see Bérubé (*Employment*); Graff (*Beyond*, *Clueless*, and *Professing*); Nelson; Schell; Schell and Stock; Shumway and Dionne; Sosnoski; and Williams.

20. Many of the most recent secessions of rhetoric and writing programs from English departments are chronicled in Peggy O'Neill, Angela Crow, and Larry W. Burton's edited collection *A Field of Dreams: Independent Writing Programs and the Future of Composition Studies*. And in an *ADE Bulletin* article titled "After Composition," Karyn Z. Sproles, then chair of the English department at James Madison University, describes her own experience of rhetoric and composition's secession from the perspective of literary studies.

21. Ohmann's critique of composition was based, by the way, on a group of 1965 first-year English textbooks, not on the interesting work that was starting to be published in the field's professional journals. The 1996 reissue of *English in America* includes revised and new sections that argue for the full disciplinary status of previously marginalized fields such as rhetoric and composition.

22. Interestingly, the problem that Ohmann (in his 1976 text) and Fish represent for English studies (i.e., valuing only literature and nothing else) is "generational" in many departments, including my own. Faculty members who were educated in English studies from the mid-1980s on (in my own department, this would include all of our assistant professors and most of our newer associate professors) have almost all taken graduate courses in composition theory and practice, often required as preparation for teaching assistantships, and they emerged into the discipline of English when composition was a thriving intellectual field. On the other hand, faculty members who were educated before the 1980s (more experienced associate and full professors, including, in my own case, the chair of my department) know nothing of composition's disci-

plinary status, since, in most cases, their only encounter with writing studies has been restricted to the first-year composition courses they occasionally have to teach (or successfully avoid teaching).

23. I want to make it clear that the exclusive focus on literature that Ohmann and Fish propose for English studies is *not* what North would call corporate compromise because there simply is no compromise involved. Literature, within this limited framework, is not a discipline that manages other disciplines; instead, for Ohmann and Fish, literature is the only important discipline, and the others are treated as cavities, as problems that could have been prevented long ago, but now they're here. The only solution? Drill.

24. This question was posed to me in an e-mail message from Amy Elias, author of the "Critical Theory and Cultural Studies" chapter in this book.

Works Cited

ACLS (American Council of Learned Societies). *Report of the Commission on the Humanities*. New York: ACLS, 1964.

Anderson, Benedict. *Imagined Communities: Reflections on the Origin and Spread of Nationalism*. 1983. Rev. ed. London: Verso, 1991.

Andresen, Julie Tetel. *Linguistics in America, 1769–1924: A Critical History*. London: Routledge, 1990.

Applebee, Arthur N. *Tradition and Reform in the Teaching of English: A History*. Urbana, IL: NCTE, 1974.

Aronowitz, Stanley, and Henry A. Giroux. *Education under Siege: The Conservative, Liberal, and Radical Debate over Schooling*. South Hadley, MA: Bergin, 1985.

Bate, W. Jackson. "The Crisis in English Studies." *Scholarly Publishing* 14 (1983): 195–212.

Benjamin, Walter. "Theses on the Philosophy of History." *Illuminations*. Trans. Harry Zohn. Ed. Hannah Arendt. London: Fontana, 1973. 253–64.

Berlin, James A. *Rhetorics, Poetics, and Cultures: Refiguring College English Studies*. Refiguring English Studies. Urbana, IL: NCTE, 1996.

Bérubé, Michael. *The Employment of English: Theory, Jobs, and the Future of Literary Studies*. New York: New York UP, 1998.

———. *Public Access: Literary Theory and American Cultural Politics*. New York: Verso, 1994.

Bloom, Allan. *The Closing of the American Mind: How Higher Education Has Failed Democracy and Impoverished the Souls of Today's Students*. New York: Simon, 1987.

Brantlinger, Patrick. *Crusoe's Footprints: Cultural Studies in Britain and America*. New York: Routledge, 1990.

Brooker, Peter. "Post-Structuralism, Reading and the Crisis in English." *Re-Reading English*. Ed. Peter Widdowson. London: Methuen, 1982. 61–76.

Burke, Kenneth. *The Philosophy of Literary Form: Studies in Symbolic Action*. 3rd ed. Berkeley: U of California P, 1973.

———. *A Rhetoric of Motives*. New York: Prentice, 1950.

Bush, Douglas. "Science and the Humanities." *Education in the Age of Science*. 1959. Ed. Brand Blanshard. Freeport, NY: Books for Libraries, 1971. 167–87.

Cain, William E. *The Crisis in Criticism: Theory, Literature, and Reform in English Studies*. Baltimore: Johns Hopkins UP, 1984.

Charlton, William. "Greek Philosophy and the Concept of an Academic Discipline." *History of Political Thought* 6 (1985): 47–61.

Cheney, Lynne V. *Telling the Truth: Why Our Culture and Our Country Have Stopped Making Sense—and What We Can Do about It*. New York: Simon, 1995.

Connors, Robert J. "Composition History and Disciplinarity." Ede and Lunsford 405–22.

———. "Overwork/Underpay: Labor and Status of Composition Teachers since 1880." Ede and Lunsford 181–98.

———. *Selected Essays of Robert J. Connors*. Ed. Lisa Ede and Andrea A. Lunsford. Boston: Bedford; Urbana, IL: NCTE, 2003.

———. "Writing the History of Our Discipline." Ede and Lunsford 202–20.

Cushman, Ellen. "Service Learning as the New English Studies." Downing, Hurlbert, and Mathieu 204–18.

Dewey, John. "Context and Thought." 1931. *John Dewey: The Later Works, 1925–1953.* Ed. Jo Ann Boydston. Vol. 6: 1931–1932. Carbondale: Southern Illinois UP, 1985. 3–21.

———. *The Educational Situation.* 1901. *John Dewey: The Middle Works, 1899–1924.* Ed. Jo Ann Boydston. Vol. 1: 1899–1901. Carbondale: Southern Illinois UP, 1976. 257–313.

———. "Pedagogy as a University Discipline." 1898. *John Dewey: The Early Works, 1882–1898.* Ed. Jo Ann Boydston. Vol 5: 1895–1898. Carbondale: Southern Illinois UP, 1972. 281–89.

Downing, David B. "Beyond Disciplinary English: Integrating Reading and Writing by Reforming Academic Labor." Downing, Hurlbert, and Mathieu 23–38.

Downing, David B., Claude Mark Hurlbert, and Paula Mathieu, eds. *Beyond English, Inc.: Curricular Reform in a Global Economy.* Portsmouth, NH: Boynton, 2002.

"The Dream of the Rood." *The Vercelli Book.* Ed. George Philip Krapp. New York: Columbia UP, 1932. 61–65.

D'Souza, Dinesh. *Illiberal Education: The Politics of Race and Sex on Campus.* New York: Free, 1991.

Eagleton, Terry. "The End of English." *Textual Practice* 1 (1987): 1–9.

———. *Literary Theory: An Introduction.* 2nd ed. Minneapolis: U of Minnesota P, 1996.

Easton, David. "The Division, Integration, and Transfer of Knowledge." *Divided Knowledge: Across Disciplines, across Cultures.* Ed. David Easton and Corinne S. Schelling. Newbury Park, CA: Sage, 1991. 7–36.

Elbow, Peter. *What Is English?* New York: MLA; Urbana, IL: NCTE, 1990.

Fish, Stanley. "Them We Burn: Violence and Conviction in the English Department." Raymond 160–73.

Fowler, Roger. "Linguistic Theory and the Study of Literature." *Essays on Style and Language: Linguistic and Critical Approaches to Literary Style.* Ed. Fowler. London: Routledge, 1966. 1–28.

Franklin, Phyllis. "English Studies in America: Reflections on the Development of a Discipline." *American Quarterly* 30 (1978): 21–38.

Freeman, Donald C. "Linguistic Approaches to Literature." *Linguistics and Literary Style*. Ed. Donald C. Freeman. New York: Holt, 1970. 3–17.

Goggin, Maureen Daly. "The Tangled Roots of Literature, Speech Communication, Linguistics, Rhetoric/Composition, and Creative Writing: A Selected Bibliography on the History of English Studies." *Rhetoric Society Quarterly* 29 (1999): 63–88.

Graff, Gerald. *Beyond the Culture Wars: How Teaching the Conflicts Can Revitalize American Education*. New York: Norton, 1992.

———. *Clueless in Academe: How Schooling Obscures the Life of the Mind*. New Haven: Yale UP, 2003.

———. "Is There a Conversation in This Curriculum? Or, Coherence without Disciplinarity." Raymond 11–28.

———. *Professing Literature: An Institutional History*. Chicago: U of Chicago P, 1987.

Greenblatt, Stephen, and Giles Gunn. Introduction. *Redrawing the Boundaries: The Transformation of English and American Literary Studies*. Ed. Greenblatt and Gunn. New York: MLA, 1992. 1–23.

Gutierrez, Nancy. "An Identity Crisis?" *PMLA* 115 (2000): 1274.

Hall, Stuart. "On Postmodernism and Articulation: An Interview with Stuart Hall." Ed. Lawrence Grossberg. *Stuart Hall: Critical Dialogues in Cultural Studies*. Ed. David Morley and Kuan-Hsing Chen. London: Routledge, 1996. 131–50.

Halliday, M. A. K., and Ruqaiya Hasan. *Cohesion in English*. London: Longman, 1976.

Hayes, Curtis W. "Linguistics and Literature: Prose and Poetry." *Linguistics Today*. Ed. Archibald A. Hill. New York: Basic, 1969. 173–87.

Henry, George H. "What Is the Nature of English Education?" *English Education* 18 (1986): 4–41.

Higham, John. "The Matrix of Specialization." *The Organization of Knowledge in Modern America, 1860–1920*. Ed. Alexandra Oleson and John Voss. Baltimore: Johns Hopkins UP, 1979. 3–18.

Holman, C. Hugh. *A Handbook to Literature: Based on the Original Edition by William Flint Thrall and Addison Hibbard*. 4th ed. Indianapolis: Bobbs, 1980.

Hough, Graham. "Crisis in Literary Education." *Crisis in the Humanities.* Ed. J. H. Plumb. Baltimore: Penguin, 1964. 96–109.

Kermode, Frank. "The New Apocalyptists." *Partisan Review* 33 (1966): 339–61.

Kijinski, John L. "Securing Literary Values in an Age of Crisis: The Early Argument for English Studies." *English Literature in Transition, 1880–1920* 31 (1988): 38–52.

Kimball, Roger. *Tenured Radicals: How Politics Has Corrupted Our Higher Education.* New York: Harper, 1990.

Kramnick, Jonathan Brody. "Origins of the Present Crisis." *Profession 1997.* New York, MLA, 1997. 84–92.

Kress, Gunther. "Representational Resources and the Production of Subjectivity: Questions for the Theoretical Development of Critical Discourse Analysis in a Multicultural Society." *Texts and Practices: Readings in Critical Discourse Analysis.* Ed. Carmen Rosa Caldas-Coulthard and Malcolm Coulthard. New York: Routledge, 1996. 15–31.

———. *Writing the Future: English and the Making of a Culture of Innovation.* Sheffield, Eng.: National Association for the Teaching of English, 1995.

Kruisinga, E. "A Guide to English Studies." *English Studies* 7 (1925): 1–4.

Lauer, Janice. "The Spaciousness of Rhetoric." *Beyond Postprocess and Postmodernism: Essays on the Spaciousness of Rhetoric.* Ed. Theresa Enos and Keith D. Miller. Mahwah, NJ: Erlbaum, 2003. 3–21.

Leech, G. N. "Linguistics and the Figures of Rhetoric." *Essays on Style and Language: Linguistic and Critical Approaches to Literary Style.* Ed. Roger Fowler. London: Routledge, 1966. 135–56.

Levin, Harry. "Interpreting the Interpreters: The Crisis of Interpretation." *Teaching Literature: What Is Needed Now.* Ed. James Engell and David Perkins. Cambridge, MA: Harvard UP, 1988. 29–47.

Malinowski, Bronislaw. "The Problem of Meaning in Primitive Languages." *The Meaning of Meaning: A Study of the Influence of Language upon Thought and of the Science of Symbolism.* C. K. Ogden and I. A. Richards. New York: Harcourt, 1923. 296–336.

Miller, Thomas P. *The Formation of College English: Rhetoric and Belles Lettres in the British Cultural Provinces.* Pittsburgh: U of Pittsburgh P, 1997.

Moran, Joe. *Interdisciplinarity*. New York: Routledge, 2002.

Myers, D. G. *The Elephants Teach: Creative Writing since 1880.* Englewood Cliffs, NJ: Prentice, 1996.

Nelms, Ben. "Toward a New Professionalism: *English Education* in the Mid-1970s." *English Education* 28 (1996): 183–201.

Nelson, Cary. *Manifesto of a Tenured Radical*. New York: New York UP, 1997.

North, Stephen M., et al. *Refiguring the Ph.D. in English Studies: Writing, Doctoral Education, and the Fusion-Based Curriculum.* Refiguring English Studies. Urbana, IL: NCTE, 2000.

Ogden, C. K., and I. A. Richards. *The Meaning of Meaning: A Study of the Influence of Language upon Thought and of the Science of Symbolism.* New York: Harcourt, 1923.

Ohmann, Richard. *English in America: A Radical View of the Profession.* New York: Oxford UP, 1976.

———. *Politics of Letters*. Middleton, CT: Wesleyan UP, 1987.

O'Neill, Peggy, Angela Crow, and Larry W. Burton, eds. *A Field of Dreams: Independent Writing Programs and the Future of Composition Studies.* Logan: Utah State UP, 2002.

Parker, William Riley. "Where Do English Departments Come From?" *College English* 28 (1967): 339–51.

Pradl, Gordon M. "Democracy and *English Education*." *English Education* 28 (1996): 217–23.

Pratt, Mary Louise. "Arts of the Contact Zone." *Profession 1991*. New York: MLA, 1991. 33–40.

———. *Toward a Speech-Act Theory of Literary Discourse.* Bloomington: Indiana UP, 1977.

Raymond, James C., ed. *English as a Discipline: Or, Is There a Plot in This Play?* Tuscaloosa: U of Alabama P, 1996.

———. "The Play's the Thing: English as Theater." Introduction. Raymond 1–10.

Sampson, Geoffrey. *Schools of Linguistics*. Stanford: Stanford UP, 1980.

Schell, Eileen E. *Gypsy Academics and Mother-Teachers: Gender, Contingent Labor, and Writing Instruction.* Portsmouth, NH: Boynton, 1997.

Schell, Eileen E., and Patricia Lambert Stock, eds. *Moving a Mountain: Transforming the Role of Contingent Faculty in Composition Studies and Higher Education*. Urbana, IL: NCTE, 2001.

Scholes, Robert. *Textual Power: Literary Theory and the Teaching of English*. New Haven: Yale UP, 1985.

Shumway, David R., and Craig Dionne, eds. *Disciplining English: Alternative Histories, Critical Perspectives*. Albany: SUNY P, 2002.

Sinfield, Alan. "Literary Theory and the 'Crisis' in English Studies." *Critical Quarterly* 25 (1983): 35–48.

Small, Ian, and Josephine Guy. "English in Crisis?" *Essays in Criticism* 39 (1989): 185–95.

Sosnoski, James J. *Token Professionals and Master Critics: A Critique of Orthodoxy in Literary Studies*. Albany: SUNY P, 1994.

The South English Legendary. Ed. Charlotte D'Evelyn and Anna J. Mill. London: Oxford UP, 1967.

Sproles, Karyn Z. "After Composition: Using Academic Program Review to Redefine Departmental Identity and Create Community." *ADE Bulletin* 127 (2001): 23–26.

Warnock, Tilly. "Making Do, Making Believe, and Making Sense: Burkean Magic and the Essence of English Departments." Raymond 143–59.

Widdowson, Peter. "The Crisis in English Studies." Introduction. *Re-Reading English*. Ed. Peter Widdowson. London: Methuen, 1982. 1–14.

Williams, Jeffrey J., ed. *The Institution of Literature*. Albany: SUNY P, 2002.

CHAPTER ONE

Linguistics and Discourse Analysis

ELLEN BARTON
Wayne State University

Disciplines are entwined and entangled in intellectual, curricular, social, and political ways, as described by Ellen Messer-Davidow, David Shumway, and David Sylvan:

> [W]e are disciplined by our disciplines. First, they help produce our world. They specify the objects we can study and the relations that obtain among them. They provide criteria for our knowledge (truth, significance, impact) and methods (quantification, interpretation, analysis) that regulate our access to it. Second, disciplines produce practitioners, orthodox and heterodox, specialist and generalist, theoretical and experimental [. . .]. Third, disciplines produce economies of value. They manufacture discourse in abundance [. . .]. They provide jobs [. . .]. They secure funding [. . .]. They generate prestige [. . .]. Finally, disciplines produce the idea of progress [. . .]. They tell stories of progress, showing how knowledge advances within existing disciplines and by the establishment of new ones. (vii–viii)

Disciplines and their relations can be paradoxical, as in the case we will examine here—linguistics, discourse analysis, and English studies.

On the one hand, linguistics is emphatic in representing its disciplinary autonomy and relations. For well over a century, it has defined itself as the science of language, presenting what Messer-Davidow, Shumway, and Sylvan call a story of progress. John Joseph writes,

> [The history of linguistics] is the gradual realignment of the study of language away from moral science, philosophy, aesthetics, rhetoric, and philology, and in the direction of the natural sci-

ences—first botany, biology, chemistry, and comparative anatomy; and finally physics, by way of mathematics [. . .]. [F]or linguists progress came to be equated with scientificization [. . .]. In other words, progress was defined as the acquisition of autonomous status for linguistic science. ("Trends" 221)

As we will see, linguists aggressively seek to maintain their disciplinary autonomy in intellectual and curricular ways in the terms of the rhetoric of science. On the other hand, when we follow Messer-Davidow, Shumway, and Sylvan to consider the economies of value in linguistics, we find the following paradoxical social and political (and potentially intellectual and curricular) situation: in the contemporary American university, at least one-third of linguistics programs are headquartered in or are otherwise closely connected to English departments (Reynolds). Full disciplinary autonomy, at least as measured by the currency of departmental status, has eluded the field as a whole. My own situated context is a case in point: the linguistics program at Wayne State University is an independent and interdisciplinary degree-granting program, with its own curriculum and degrees (a BA and an MA in linguistics), but the core faculty—that is, those who routinely teach the required curriculum in the undergraduate and graduate program—have their faculty lines in the Department of English. Many linguists explain this paradox away in superficial ways: linguistics is a small discipline that sometimes still resides in historically remaindered and intellectually incompatible places, but the ideal for linguistics is departmental status. As anecdotal evidence, I can point to an event at a neighboring institution—the two-day 2001 Celebration Symposium held by the University of Michigan in honor of linguistics' return to departmental status after a short and unhappy demotion to an interdisciplinary program.

The English department, then, is indeed an attic for some linguists looking out at the greener grass of a linguistics department. Graduate students are routinely advised to "write their way" out of English departments or interdisciplinary programs and into linguistics departments, where the theoretical atmosphere is not "tainted," as one colleague once said to me. For other linguists, though, English departments have become comfortable homes, although the extent to which they participate in disciplinary conversations varies. In this chapter, I look at some of the ways in which linguistics and discourse analysis have made themselves at home in English departments, joining the conversation of English studies and bringing some of this conversation back to linguistics. To do so, I provide a brief disciplinary look at contemporary linguistics and argue for some ways I have found linguistics, discourse analysis, and English studies to interact in intellectually productive ways for research and teaching: my experience leads me to argue that linguistics provides a substantive and robust theory of language as an object of study and offers discourse analysis as an empirical method for describing the organization of language in context; English studies provides an equally substantive and robust understanding of discourses as configurations of power and knowledge and offers a range of interpretive and critical methods for theorizing discourses. I make this argument by considering a recent investigation of my own on the topic of prognosis in the discourse of medicine, showing how linguistic discourse analysis can be enriched through the theorizing practices of English studies.

Linguistics in a Disciplinary Sense

Some historians argue that the origin of contemporary linguistics can be dated in Europe to 1916, with the publication of Ferdinand de Saussure's *Cours de Linguistique Générale,* and in America to roughly the same time period, with the publication of Franz Boas's *Handbook of American Indian Languages* in 1911 and Edward Sapir's *Language* in 1921. Others suggest that contemporary linguistics should be dated somewhat later in America—to 1933, with the publication of Leonard Bloomfield's *Language,* or to 1957, with the publication of Noam Chomsky's *Syntactic Structures.*[1]

Saussure broadened the attention of the field to encompass synchronic as well as diachronic linguistics, in other words, the study of languages in their contemporary forms as well as in their historical development. Saussure developed the theoretical framework of structuralism in order to conceptualize the linguistic sign (i.e., the word) in terms of *langue* (the system of language) and *parole* (an instance of speech). *Langue* is the framework of the linguistic system of a language at a synchronic point in time, where signs acquire their meaning and use through contrast with other signs (consider, for example, the subtly different meanings of different members of the modal system of English, which ranges across *must, may, might, can, could, will, would, shall,* and *should;* each member in this set is defined in terms of the other members of the set). Langue, roughly speaking, is a system that resides in the minds of speakers, their linguistic knowledge, so to speak. *Parole* is an individual act of speech, which is always anchored in a social context, a particular time and place. Saussure likened langue and parole to a symphony—langue is the score that stays constant, parole is an individual performance of that score, with a certain amount of variation. To look ahead to the arguments later in this chapter, Saussure draws attention to the ways in which language is a structure with both cognitive and social dimensions.

In America, at roughly the same time, the work of Boas and Sapir turned the attention of linguistics to the need for learning and describing the rapidly disappearing indigenous languages of native America. Boas and Sapir were founding figures in linguistic and cultural anthropology, developing field methods for learning and describing languages that existed only in oral form and for studying the interaction of language and culture by participating in the life of a group. The linguistic description of native American languages enriched the field of linguistics immensely by highlighting the structural diversity of languages in the world: native American languages were shown to use a previously unknown variety of sounds, word formations, and grammatical constructions, challenging uninformed assumptions about the linguistic superiority of better-known European languages. More controversially, when Benjamin Lee Whorf, a student of Sapir's, considered the implications of this structural diversity of languages in terms of thought, culture, and worldview, he formulated what has come to be called the Sapir-Whorf hypothesis, which holds that, to a greater or lesser extent, the structure of a language (its system of color terms, for example) shapes the worldview of its users (the concept of color for speakers of a particular language).

Although the Sapir-Whorf hypothesis has been debated extensively and discredited in its simplest form of linguistic determinism (that language *determines* thought), the question of linguistic relativism (that language *influences* thought) is regarded as an open question in linguistics, and it draws attention to the ways in which language is intricately interrelated with thought as well as culture, again pointing to the nature of language as a cognitive and social object (Lucy; Gumperz and Levinson).

With a similar focus on the diversity of structure across languages and on the importance of describing disappearing languages, Bloomfield developed a set of rigorous methods for the description of languages. Bloomfield's approach to linguistics has been termed structuralist because its methods were meant to develop a grammar of a language by progressing through its structural levels in order to build a description moving up from sounds (phonetics and phonology) to words (morphology) to sentences (syntax) and discourse (extended stretches of language). Within structuralist methods, the levels of language and the order of analysis were assumed to be autonomous and absolute: the description of the sound system of a language was primary, and its analysis was to take place without reference to the morphological system of word construction, the syntactic system of sentence grammar, or the relations among sentences in discourse. This methodological progression focused linguistics primarily upon phonological and morphological analysis, only rarely progressing to the syntactic analysis of languages or to the investigation of discourse, and this progression also led to a strong reluctance to study meaning (semantics) as a part of the analysis of languages. Bloomfield is famous for noting that the ability of linguistics to study meaning scientifically was doubtful, if not impossible (139). These methodological constraints came from Bloomfield's use of the reigning theoretical framework in psychology at the time—stimulus-response behaviorism, which followed a very strong form of empiricism (an approach that, roughly speaking, holds that findings in research must be based on direct observation and on defined procedures for formulating generalizations).

In the late 1950s, Chomsky challenged both the theoretical framework of behaviorism and the lack of focus on syntax and semantics in linguistic analysis. In 1959, he published a scathing review of B. F. Skinner's *Verbal Behavior,* a volume meant to be a comprehensive treatment of language within behaviorism. In what is still regarded as an intellectual *tour de force,* Chomsky argued that behaviorism is incapable of providing a theory or description of language, particularly its acquisition, because language is not learned by imitation, correction, stimulus-response, or any of the other constructs of behaviorism. Instead, Chomsky argued in his review and in other early publications, including *Syntactic Structures* and *Aspects of the Theory of Syntax,* that language acquisition must be explained as a part of human cognition and development, and, further, that the description of this cognition and its development is the proper object of study for the field of linguists. Linguistic theory, in other words, goes beyond the description of individual languages to describe the principles universal to human language in general and to explain how the variation of particular languages can be predicted and explained on the basis of these principles, sometimes called universal grammar. Linguistic theory, in this sense, is a tightly knit set of abstract generalizations that interact to predict properties of the grammars of individual languages. In this view, the grammars of particular languages are rule-based: the rules of a language are deeply internalized and highly abstract generalizations worked out in the process of language acquisition.[2]

An example of this interaction between linguistic theory and grammars of languages is word order. Some languages (English, for example) structure their sentences with a subject-verb-object order, but other languages use different word orders: Japanese, for instance, structures sentences with a subject-object-verb order. No native speaker, especially a child learning language, is ever consciously directed to follow this rule or even positively reinforced for imitating this structure, as behaviorism would have it. No one tells a toddler learning English, for example, "Now the rule is to put the object after the verb; obey it, and apply that to the order of preposition-object, too." Nor is the opposite version of this rule told to toddlers learning Japanese. Children learning language are neither explicitly praised nor reinforced for getting the structure of a verb phrase or prepositional phrase correct (toddlers receive many compliments, but usually not ones that praise the specific order of words in a verb phrase). But every native speaker internalizes the word order rules for the language(s) that he or she speaks, and uses these rules again and again to produce and understand new phrases, clauses, and sentences. Within this view, the principles of linguistic theory predict and describe the clustering of word order properties in language (for example, that languages where the object follows the verb will also have objects following prepositions, or vice versa), while the rules for languages set the particular order (for example, that the order is subject-verb-object in English or subject-object-verb in Japanese). In generative linguistics, the interaction of principles of linguistic theory and the rules of grammars has far-reaching consequences, such as the differences between a language like English and a language like Potowatomi, Swahili, Inuit, or Japanese.

Within this theory of the interaction of linguistics as a description of language in general and grammars as a description of the rules of particular languages, the place of syntax and semantics (sentence structure and meaning) is central to the construction of the grammar of a language. Chomsky called this kind of grammar a generative grammar, because its task, so to speak, is to generate all of the sentences in a language that are grammatical, and only those sentences. Based on principles of linguistic theory, a grammar consists of the abstract rules of language that describe speakers' linguistic competence, that is, their ability to produce and understand novel sentences that they have never heard or uttered before. It is important to note here that both the principles of linguistic theory and the abstract rules of grammar are both predictive and falsifiable: in linguistic theory, principles can be falsified if they make inaccurate predictions about the properties of languages; in grammars, rules can be falsified if they make incorrect predictions about the grammaticality of the sentences they generate. In other words, if a rule predicts that a sentence is grammatical when it is judged ungrammatical by native speakers, the rule must be modified; and if a grammatical sentence cannot be generated by the rules of the grammar, the grammar must be modified. Linguists like to sum up this sense of the relationship between theory-building and grammar construction with the saying, "That's an empirical question." In other words, a theoretical construct or a grammatical rule must be formulated and tested with data; data, in turn, consist of native speakers' judgments of grammaticality. In contrast to the structuralist grammar of Bloomfield, this was a radical reconceptualization of linguistic theory, grammatical description, and linguistic analysis, but, Chomsky and others were careful to point out, one that was aligned with other kinds of scientific theorizing in abstract fields such as physics and mathematics.

Like Saussure, Chomsky established a distinction between language as a cognitive object and the use of language on a specific occasion. Although the terms are not precisely the same in definition, Saussure's *langue* and *parole* are similar to Chomsky's *competence* and *performance*. In generative linguistics, competence is defined as the ability of a native speaker to produce and understand new utterances in his or her language; under this view, competence is a cognitive construct, one that is the central focus of research in the field. Further, competence is defined primarily as autonomous; that is, in this view, the structure of language is not driven by external factors such as the functions of communication or the sociocultural context of speakers and languages. Chomsky's distinction between competence and performance, however, as well as his focus on an autonomous competence as the primary object of study in the field, was immediately and vigorously challenged by linguists developing competing theories of grammar as well as emerging fields and areas within linguistics. In grammar, for instance, linguists such as M. A. K. Halliday began to argue that the structure of language is not primarily cognitive and autonomous but is a closer interaction between structure and the various social and communicative functions language performs. Recent work in pragmatics, the study of the interaction of grammar and context, has argued for the concept of pragmatic intrusion, defined as the ways that the grammar necessarily incorporates contextual information, including deixis and reference, speech acts and intentionality, and inference and interpretation (see Levinson; work in linguistic pragmatics followed early work on natural language philosophy by Austin and Searle). In emerging fields like sociolinguistics, researchers also argued against the assumption of a distinct separation between competence and performance: William Labov

conducted pioneering studies of dialectal variation with respect
to social dimensions such as age, gender, ethnicity, and class and
claimed that language is inextricably bound up in the social context of its speakers. Continuing work in linguistic anthropology,
Dell Hymes coined the term *communicative competence* to describe speakers' ability to use language appropriately in sociocultural situations ("Models"); this concept became central to
the emerging field of discourse analysis, which looks at the intricate ways in which extended stretches of language are organized
within social and cultural contexts. In sociolinguistics, linguistic
anthropology, and discourse analysis, work focuses on the complexities of language as a social object.

At the same time that fields like sociolinguistics and discourse
analysis were emerging as areas of linguistics that investigated
language in use, the field of applied linguistics also began to draw
upon research in contemporary linguistics. *Applied linguistics* is
a term that has been in use to refer to language teaching since the
1940s, but is defined today more broadly as the use of linguistics
in addressing specific areas and problems in real-world communication (AILA). The central area in applied linguistics is second
language learning and teaching, including English as a Second
Language (ESL) as well as foreign language teaching in general,
but applied linguistics also investigates a variety of other theoretical and applied topics, conducting research on second language acquisition, bilingualism, and language loss (see the journal
Applied Linguistics). Contemporary applied linguistics focuses
not only on language as a cognitive object but also as a social
object, and pedagogical practices in language teaching have shifted
from a primary focus on vocabulary, grammar, and error to a
focus on the cognitive processes involved in language learning
and the pedagogical processes involved in working toward the
effective use of language in a variety of social settings, including
classrooms and workplaces (see the overview essay by D. A.
Wilkins as well as the variety of recent handbooks in applied
linguistics, including Davies and Elder; Spolsky; Kaplan; and
Bhatia and Ritchie). Applied linguistics has developed a number
of specialized areas within language learning and teaching, including second language writing (Matsuda and Silva; see the *Journal of Second Language Writing*), and English as a research

language (Swales and Feak; see the journal *English for Specific Purposes*). Much of this work arose from a concern about the situation of many speakers of English as a second language who are working as researchers and graduate students who wish to (or have to) publish their work in English as the dominant language of academic research. Some research on academic writing uses discourse analysis as its primary methodology, and a seminal text here is John Swales's *Genre Analysis*, which looks at the general organization of the research article as well as the discipline-specific conventions that operate in fields as diverse as botany, psychology, and literary criticism across a variety of genres, including research articles as well as abstracts, posters, and dissertations. Other research on academic writing uses systemic linguistics as its theoretical and methodological framework (Halliday, *Introduction* and *Language*). In *Writing Science: Literacy and Discursive Power,* for example, Halliday and J. R. Martin look in great detail at the sentence-level conventions of writing in the sciences in order to explore its considerable social power. Other work in this area looks at academic discourse cross-linguistically: Ulla Connor's *Contrastive Rhetoric: Cross-Cultural Aspects of Second-Language Writing,* for example, compares the preferred conventions of presentation and persuasion across a variety of languages and cultures. Yet more work looks at second language writing in the classroom: Ann Johns looks at the genres of academic discourse in *Text, Role, and Context: Developing Academic Literacies* and in *Genre in the Classroom* (see also Belcher and Braine as well as Lauer, this volume).

What unites all of the stories of the discipline (told too briefly above) is that they all regard language as a complex structure, in the classic (or, if you prefer, the scientific) sense of structure: a structure consists of units or features and their interaction, described by rules, generalizations, or conventions; the structure of language consists of some number of interacting structural levels (at the least, phonology, morphology, syntax, semantics, and, arguably, discourse and pragmatics). A linguistic analysis, then, consists of identifying the units or features and formulating claims that describe their interaction within a level, as well as exploring the interaction of levels. Even at this moment in intellectual time, then, linguistics remains ardently structuralist. The core assumption of almost all linguists is that language simply cannot work if it is not a structure: the wonderful complexities of language, in its internal structure and in its intricate organization in an endless variety of social contexts, cannot operate to communicate, to work toward intersubjectivity, to form discourse or discourses, without the common basis of linguistic structure.

Within this view, contemporary linguistics can thus be characterized as the study of the structure of language as a cognitive and social object. This characterization, however, would not go unchallenged by many linguists, and the stories recounted above elide considerable internecine tensions, particularly with respect to the primacy and autonomy of language as a cognitive object, as assumed in generative linguistics, and the highly contested assumption that cognitive structure is primary in comparison to social function. A broader, though still controversial, characterization of the field might be to say that linguistics investigates language as both a cognitive and social object, viewing language as a set of structures and a variety of functions. Under this view, speakers have internalized both the rules of grammatical structure and the conventions that underlie the situated and communicative functions of language in context. Focus on the former leads to the study of language as a cognitive object; focus on the latter leads to the study of language as a social object; study of the interaction of cognitive and social aspects of language is one of the most controversial areas of linguistic research.[3]

Linguistics in an Interdisciplinary Sense

I wish now to consider another paradoxical way in which linguistics, particularly generative linguistics, is situated within the academy, this time with respect to funded research (another way to look at what Messer-Davidow, Shumway, and Sylvan term the economies of value situating a field). Linguistics with a focus on language as a cognitive object is funded through the National Science Foundation (NSF). The NSF Web site is organized according to scientific fields: "The National Science Foundation funds research and education in most fields of science and engineering [. . .]. Most NSF funding opportunities are divided into broad program areas: Biology; Computer and Information Sciences; Crosscutting Programs; Education; Engineering; Geosciences; International; Math, Physical Sciences; Polar Research; Science Statistics; [and] Social, Behavioral Sciences" (NSF, "About"). The linguistics program, housed within the Behavioral and Cognitive Sciences division of the Social, Behavioral, and Economic Sciences directorate of NSF,

> [s]upports scientific research of all types that focus on human language as an object of investigation. The program supports research on the syntactic, semantic, phonetic, and phonological properties of individual languages and of language in general; the psychological processes involved in the use of language; the development of linguistic capacities in children; social and cultural factors in language use, variation, and change; the acoustics of speech and the physiological and psychological processes involved in the production and perception of speech; and the biological bases of language in the brain. (NSF, "Linguistics")

This representation of disciplinarity follows the rhetoric of science straightforwardly: it identifies a specific object of study in the first sentence, and it divides that object of study into precisely defined areas in the rest of the description. Research in any of these areas would be presumed to follow shared methods in order to contribute to the disciplinary research literature. Contribution, significance, and value of research would be determined with respect to the ways it illuminates the object of study with the methods of the field. In this disciplinary statement, the predominance of language as a cognitive object is well-established: of six areas, five are cognitive and only one (social and cultural factors in language use) is social. Lore among linguists, especially those who investigate language as a social object, is that the NSF is not the place to go for projects that are at the "softer," less quantitative end of the continuum of investigations of language as a social object, such as projects in discourse analysis. My own experience is a case in point: when I talked to two different program officers at the NSF about work in the discourse analysis of interaction in medical encounters, I was told by both that the project would be problematic for funding because it did not seem to make an obvious contribution to theoretical linguistics. Although this was hard to hear, it is consistent with the enactment of a strong sense of disciplinarity in the field of linguistics and the way that the field carefully protects its priorities, particularly with respect to the dominance of the study of language as a cognitive object.

Fortunately, however, for those who investigate language primarily as a social object, the National Endowment for the Humanities (NEH) also funds projects in linguistics, reminding us of the paradoxical situatedness of the field, with fortunate effects with regard to funding. Linguistics is listed as one of the areas that the NEH funds:

> The act that established the National Endowment for the Humanities says, "The term 'humanities' includes, but is not limited to, the study of the following: language, both modern and classical; linguistics; literature; history; jurisprudence; philosophy; archaeology; comparative religion; ethics; the history, criticism, and theory of the arts; those aspects of social sciences which have humanistic content and employ humanistic methods; and the study and application of the humanities to the human environment with particular attention to reflecting our diverse heritage, traditions, and history and to the relevance of the humanities to the current conditions of national life." (NEH, "Who We Are")

But there are no separate sites for the disciplines of the humanities, as there are for the disciplines of science. Instead, the NEH Web site is organized in terms of broad programs and initiatives, presented in the rhetoric of the humanities, as in this excerpt from the Fellowship and Faculty Research Awards page, which is the main mechanism through which the NEH supports individual research projects:

> Fellowships and Faculty Research Awards support individuals pursuing advanced research in the humanities that contributes to scholarly knowledge or to the general public's understanding of the humanities. Recipients usually produce scholarly articles, monographs on specialized subjects, books on broad topics, archaeological site reports, translations, editions, or other scholarly tools [. . .]. Knowledgeable persons outside NEH will read each application and advise the agency about its merits. (NEH, "Fellowships")

If there are statements or definitions of objects of study here, they are by implication only, framed in the most general terms of scholarship (e.g., "advanced research," "scholarly knowledge") or in the careful exclusion of the nonhumanistic social sciences (in another place on the NEH Web site, projects that would be primarily pedagogical are also specifically excluded; see "Common Questions"). However, there are no definitive statements of the object(s) of study in the disciplines, nor any implications of agreed-upon methods for investigation or of recognized standards for assessing the contribution, significance, or value of research other than general statements about peer review. The site, in short, is not organized by disciplinarity and all that disciplinarity entails and implies in the rhetoric of science; instead, it is organized by initiatives and programs that cross broad swaths of scholarly effort, with what appears, nominally at least, to be an equal relationship between the contribution of research to knowledge and to the understanding and edification of the public. Incidentally, the lore among linguists is that the NEH most often funds reference and archival projects, particularly dictionaries, descriptive grammars, and collected materials of endangered languages; in this way, its funding represents a valuation of its origins as a historical field, connected with history as one of the central endeavors of the humanities.

Nevertheless, there are interdisciplinary opportunities in this situation, intellectual and curricular, specifically for linguists who are in departments and programs that have connections to both science and the humanities, linguists who might be, say, situated in departments of English and interested in the project that the editor of this volume, Bruce McComiskey, sets out for English studies defined as a complementarity of disciplines working together on the analysis, critique, and production of discourse in social context.

Such an endeavor is actually actively underway in many configurations. Literary stylistics is one of the oldest relations between linguistics and literature (Verdonk and Weber). More recently, discourse analysis has figured prominently in the formation and development of the field of composition-rhetoric (Barton and Stygall, "Linguistics and Composition"). Most recently, the emerging and interdisciplinary field of discourse studies has incorporated a variety of theories, methods, and areas of interest from both linguistics and English, including a great deal of attention to the emerging approach called critical discourse analysis (van Dijk, *Ideology;* Fairclough, *Critical* and *Language;* Hodge and Kress). Also, in a recent text entitled *Discourse Analysis,* Barbara Johnstone compares discourse analysis to close reading, making connections to both literary analysis and contemporary literary theory (see chapters by Richard Taylor and Amy Elias, this volume). To illustrate my own particular configuration of disciplinarity and interdisciplinarity in English studies, what I will do in the rest of this chapter is look at one of my own recent discourse studies projects, with the idea of explaining its formation, development, and implications in terms of linguistics, discourse analysis, and English studies.

One of my areas of research is the discourse of medicine. In the humanities, the language of medicine has also been an area of investigation in a variety of fields. One of the central works of theory in the humanities—Michel Foucault's *The Birth of the Clinic*—used medicine as an exemplar of the history and development of a professionalized discourse as a configuration of knowledge and power. In English studies, there is a small area on literature and medicine and a small body of research on literary features of the language of medicine, such as metaphor (Fleischman). In addition, medicine has a scholarly literature in history (Porter; Starr; Wells), anthropology (Kleinman, *Writing*), sociology (Mishler), and what is called the medical humanities (Brody; Cassell, *Place*; Katz; Kleinman, *Illness*). In linguistics, the language of medicine has been an object of investigation for over twenty years (Ainsworth-Vaughn), primarily using the methods of discourse analysis to investigate the interaction that takes place in a wide variety of medical encounters.

Discourse analysis, as noted above, investigates language primarily as a social object; in terms of a more specific object of study, discourse analysis describes the ways that extended stretches of language are structured and organized in sociocultural contexts. Take, as a simple example, the way greetings are organized in medical encounters: until fairly recently, it was typical for physicians to address patients, adults as well as children, with first names, while patients addressed physicians with titles plus last

names. This organization of language in context, or to use another expression, these discourse practices of greetings, are expressions that conventionally reflect the traditional social roles
and relationships in the medical encounter and create them anew
in each particular encounter. The asymmetry in greetings functions in several ways: the physician's professionalized role, with
its attendant expertise and authority and its social contract to
deliver such expertise ethically, is recognized, along with his or
her control of the interaction and discourse in the encounter.
Greetings are thus one specific linguistic means of the interactional co-construction of the institutional discourse of medicine
(Drew and Heritage; Maynard; ten Have). Discourse analysts look
for the features and patterns in extended stretches of language
that make connections to the sociocultural context. Many of these
connections could be termed conventions of discourse, that is,
the regular connection between the use of a discourse practice or
set of practices and their meaning and significance in context.
Discourse analysis is an empirical method: it looks for features
and patterns that occur with regularity across a body of data in
order to describe the conventional relationships between the way
the language is organized and the meaning, significance, or interpretation of that language in context (Barton, "Inductive" and
"Linguistic"; Cameron; Johnstone, *Discourse* and *Qualitative;*
van Dijk, *Discourse;* Schiffrin; Schiffrin, Tannen, and Hamilton).[4]

In the project described briefly here, I developed an analysis
of the discourse of prognosis in medical oncology encounters
between physicians and patients who have recently been diagnosed with cancer, focusing in particular on the treatment discussion—that portion of the encounter in which treatment options
are presented, treatment decisions made (ideally collaboratively),
and treatment plans established. The treatment discussion is, by
far, the most interactional portion of the initial medical oncology
encounter, with patients and families asking many questions,
sometimes working from a list for, as they often say with a ritu-
alistic acknowledgment of the professional and institutional context, "the doctor." The full study is published elsewhere (Barton,
"Discourse"), but I discuss one specific encounter here in order
to give an idea of how linguistic discourse analysis works.

For the framing theoretical construct of this work, I used the ethnomethodologist Erving Goffman's distinction between front-stage and back-stage regions in institutions. On the front stage, professionals deliver a performance to an audience: "The performance of an individual in a front region may be seen as an effort to give the appearance that his activity in the region maintains and embodies certain standards" (107). The back stage, however, is a region for insiders: "[In the back-stage region], suppressed facts make an appearance [. . .]. A back stage may be defined as a place, relative to a given performance, where the impression fostered by the performance is knowingly contracted as a matter of course" (112). Goffman's distinction captures the contextual situation of the discourse of medicine in a powerfully intuitive way: on the front stage in a clinical encounter, physicians deliver the professionalized discourse of medicine; on the back stage, in the hallway or the clinical work area, physicians and other medical professionals talk as co-workers, co-constructing an insider discourse of medicine. As a heuristic, this distinction suggests that we look with interest at matters with different front-stage and back-stage discourses.

Prognosis is one such discourse in medicine. Prognosis is defined as the probable course or outcome of a disease and the patient's chance of recovery (Chabner). Intuitively, prognosis would seem to be an important part of any treatment discussion, particularly in oncology, where treatment plans can set up long and difficult courses with the risk of serious side effects. Counterintuitively, however, the front-stage discourse of prognosis varied widely across the corpus of twelve encounters that I observed, recorded, transcribed, and analyzed for this research. Further, the features of the discourse of prognosis on the back stage were almost exactly the opposite of the front-stage discourse, pointing to its problematic status on the front stage. In this study, I argued that the front-stage presentation of prognosis was organized to allow physicians to do, not do, or avoid the difficult interactional work of presenting a prognosis, particularly a poor one.

Through the methods of discourse analysis, I found, first, that prognosis was not predictable: of the twelve encounters observed, four contained no physician-initiated mention or discussion of prognosis at all, indicating that presenting a prognosis does not have a consistent and stable status as a discourse feature of the treatment discussion. The possible absence of prognosis, for example, contrasts with the obligatory presence of diagnosis, which was mentioned in all twelve of the encounters in the study. Sometimes, as in the case of patients whose cancer has not been definitively staged and diagnosed, the omission of prognosis is appropriate. At other times, however, as we will see in the following case, the presentation of a poor prognosis might be avoided in a more problematic way.

Consider, then, the following treatment discussion from one of the encounters in the corpus; the patient received a diagnosis of colon cancer:

> PHYSICIAN: When they did the liver biopsy in March, it showed that there were multiple lesions of the liver. And that means that we can't cut it out. It has to be treated by some kind of chemotherapy to try to control it. Now, we have a number of different drugs that we use for that kind of treatment.

This treatment discussion is notable for its indirect and vague front-stage language, particularly with respect to prognosis. In starting the discussion with the results of the liver biopsy, the physician does not directly state that the colon cancer that metastasized to the liver is Stage IV, which, in the professional discourse of medicine, is associated with a prognosis of incurable disease. In presenting the treatment recommendation for chemotherapy, the physician uses the vague expression "to try to control it"; again, in the professional discourse of medicine, controlling a tumor also carries the unmistakable implications of incurable disease. I would argue, however, that neither of these prognostic implications (either the staging of the tumor or the ultimately futile attempts to control it) would be shared by patients and families without rather sophisticated knowledge of or previous experience with cancer. Further, this vague expression that hints at a prognosis ("to try to control it") is deeply embedded within the foregrounded movement of a treatment discussion from treatment recommendation ("It has to be treated by some sort of chemotherapy") to treatment plan ("Now, we have a number of drugs that we use for that kind of treatment"). Prognosis, in other words, is not given topic status or potential topic status in the discussion; its deep embedding functions effectively to background it. In sum, indirect and vague language as well as embedding are discourse practices by which physicians are able to avoid the foregrounded delivery of a poor prognosis.

Contrast, however, the backgrounding of prognosis on the front stage with the foregrounding of prognosis on the back stage for this encounter. As the physician and I left the examination room, we had a short exchange:

ELLEN: Sweet lady.

PHYSICIAN: Bad disease.

ELLEN: Because they didn't catch it before it went to the liver?

PHYSICIAN: Yeah. She's a hard one to know what to do with in terms of protocol [clinical trial]. She's an older, frail lady. But she has bad disease.

This back-stage discussion of prognosis has features that are almost exactly opposite to those of the front-stage presentation. First, it is predictable, not unpredictable. Of twelve encounters in this study, three were with patients who had been diagnosed with early-stage disease (Stage I or II), and nine were with patients who had been diagnosed with late-stage disease (Stage III or IV). Back-stage, physicians commented upon prognosis for six of the nine patients with late-stage disease, indicating that prognosis has a prominent, even predictable, topic status in the case of bad news when it is discussed back-stage. Second, back-stage discussions of prognosis use direct, not indirect language: compare "try to control it" to the repetition of "bad disease."

Two other interesting contrasts between the front-stage and back-stage discourses of prognosis are communicative initiative and the representation of prognostic information. On the back stage, physicians themselves typically initiate the topic of prognosis and speak about it directly, especially in cases of bad news, as shown in the excerpt above. This direct statement of prognosis also presents the information as reliable; "bad disease" is not mitigated or qualified. On the front stage, however, prognosis is often a topic that is initiated by families. In the twelve encounters in the study, patients or families asked for information about prognosis in six. Consider the continuation of the encounter excerpted above: as noted, the indirect reference to prognosis was backgrounded effectively, so it was not developed as a topic during the treatment discussion. During the question portion of the encounter, however, the patient's husband initiated the topic of prognosis and the patient herself asked direct questions about it. Note below that the husband's question introducing the topic is a general one, but the patient's question goes back to the first (and, in a sense, the most telling) sentence in the treatment discussion about the liver:

> HUSBAND: Overall, what success rate do you have?
>
> PHYSICIAN: Well, the chemotherapy, in most people, will help slow the growth of the tumor. In all probability, depending on what regimen you select, anywhere from 20 to 50 percent of the time it will help shrink it down substantially. But it's unlikely to get rid of it entirely.
>
> PATIENT: The liver has tumors, right?
>
> PHYSICIAN: Right. The chemotherapy hopefully will keep it under control for a time, but it won't prevent it. And eventually it'll grow despite treatment. The tumors become resistant to treatment. But that could be months from now, it could be weeks from now, it could be years from now.
>
> PATIENT: Well, I'm glad you were straightforward with that because I was wondering, you know—

Once the topic has been introduced to the discourse of the encounter, the physician provides a front-stage presentation of prognosis, with two notable features. First, there is specific information about the probable course of treatment, complete with percentages of success ("[T]wenty to 50 percent of the time [treatment] will shrink [the tumor] down considerably") and a direct statement that chemotherapy will not be curative ("[E]ventually it'll grow despite treatment"). Second, there is a specific warning that prognostic information is unreliable to predict the course for a specific individual patient ("But that could be months [. . .] weeks

[. . .] years from now"). Again, these features contrast with the back-stage discussion of prognosis: on the front stage, the communicative burden for initiating the topic of prognosis is shifted to the patient, and when specific information about prognosis is presented, it is represented as unreliable with respect to that individual patient. On the back stage, the physician him- or herself initiates the topic of prognosis, and speaks of it directly, with no mitigations or representation of the information as unreliable. In the reality accompanying this discourse, the physician was right in his back-stage assessment of "bad disease"; the patient died within a few months despite treatment.

Before continuing the discussion of prognosis in the discourse of medicine, it is important to note that the presentation of the research here used a single case for expository efficiency. In the full publication, all of the features mentioned above were shown to appear with a stated degree of regularity across the corpus of data, thereby establishing the pattern of the discourse of prognosis empirically (cf. Note 4). In other words, the claim and argument of the research—that the discourse of prognosis is organized to allow physicians to do, not to do, or to avoid the presentation of prognosis through discourse practices of foregrounding and backgrounding—is one that was revealed empirically through the inductive analysis of the data and the confirmation of the generalizations of that analysis across the corpus.

Describing versus Theorizing Language in Context

So the organization of the discourse of prognosis was developed through discourse analysis, identifying specific features and their occurrence across the data. The discourse analysis answers "what" and "how" questions about the discourse of prognosis: I described what was being done (doing, not doing, or avoiding prognosis) and how (via discourse practices of foregrounding and backgrounding). But research also has to answer the "so what" question—what is the contribution and significance of the research? What I will explore in this section is the way that researchers in linguistics and discourse analysis and scholars in English studies answer this question somewhat differently. For linguists, the disciplinary interest in this research is satisfied by its description of the organization of language in context (prognosis in the discourse of medicine) and in its identification of the specific discourse practices through which it is organized (foregrounding and backgrounding, and topic initiation and development). The contribution of the research, in other words, would remain closely connected to the language: To answer the "so what" question, or in the genre terms of the research article, to develop the discussion section of an article, I could argue that this aspect of the discourse of medicine points to a general understanding of foregrounding and backgrounding as discourse practices as one of the means by which institutional discourse is organized asymmetrically (Drew and Heritage). I also could argue that contrast between the front-stage and back-stage discourse points to a methodological direction in working on institutional discourse (Sarangi and Roberts). I could point to the implications of this research in terms of its contribution to understanding how discourse practices of physicians maintain control over the interaction in ways that might be contrary to the interests and expectations of patients and families, with prognosis as an exemplar of a problematic discourse of avoidance (Fisher and Todd). Finally, I could suggest that the findings of this research be brought to physicians for their consideration of and improvement upon physician-patient interaction. All of these possibilities, however, remain very close to the analysis of language, which reflects the disciplinary interest of the field of linguistics. The "so what" question for linguistics is answered in terms of the field's disciplinary interest in the organization of language in context.

Note that the previous paragraph was written in the conditional. I could have, and probably would have, discussed the contributions and significance of this research primarily in terms of the study of language in institutional contexts if I had sought to publish this article in a linguistics journal such as *TEXT,* or *Discourse Studies,* or even *Discourse and Society.* But disciplinary situatedness worked in a funny way here: I actually submitted the first version of the essay in response to a call for articles on critical practices in professional communication to appear in the *Journal of Business and Technical Communication,* a journal in the fields of composition studies and professional-technical writing. In other words, the paper went out to an audience defined more in terms of English studies than of linguistics. I have no principled explanation for this set of circumstances, other than that I have a career in both fields and a vague professional goal of publishing roughly equal amounts in both. But the most salient feature of the review process for this article does point to a way to think about the different disciplinary interests of linguistics and English and the ways they expect their practitioners to answer the "so what" question. To put the matter most simply, while linguistics encourages its practitioners to remain close to the description of language, English studies encourages its practitioners to use broader categories like professions and professionalism in order to theorize the discourse.

The most salient point of the review process for the publication of my research on the discourse of prognosis was the editor's request that I add "at least a nod" to the word *critical* in the title of the special issue. Dutifully, I developed a final section for the paper entitled "Critical Questions." In order to write this section, I tried to answer the "so what" question by posing a series of "why" questions, asking why the discourse of prognosis in medicine might be arranged as it is, particularly with respect to the readily available means for avoiding it. By looking at historical, pedagogical, and reflective sources in the literature of medicine, I formulated a claim that the reasons that the front-stage and back-stage discourse of prognosis were in such stark contrast had to do with the connections between the discourse of prognosis and complex and conflicted categories deeply embedded in the received wisdom of the profession of medicine. I developed this argument by comparing the way that the language of prognosis was unsettled in comparison to the language of diagnosis and by looking at the way prognosis was presented in medical textbooks and discussed in the reflective writings of the field (for example, Sherwin Nuland's *How We Die* and Jerome Groopman's "Dying Words"). To make a long theorizing story short, I argued that the language of prognosis is unsettled in medicine for multiple reasons buried deeply in the profession's sense of itself. I argued that prognosis is disruptive language in medicine because it challenges the profession's orientation to treatment and cure in an idealized doctor-patient relationship. This argument can be made by looking at the textbooks of medicine, which specifically warn physicians in training to be careful about disclosing prognosis; the following quotation is from the very first section of the massive and venerable *Harrison's Principles of Internal Medicine:*

> No problem is more distressing than that presented by the patient with an incurable disease. Although some would argue otherwise, there is no ironclad rule that the patient must immediately be told "everything." [. . .] How much the patient is told should depend upon the patient's ability and capacity to deal with the possibility of imminent death; often this capacity grows with time, and, whenever possible, gradual rather than abrupt disclosure is the best strategy [. . .]. The patient must be given an opportunity to talk with the physician and ask questions. (Wilson et al. 4)

This position is also articulated in the reflective stories written by physicians:

> As an oncology fellow, I began my career believing that it was essential to provide details to my patients. Sharing statistics seemed like the obvious thing to do: surely a patient should have access to everything I knew [. . .]. [I met with my patient Claire] in my clinic office, and she looked at me expectantly.
> "Claire, with this disease, a remission would ordinarily last three to six months," I told her bluntly. "A person could expect to survive between one to two years."
> She appeared to take the news stalwartly, but I later learned from her husband that she had left the appointment deeply shaken [. . .]. Her face was full of despair whenever I saw her. And yet Claire lived for nearly four years. She was able to travel, work part time, and take care of her children, but was unable to stop thinking that she could die at any moment. (Groopman 64)

The textbooks and reflections thus offer an explanation for the reasons the discourse of prognosis is constructed to allow avoidance: physicians routinely shift the burden of communication about prognosis to patients and families under the assumption that these questions will reflect what they truly wish to know about prognosis in a gradual understanding of their condition.

But this explanation went only so far. It explained avoidance in broader terms of pedagogy and practice, but that raises yet another "why" question: why would gradual disclosure be so important as to displace other important communicative values such as the frank provision of medical information? Digging more deeply into the medical sources, I argued that the discourse of prognosis is problematic in medicine because it conflicts with the profession's conceptualization of and commitment to hope. The medical humanist Eric J. Cassell defines hope as essential to life itself: "Every person has a perceived future [. . .]. Intense unhappiness results from a loss of that future—the future of the individual person, of children, and of other loved ones. It is in this dimension of existence that hope dwells [. . .]. No one has ever questioned the suffering that attends the loss of hope" (*Nature* 43). The loss of hope is thus connected to the worst of human suffering. The connection between hope and prognosis has long been a part of medicine. A famous bit of advice about prognosis came from William Osler, widely recognized as an authoritative voice in the history and development of the profession of medicine; this advice, too, is prominently featured in *Harrison's:*

> One thing is certain; it is not for you to don the black cap and, assuming the judicial function, take hope away from any patient [. . .] hope that comes to us all. (Wilson et al. 4)

This advice is also prominent in physicians' stories and writing: Nuland notes, "A young doctor learns no more important lesson than the admonition that he must never allow his patients to lose hope" (222). This, I believe, is the basis for the profession's ambivalence about prognosis and what could be seen as its problematic delivery on the front stage of medical interaction. A poor prognosis is widely regarded by physicians as destroying (or having the potential to destroy) hope, and destroying hope is considered a breach of humane medical care. The discourse of prognosis, as problematic as it may appear superficially, is thus based on more than historical paternalism or arrogant preservation of professional power through the control of the hierarchical, asymmetrical, and problematic dispensation of knowledge in discourse and interaction. In this interpretation, the discourse of prognosis, including its avoidance, is motivated by the importance of hope.

Turning back to look at treatment discussions with the question of hope in mind actually reveals a further complexity of the discourse of prognosis, which is the creation of false hope. In the encounters, patients and families appear to define hope differently than do physicians. In formulating questions about prognosis, for example, they express a sense of hope in general terms of survival or in more specific terms of time left:

> HUSBAND: Overall what success rate do you have?
>
> PATIENT: In looking at chemo and radiation. Does it set it back for a year?
>
> PATIENT: I know this is very serious, yet I don't have a clear picture about how much time I have. Is there any way I can—
>
> PATIENT: They told me that if I didn't have the chemo, that I have six months to a year.

If hope is present within these utterances, it seems to be conceptualized in the material binary of survival until death.

But physicians, especially in the face of advanced disease, conceptualize hope not in general terms of survival but in more limited terms of control of the tumor. Their presentation of prognosis is connected to treatment, as in the following examples from five different encounters:

> PHYSICIAN: It has to be treated by some sort of chemotherapy to try to control it.
>
> PHYSICIAN: We have some drugs that sort of work for abdominal cancer.
>
> PHYSICIAN: [W]e have approximately a 20 to 25 percent chance of a long-term cure. Despite doing all this [treatment].
>
> PHYSICIAN: [T]here are a few patients [. . .] that have been fortunate enough to respond to treatment very dramatically and have had good outcomes for the long haul.
>
> PHYSICIAN: And the real test is how much does it shrink, and can we get it to disappear entirely?

For physicians, this more limited conceptualization of hope supports the decision to treat. And when treatment works, it is the right material decision: Groopman's patient Claire, for instance, lived to care for her children for four more years, and every oncologist has stories of patients who defied prognostic odds, went into remission, or even were cured of advanced disease. "We cured him" is not an unusual back-stage comment from a physician after seeing a patient who is disease-free some years after treatment.

But treatment does not always work to control cancer. One of the unfortunate material consequences of physicians' conceptualization of hope is that it can support the decision to undertake futile treatment, as Nuland argued: "Sometimes it is really to maintain his own hope that the doctor deludes himself into a course of action whose odds of success seem too small to justify embarking on it [. . .]. [H]e indulges a very sick person and himself in a form of medical 'doing something' to deny the hovering presence of death" (223–24). The hope of physicians to achieve control over cancer can thus result in excessive treatment at the end of a patient's life.

I would tentatively suggest that this study points to some of the strengths of considering research from the disciplinary perspectives of linguistics, discourse analysis, and English studies. From linguistics, this project gains its close focus on language— it captures as data what physicians actually do in the presentation of prognosis (rather than what might be thought to be done), and thus proceeds from a solid empirical base. Discourse analysis thus incorporates a strong methodological constraint: analysis uncovers the discourse practices that participants themselves use to drive the discourse (Drew and Heritage). In other words, the contextual categories proposed in an analysis (doing, not doing, or avoiding prognosis, as proposed here) must be shown to operate technically within the language in terms of specific discourse features and practices (foregrounding and backgrounding). From linguistics, then, this project formulates its analysis within a claim about discourse practices—that the discourse of prognosis is organized to allow physicians to deliver prognostic news in a variety of foregrounded and backgrounded ways.

Turning to English studies, however, encourages questions that range widely and freely in constructing an interpretation of discourse that is based on multiple sources. Interpretation, in other words, is not necessarily based closely on the language; the relationship of theoretical constructs to the discourse can be more abstract, such as the received wisdom of the field as expressed in textbooks and reflective writing. In terms of a discourse like medicine, the theorizing practices of English studies create a means for discovering very deeply embedded constructs—like hope—that may motivate and drive a discourse in indirect but powerful ways. These are constructs that are not apparent to a strictly linguistic analysis, although they are constructs that can be used to return to the data, to develop a reading of the discourse of prognosis in terms of hope, which is the disciplinary interest of English studies. These are also constructs that can be used to deepen the discourse analysis, as shown above in the ways that a consideration of hope found that families and physicians seem to follow different discourse practices reflecting different conceptualizations of hope.

Conclusion

The analysis of the discourse of medicine above is an example from my own research, which focuses on the discourse of professions and institutions, but there are a number of other lines of interdisciplinary research in linguistics, discourse analysis, and English studies, particularly in composition/rhetoric. One of the best known of these is genre analysis (Swales), mentioned above as an area of applied linguistics. Following the seminal work of Carolyn Miller, who defined genre as rhetorical and social action, researchers have looked at genre in a wide variety of academic and professional settings, from banks to social work (Freedman and Medway), focusing most recently on the ways that genres are organized into complex activity systems (Russell; Bazerman and Prior). Another line of research is critical discourse analysis (Fairclough, *Critical* and *Language*; Hodge and Kress; van Dijk, *Ideology*), an approach that analyzes texts primarily in terms of conventions that encode relations of power (Huckin). Critical discourse analysis often addresses political issues such as discrimination in public texts and settings like journalism and political debate (Reisigl and Wodak; Wodak and van Dijk). In composition/rhetoric, Ellen Cushman's work on minority women negotiating social services is an example of a study that uses critical discourse analysis to explore interrelated issues of race, gender, and class. A number of other topics and approaches in interdisciplinary research in linguistics, discourse analysis, and English studies are described in the collection entitled *Discourse Studies in Composition* (Barton and Stygall).

What I have tried to argue in this chapter is that linguistics has the potential to make an important contribution to English studies, and English studies has the potential to make an important contribution to linguistics, most specifically in discourse analysis. To use the terminology of English studies, linguistics has the potential to complicate the understanding of language; English studies, in turn, has the potential to theorize the findings of discourse analysis. I believe that the field of discourse studies has strong ties to both fields and represents a truly interdisciplinary endeavor between them. This particular interdisciplinary configuration is my own, but I believe that it points to a common intellectual area for those who are interested in detailed descriptions of the organization of language in context enriched by theorizing practices of interpretation. However, this is not the only possible interdisciplinary configuration of linguistics and English studies. Some other possibilities include work on texts written in older forms of English by historical linguists and literary scholars, pedagogical research by applied linguists and composition scholars, and even a look at the growth of linguistics and English as different fields by disciplinary historians of linguistics as well as English studies. Should these interdisciplinary areas prove rich in their research findings and implications, perhaps new social and political relations that are not quite so paradoxical and contradictory may emerge for linguistics and English studies, especially when they share the same departmental home.

I would like to close by making a brief curricular argument, because it is possible that curriculum can drive interdisciplinarity in these endeavors, as Bruce McComiskey suggests in the introduction. At the moment, the curricula in linguistics and English studies are almost completely separate entities, at least in the example of my own department, but there are many possible points of interdisciplinary interest. For scholars and students in

linguistics and English studies, conversation in the Burkean parlor may become animated and productive if these overlap courses
are taught as truly interdisciplinary courses, ones that draw upon
the literatures of both fields. In my own experience, though, I
must admit that I find this very hard to do. When I teach courses
in the undergraduate or graduate curriculum in linguistics, I feel
a disciplinary responsibility to introduce primarily, if not exclusively, the "linguistic" ways of investigating and exploring topics. So to teach a course on language and gender, say—certainly a
possible crossover course since linguistics has an extensive research literature on gender in interaction and English studies has
an extensive theoretical literature in gender studies—I usually
don't make the brave decision to teach from both disciplines. It is
somewhat easier to be more interdisciplinary when teaching
courses that combine discourse analysis and composition-rhetoric, my area in English studies. To teach a course on research
methods, for example, I can comfortably justify a unit on discourse analysis, but I might even be able to take a more interdisciplinary step here by teaching in terms of discourse studies rather
than discourse analysis (Johnstone, *Discourse*). I can also imagine interdisciplinary seminars taught by historical linguists and
disciplinary historians and theorists—a seminar on Ferdinand de
Saussure, for example, could look productively at the different
ways that this intellectual figure has contributed to the development of the fields of linguistics and English studies. Beyond these
hypotheticals, though, it seems that English studies may in fact
be moving toward the complementarity of disciplines that is suggested in this volume. The publication of this volume reflects the
fact that English departments nationwide are looking for resources
to teach classes that introduce students to an interdisciplinary
view of English studies. Further, this volume reflects the ways
English departments nationwide are working toward interdisciplinary curriculum redevelopment. In my own department, for
example, we are in the process of revising our undergraduate
and graduate curricula to an English studies model, and faculty
in the linguistics program have designed two new courses for
these curricula, one aimed at interdisciplinarity more generally
and one aimed at the specific interdisciplinary area of linguistics
and English education. The interdisciplinary course for the un-

dergraduate major is entitled The Structure of English, and it is designed not only to cover current views from linguistics of language as a cognitive and social object but also to explore their importance in terms of a revised English major, with topics such as the relationship between oral and written language, including spelling and writing, for English education majors, and the history of the English language for literature majors. The specifically interdisciplinary course for English education majors and MA students is entitled Linguistics and Education, and it is designed to provide in-depth coverage of issues such as the differences between prescriptive and descriptive grammar; the standard and nonstandard varieties of English, with special attention to African American English; the different kinds of language acquisition in speech, reading, and writing in native and nonnative languages; and the role of language in establishing identity and maintaining culture. It is, perhaps, through curricular efforts like these that there will be more talk in the English studies parlor that will move us toward generative and productive intellectual and collegial interdisciplinarity in the English department as a common home.

Notes

1. In the brief description of contemporary linguistics presented here, I draw heavily upon Frederick Newmeyer's *Linguistic Theory in America, The Politics of Linguistics,* and *Language Form and Language Function.*

2. For a very clear discussion of the interaction of universal grammar and the grammars of particular languages, see Lydia White's *Universal Grammar and Second Language Acquisition.*

3. For a much more detailed account of these tensions, see the work of Newmeyer noted above: Newmeyer focuses on the history and development of linguistics in *Linguistic Theory in America* and *The Politics of Linguistics,* and he covers the controversy surrounding the concept of autonomous competence in *Language Form and Language Function.* Other sources on the history and development of the field include Randy Harris's *The Linguistic Wars,* and a small industry of books about Noam Chomsky and his work (e.g., McGilvray; Smith; Antony and Hornstein;

Postal). For histories of the field of linguistics, see Dell Hymes's *Studies in the History of Linguistics* as well as Geoffrey Sampson's *Schools of Linguistics*, Julie Tetel Andresen's *Linguistics in America, 1769–1924*, and John Joseph's *From Whitney to Chomsky: Essays in the History of American Linguistics*. For an excellent overview of generative linguistics written for the general public, see Steven Pinker's *The Language Instinct*. For technical introductions to generative linguistics, see Thomas Stewart and Nathan Vaillette's *Language Files*, a text often used in undergraduate courses, or Victoria Fromkin and her colleagues' *Linguistics*, a text for graduate courses. David Crystal's *Cambridge Encyclopedia of Language* is an excellent overall reference for topics within the field of linguistics.

4. The term *empirical* here must be distinguished from the term *empiricism* used above in the discussion of Bloomfield's structuralist linguistics. *Empiricism* is an earlier term used to refer to the strong constraint of assuming that knowledge and theory are built upon direct observation only, as, for example, in behaviorism. *Empirical* is a more contemporary term used to refer to systematic data collection and analysis. For our purposes, it might be useful to point out that one of the key characteristics of empirical research in discourse analysis is that its findings are based on an analysis of the entire body of data using defined categories and systematic coding (in other words, data analysis is not as freely selective as interpretive analysis). Another key characteristic of empirical research is that its findings can be replicated and falsified; in other words, given the data and defined categories, other researchers should be able to arrive at the same results (replicability), and given counterexamples the generalizations from the findings can be shown to be incorrect, inaccurate, or in need of further refinement (falsifiability). For more discussion of the nature and place of empirical research in English studies, particularly in composition-rhetoric, see Charney; Barton, "More"; Johanek; and MacNealy.

Works Cited

AILA (Association Internationale de Linguistique Appliquée). 3 Jan. 2006. http://www.aila.info.

Ainsworth-Vaughn, Nancy. "The Discourse of Medical Encounters." Schiffrin, Tannen, and Hamilton 435–69.

Andresen, Julie Tetel. *Linguistics in America, 1769–1924: A Critical History*. London: Routledge, 1990.

Antony, Louise M., and Norbert Hornstein, eds. *Chomsky and His Critics*. Malden, MA: Blackwell, 2003.

Austin, J. L. *How to Do Things with Words*. Cambridge, MA: Harvard UP, 1962.

Barton, Ellen. "Discourse Methods and Critical Practice in Professional Communication: The Front-Stage and Back-Stage Discourse of Prognosis in Medicine." *Journal of Business and Technical Communication* 18 (2004): 67–111.

———. "Inductive Discourse Analysis: Discovering Rich Features." Barton and Stygall 19–42.

———. "Linguistic Discourse Analysis: How the Language in Texts Works." *What Writing Does and How It Does It: An Introduction to Analysis of Text and Textual Practice*. Ed. Charles Bazerman and Paul Prior. Mahwah, NJ: Erlbaum, 2004. 57–82.

———. "More Methodological Matters: Against Negative Argumentation." *College Composition and Communication* 51 (2000): 399–416.

Barton, Ellen, and Gail Stygall, eds. *Discourse Studies in Composition*. Cresskill, NJ: Hampton, 2002.

———. "Linguistics and Composition: A Parallel History." Barton and Stygall 1–17.

Bazerman, Charles, and Paul Prior, eds. *What Writing Does and How It Does It: An Introduction to Analyzing Texts and Textual Practices*. Mahwah, NJ: Erlbaum, 2004.

Belcher, Diane, and George Braine, eds. *Academic Writing in a Second Language: Essays on Research and Pedagogy*. Norwood, NJ: Ablex, 1995.

Bhatia, Tej K., and William C. Ritchie, eds. *The Handbook of Bilingualism*. Malden, MA: Blackwell, 2004.

Bloomfield, Leonard. *Language*. New York: Holt, 1933.

Boas, Franz. *Handbook of American Indian Languages*. 1911. *Introduction to* Handbook of American Indian Languages [Boas] *and* Indian Linguistic Families of America North of Mexico [J. W. Powell]. Ed. Preston Holder. Lincoln: U of Nebraska P, 1966.

Brody, Howard. *The Healer's Power*. New Haven: Yale UP, 1992.

Cameron, Deborah. *Working with Spoken Discourse*. Thousand Oaks, CA: Sage, 2001.

Cassell, Eric J. *The Nature of Suffering and the Goals of Medicine*. 2nd ed. New York: Oxford UP, 2004.

———. *The Place of the Humanities in Medicine*. Hastings-on-Hudson, NY: Hastings Center, 1984.

Chabner, Davi-Ellen. *The Language of Medicine: A Write-in Text Explaining Medical Terms*. 5th ed. Philadelphia: Saunders, 1996.

Charney, Davida. "Empiricism Is Not a Four-Letter Word." *College Composition and Communication* 47 (1996): 567–93.

Chomsky, Noam. *Aspects of the Theory of Syntax*. Cambridge: MIT P, 1965.

———. *Syntactic Structures*. The Hague: Mouton, 1957.

Connor, Ulla. *Contrastive Rhetoric: Cross-Cultural Aspects of Second-Language Writing*. New York: Cambridge UP, 1996.

Crystal, David. *The Cambridge Encyclopedia of Language*. New York: Cambridge UP, 1997.

Cushman, Ellen. *The Struggle and the Tools: Oral and Literate Strategies in an Inner City Community*. Albany: SUNY P, 1998.

Davies, Alan, and Catherine Elder, eds. *The Handbook of Applied Linguistics*. Malden, MA: Blackwell, 2004.

Drew, Paul, and John Heritage. "Analyzing Talk at Work: An Introduction." *Talk at Work: Interaction in Institutional Settings*. Ed. Drew and Heritage. New York: Cambridge UP, 1992. 3–65.

Fairclough, Norman. *Critical Discourse Analysis: The Critical Study of Language*. New York: Addison, 1995.

———. *Language and Power*. 2nd ed. Upper Saddle River, NJ: Pearson, 2001.

Fisher, Sue, and Alexandra Todd, eds. *The Social Organization of Doctor-Patient Communication*. 2nd ed. Norwood, NJ: Ablex, 1993.

Fleischman, Suzanne. "Language and Medicine." Schiffrin, Tannen, and Hamilton 470–502.

Foucault, Michel. *The Birth of the Clinic: An Archaeology of Medical Perception*. 1973. Trans. A. M. Sheridan Smith. New York: Vintage, 1975.

Freedman, Aviva, and Peter Medway, eds. *Genre and the New Rhetoric*. London: Taylor, 1994.

Fromkin, Victoria, et al. *Linguistics: An Introduction to Linguistic Theory*. Malden, MA: Blackwell, 2000.

Goffman, Erving. *The Presentation of Self in Everyday Life*. New York: Doubleday, 1959.

Groopman, Jerome. "Dying Words: How Should Doctors Deliver Bad News?" *New Yorker* 28 Oct. 2002: 62–70.

Gumperz, John J., and Stephen C. Levinson. *Rethinking Linguistic Relativity*. New York: Cambridge UP, 1996.

Halliday, M. A. K. *An Introduction to Functional Grammar*. London: Arnold, 1994.

———. *Language as Social Semiotic: The Social Interpretation of Language and Meaning*. London: Arnold, 1978.

Halliday, M. A. K., and J. R. Martin. *Writing Science: Literacy and Discursive Power*. Pittsburgh: U of Pittsburgh P, 1993.

Harris, Randy Allen. *The Linguistics Wars*. New York: Oxford UP, 1993.

Hodge, Robert, and Gunther Kress. *Language as Ideology*. New York: Routledge, 1993.

Huckin, Thomas. "Critical Discourse Analysis and the Discourse of Condescension." Barton and Stygall 155–76.

Hymes, Dell. "Models of the Interaction of Language and Social Life." *Directions in Sociolinguistics: The Ethnography of Communication*. Ed. John J. Gumperz and Hymes. New York: Holt, 1972. 35–71.

———. *Studies in the History of Linguistics: Traditions and Paradigms*. Bloomington: Indiana UP, 1974.

Johanek, Cindy. *Composing Research: A Contextualist Paradigm*. Logan: Utah State UP, 2000.

Johns, Ann M. *Genre in the Classroom: Multiple Perspectives*. Mahwah, NJ: Erlbaum, 2002.

———. *Text, Role, and Context: Developing Academic Literacies*. New York: Cambridge UP, 1997.

Johnstone, Barbara. *Discourse Analysis*. Malden, MA: Blackwell, 2002.

———. *Qualitative Methods in Sociolinguistics*. New York: Oxford UP, 2000.

Joseph, John E. *From Whitman to Chomsky: Essays in the History of American Linguistics*. Amsterdam: Benjamins, 2002.

———. "Trends in Twentieth-Century Linguistics: An Overview." *Concise History of the Language Sciences: From the Sumerians to the Cognitivists*. Ed. E. F. K. Koerner and R. E. Asher. New York: Pergamon, 1995. 221–33.

Kaplan, Robert B., ed. *The Oxford Handbook of Applied Linguistics*. New York: Oxford UP, 2005.

Katz, Jay. *The Silent World of Doctor and Patient*. 1984. Baltimore: Johns Hopkins UP, 2002.

Kleinman, Arthur. *The Illness Narratives: Suffering, Healing, and the Human Condition*. New York: Basic, 1988.

———. *Writing at the Margin: Discourse between Anthropology and Medicine*. Berkeley: U of California P, 1995.

Labov, William. "The Study of Language in Its Social Context." *Language and Social Context*. Ed. Pier Paolo Giglioli. Harmondsworth: Penguin, 1972. 283–307.

Levinson, Stephen C. *Presumptive Meanings: The Theory of Generalized Conversational Implicature*. Cambridge: MIT, 2000.

Lucy, John. *Language Diversity and Thought: A Reformulation of the Linguistic Relativity Hypothesis*. New York: Cambridge UP, 1992.

MacNealy, Mary Sue. *Strategies for Empirical Research in Writing*. Boston: Allyn, 1999.

Matsuda, Paul Kei, and Tony Silva. *Second Language Writing Research: Perspectives on the Process of Knowledge Construction*. Mahwah, NJ: Erlbaum, 2005.

Maynard, Douglas W. "Interaction and Asymmetry in Clinical Discourse." *American Journal of Sociology* 97 (1991): 448–95.

McGilvray, James. *Chomsky: Language, Mind, and Politics*. Malden, MA: Blackwell, 1999.

Messer-Davidow, Ellen, David R. Shumway, and David J. Sylvan, eds. Preface. *Knowledges: Historical and Critical Studies in Disciplinarity*. Charlottesville: UP of Virginia, 1993. i–viii.

Miller, Carolyn R. "Genre as Social Action." *Quarterly Journal of Speech* 70 (1984): 151–67.

Mishler, Eliot G. *The Discourse of Medicine: Dialectics of Medical Interviews*. Norwood, NJ: Ablex, 1984.

National Endowment for the Humanities. "Common Questions about Applying for an NEH Grant." N.d. 13 June 2006 http://www.neh.gov/grants/commonquestions.html.

———. "Fellowships and Faculty Research Awards." 9 Feb. 2006. 13 June 2006 www.neh.gov/grants/guidelines/fellowships.html.

———. "Who We Are." N.d. 13 June 2006 www.neh.gov/whoweare/overview.html.

National Science Foundation. "About Funding." 29 Jan. 2005. 13 June 2006 www.nsf.gov/funding/aboutfunding.jsp.———. "Linguistics." 10 Feb. 2005. 13 June 2006 www.nsf.gov/ funding/pgm_summ.jsp?pims_id=5408&org=NSF&from=fund.

Newmeyer, Frederick. *Language Form and Language Function*. Cambridge: MIT P, 1998.

———. *Linguistic Theory in America*. 2nd ed. Orlando: Academic, 1986.

———. *The Politics of Linguistics*. Chicago: U of Chicago P, 1986.

Nuland, Sherwin B. *How We Die: Reflections on Life's Final Chapter*. New York: Vintage, 1993.

Pinker, Steven. *The Language Instinct: How the Mind Creates Language*. New York: Morrow, 1994.

Porter, Roy. *The Greatest Benefit to Mankind: A Medical History of Humanity*. New York: Norton, 1999.

Postal, Paul M. *Skeptical Linguistic Essays*. New York: Oxford UP, 2004.

Reisigl, Martin, and Ruth Wodak. *Discourse and Discrimination: Rhetorics of Racism and Antisemitism*. New York: Routledge, 2000.

Reynolds, Margaret. E-mail to the author. 23 Oct. 2003.

Russell, David R. "Rethinking Genre in School and Society: An Activity Theory Analysis." *Written Communication* 14 (1997): 504–54.

Sampson, Geoffrey. *Schools of Linguistics*. Stanford: Stanford UP, 1980.

Sapir, Edward. *Language: An Introduction to the Study of Speech*. New York: Harcourt, 1921.

Sarangi, Srikant, and Celia Roberts. "The Dynamics of Interactional and Institutional Orders in Work-Related Settings." *Talk, Work and Institutional Order: Discourse in Medical, Mediation and Management Settings.* Ed. Srikant Sarangi and Celia Roberts. New York: Mouton, 1999. 1–57.

Saussure, Ferdinand de. *Course in General Linguistics.* 1916. New York: McGraw, 1966.

Schiffrin, Deborah. *Approaches to Discourse.* Malden, MA: Blackwell, 1994.

Schiffrin, Deborah, Deborah Tannen, and Heidi Hamilton, eds. *The Handbook of Discourse Analysis.* Malden, MA: Blackwell, 2001.

Searle, John R. *Speech Acts: An Essay in the Philosophy of Language.* Cambridge: Cambridge UP, 1969.

Silva, Tony, and Paul Kei Matsuda, eds. *On Second Language Writing.* Mahwah, NJ: Erlbaum, 2001.

Skinner, B. F. *Verbal Behavior.* New York: Appleton, 1957.

Smith, Neil. *Chomsky: Ideas and Ideals.* 2nd ed. New York: Cambridge UP, 2004.

Spolsky, Bernard, ed. *Concise Encyclopedia of Educational Linguistics.* Oxford: Pergamon, 1999.

Starr, Paul. *The Social Transformation of American Medicine: The Rise of a Sovereign Profession and the Making of a Vast Industry.* New York: Basic, 1982.

Stewart, Thomas W., Jr., and Nathan Vaillette, eds. *Language Files: Materials for an Introduction to Language and Linguistics.* 8th ed. Columbus: Ohio State UP, 2001.

Swales, John M. *Genre Analysis: English in Academic and Research Settings.* New York: Cambridge UP, 1990.

Swales, John M., and Christine B. Feak. *English in Today's Research World: A Writing Guide.* Ann Arbor: U of Michigan P, 2000.

ten Have, Paul. "Talk and Institution: A Reconsideration of the 'Asymmetry' of Doctor-Patient Interaction." *Talk and Social Structure.* Ed. Deirdre Boden and Don H. Zimmerman. Cambridge: Polity, 1991. 138–63.

Todd, Alexandra Dundas, and Sue Fisher, eds. *The Social Organization of Doctor-Patient Communication.* 2nd ed. Norwood, NJ: Ablex, 1993.

van Dijk, Teun A., ed. *Discourse Studies: A Multidisciplinary Introduction.* 2 vols. Thousand Oaks, CA: Sage, 1997.

———. *Ideology: A Multidisciplinary Approach.* Thousand Oaks, CA: Sage, 1998.

Verdonk, Peter, and Jean Jacques Weber, eds. *Twentieth-Century Fiction: From Text to Context.* New York: Routledge, 1995.

Wells, Susan. *Out of the Dead House: Nineteenth-Century Women Physicians and the Writing of Medicine.* Madison: U of Wisconsin P, 2001.

White, Lydia. *Universal Grammar and Second Language Acquisition.* Amsterdam: Benjamins, 1989.

Whorf, Benjamin Lee. *Language, Thought, and Reality: Selected Writings.* Ed. John B. Carroll. Cambridge: MIT P, 1956.

Wilkins, D. A. "Applied Linguistics." *Concise Encyclopedia of Educational Linguistics.* Ed. Bernard Spolsky. Oxford: Pergamon, 1999. 6–17.

Wilson, Jean, et al., eds. *Harrison's Principles of Internal Medicine.* 12th ed. New York: McGraw, 1991.

Wodak, Ruth, and van Dijk, Teun A., eds. *Racism at the Top: Parliamentary Discourse on Ethnic Issues in Six European States.* Klagenfurt, Aus.: Drava, 2000.

CHAPTER TWO

Rhetoric and Composition

JANICE M. LAUER
Purdue University

The field of rhetoric and composition is both exciting and challenging, encompassing the study and teaching of many types of writing in different contexts, including civic, workplace, academic, and cross-cultural. Using diverse composition pedagogies (teaching strategies) and research methods, rhetoric and composition specialists investigate these kinds of writing and help students develop into flexible and competent writers. The field, since its inception, has been described as "multimodal" and "interdisciplinary." *Multimodal* characterizes rhetoric and composition's use of different modes of inquiry (historical, theoretical, interpretive, critical, and observation-based) to study its many subjects for investigation. *Interdisciplinary* delineates the fact that the field has always drawn on work in other disciplines (psychology, sociology, linguistics, literary theory, etc.) as part of its initiating of questions, arguments, and ways of reasoning. This chapter introduces readers to some of the ways in which rhetoric and composition developed within English studies since its reemergence in the 1960s. It explains the initial forging of this discipline, its range of research on many aspects of writing, its multiple sites of writing and teaching composition over the last forty years, and finally some of the concerns and debates accompanying these developments. The end of the chapter offers an interpretation of where the field is now and the impact of this impressive array of scholarship on the pedagogy and practice of writing.

Students in the United States currently experience English studies in different ways. In the primary and middle grades, for example, many students take language arts curricula, learning to read and write with emphasis on traditional grammar instruction, while others work in whole language programs, reading and writing about subjects in their own cultural contexts. In high school, most students in English classes read literature, and some may write research papers, personal narratives, and book reports. Most college students take core-requirement literature courses and introductory composition courses (many of which, to this day, emphasize literature), with a few students going on to take advanced composition or business and technical writing courses. From these experiences, most students conclude that the field of English studies entails the *study* of literature and, to a lesser extent, the *teaching* of composition. In most cases, if students decide to major or even to do graduate work in English, they assume they will be studying literature. What these students often do not realize is that "English" also encompasses the discipline of rhetoric and composition, the teaching *and study* of writing and rhetoric in context. In the West, rhetoric was a prestigious academic discipline from antiquity through the Renaissance, and composition has been part of English studies since the birth of the discipline in the late nineteenth century. But only recently (in the past thirty years) has "rhetoric *and* composition" become a full-fledged discipline within English studies, with its own professional conferences, journals and monograph series, and graduate degrees and undergraduate majors.

The theory, practice, and teaching of rhetoric (written and oral discourse) had been a part of the *trivium* (rhetoric, philosophy, and grammar) in Western education from the time of the ancient Greeks and Romans down through the Renaissance, including the arts of invention, arrangement, style, memory, and delivery. During these centuries, students from elementary years through higher education received a thorough rhetorical education. By the twentieth century, however, rhetorical scholarship on written discourse and the graduate study of rhetoric had disappeared from English studies. What remained was the teaching of composition, limited to the arrangement and style of finished products and grammar instruction.[1] Below is a discussion of the reemergence of rhetoric in English studies and its link with composition to form a new discipline, "rhetoric and composition."

The Relationship between Rhetoric and Composition

In the mid-twentieth century, a small group of scholars within the field of English became interested in the history of written discourse (rhetoric) and its importance for understanding the nature, contexts, and practices of composition. In 1964, Robert Gorrell and others convened a meeting at the annual Conference on College Composition and Communication (CCCC) to discuss this new interest in rhetoric and its linkage with composition (Gorrell). Following this watershed event, other scholars began pointing out the importance of the ancient discipline of rhetoric as the historical inheritance of a new field, maintaining that rhetoric had benefits for teaching composition, such as helping students develop the arts of invention, sensitivity to rhetorical situations and diverse audiences, and informal reasoning powers, including appealing to ethos and pathos. These scholars pointed out that the use of *topics* ("places" for discovering arguments) and *status* (finding the type of issue in dispute) helped students raise and investigate compelling questions in rhetorical situations; that employing informal enthymemes and examples rather than formal syllogistic reasoning strengthened students' arguments; and that introducing the notion of *kairos* (the right or opportune moment for certain arguments) encouraged the construction of a full composition curriculum with different aims of writing.[2] These early scholars also conducted revisionary studies of past rhetorical texts like Aristotle's *Rhetoric*, Cicero's *De Oratore*, and Quintilian's *Institutio Oratoria* in order to offer new understandings of how this discipline had functioned as the center of civic culture.

More recently, rhetoric and composition scholars have revisited the history of rhetoric, attempting to update our understanding of the birth of the discipline and women's and minorities' roles in its long history. Some of these scholars argued that the Sophists (fifth- and fourth-century BCE traveling teachers) offered a more appropriate rhetorical epistemology for the postmodern world than many other ancient rhetoricians, including Plato and Aristotle. Others recovered the rhetorical work of women and minorities who had been marginalized. In addition, collections of historical essays were beginning to be published, as were bibliographical tools for historical scholarship, such as those of Win Horner.[3] Rhetoric and composition scholars conducted the above studies from a new perspective based on issues pertinent to the emerging field, examining such matters as whether writing constructs or only transmits knowledge, whether writing is social or individual, what the province of rhetoric is, who can be a writer or rhetor, and what the relative importance is of ethos, pathos, and logos today.[4]

Disciplinary Status

What initiated this disciplinary effort to restore rhetoric's relationship to writing in the 1960s? One factor was the founding of the interdisciplinary Rhetoric Society of America (RSA). At early meetings of this organization, some members of English departments, including Edward Corbett, Ross Winterowd, Richard Young, Janice Lauer, and Richard Larson, began discussing the development of a field within English studies that connected rhetoric and composition (Lauer, "Getting"). Because at that time composition was considered only a teaching practice, it did not have a place in the academy as a full-fledged discipline; writing was taught by contingent or part-time faculty and graduate students with little training in or knowledge of the history, the arts, or the nature of writing processes. During the next two decades (the 1970s and 1980s), the discipline of rhetoric and composition saw an explosion of theory building, research, and historical studies (Lauer, "Composition"). Scholars started teaching undergraduate and graduate courses in rhetoric and composition theory and research at their colleges and universities, while at professional conferences sessions devoted to this scholarship increased. Summer and yearlong seminars in rhetoric and composition, like those sponsored by the National Endowment for the Humanities (NEH), were taught by Edward Corbett, Ross Winterowd, and Richard Young. A two-week Summer Rhetoric Seminar at the University of Detroit (and later at Purdue University) offered graduate credit for those wishing formally to study in this field

(Lauer, "Disciplinary"). Degree programs, such as the DA at the University of Michigan, directed by Young, and courses like those taught at the Ohio State University by Edward Corbett provided new opportunities for graduate study in this emerging discipline. Near the end of the 1970s, doctoral programs were founded in rhetoric and composition, including the ones at the University of Southern California, Rensselaer Polytechnic Institute, and the University of Louisville. In the early 1980s, several other doctoral programs emerged (e.g., at Carnegie Mellon and Purdue universities), and undergraduate majors and MA degrees also sprang up across the country. From these seminars and programs emerged people who began to identify themselves as rhetoric and composition specialists.

Also in the 1980s, new professional conferences that showcased this field's work were established, including the Penn State Conference on Rhetoric and Composition, the International Society for the History of Rhetoric Conference, the University of New Hampshire's Biennial Composition Studies Conference, the Conference of the Association for Business Communication, the Rhetoric Society of America Conference, the Writing Centers Association conferences, and the Writing Program Administration Summer Workshop and Conference. Further, the Modern Language Association created two new divisions, The Teaching of Writing and The History and Theory of Rhetoric and Composition, formally recognizing rhetoric and composition as a legitimate English studies discipline. Important new journals included *Rhetoric Review, Rhetorica, Written Communication, The Writing Instructor, Focuses, PRE/TEXT, Argumentation, Readerly/ Writerly Texts,* and *Writing on the Edge.* And the first bibliography of rhetoric and composition scholarship, the *Longman (later CCCC) Bibliography of Composition and Rhetoric,* was started by Erika Lindemann, involving members of the field as annotators. Finally, throughout the 1980s many new graduate programs in rhetoric and composition continued to be established.

At the end of the 1980s, Louise Wetherbee Phelps characterized this newly emerging discipline of rhetoric and composition as a "human science" (*Composition*), and a decade later she captured the already extremely complex nature of the field in terms of its multiple titles, notions of teaching and learning in society, various classrooms, literate practices, uses of technology, and range of sites: workplace, political, and academic, among many others ("Composition Studies" 126–27). Despite this diversity, Phelps contended that the field had distinctive features (or family resemblances) shared among different groups within the discipline:

- the conception of writing as *mediating* complex dynamics (for example, various symbol systems and media) [. . .]

- a generalized attention to *composing* both language and action, through an inscribed medium that allows planning, self-reflection, and revision

- a democratic, perhaps utopian, *commitment* to literacy

- *a rhetorical (functional or strategic) perspective* on language (as distinct from, say, a formalist or structuralist one)

- *a developmental orientation* and a focus on the concrete individual, even when the person is conceived as a nexus for heteroglossic social forces; similarly, a focus on concrete, particular discourses or *"utterances"*

- historically special issues and concerns of earlier composition practice becoming *thematic* within an expanded subject matter [. . .]

- *reflexivity* about the professional activities of members of the discipline

- a generalized interest in *practices,* especially reflective practice mediated by writing about an activity. ("Composition Studies" 131)

Now in the new millennium, a Consortium of Doctoral Programs in Rhetoric and Composition includes over seventy-four programs. The discipline has become extremely complex and networked with other organizations in which members conduct research on writing.[5] Also, two important online bibliographies have been established: the CCCC Bibliography, constructed by Todd Taylor, and CompPile, provided by Richard Haswell and Glen Blalock.

Studies of Composing Processes

During the early decades—the 1960s and 1970s—a groundswell of theory and research on writing took place. From the mid-1960s, members of the emerging field of rhetoric and composition began to challenge the teaching of writing as a "product" in which papers were assigned, handed in, and graded. Such teaching also focused on reading and discussing essays, completing exercises on style, and repeating drills on grammar. Little, if any, attention was paid to helping students get started, investigate ideas, consider readers, receive feedback on drafts, or revise. Richard Young, using Daniel Fogarty's term, dubbed this kind of teaching the *current-traditional* paradigm.

To counteract this stifling pedagogy, scholars began publishing research on composing processes. Gordon Rohman and Albert O. Wlecke, for example, introduced the concept of *prewriting*, citing the

> fundamental misconception which undermines so many of our best efforts in teaching writing: if we train students how to recognize an example of good prose, ("the rhetoric of the finished word") we have given them a basis on which to build their own writing abilities. All we have done, in fact, is to give them standards by which to judge the goodness or badness of their finished effort. *We haven't really taught them how to make that effort.* (106)

Janet Emig, studying the writing of twelfth graders, explained that these students engaged in prewriting and planning, including jottings, lists, and topic outlines. She described *prewriting* as "that part of the composing process that extends from the time a writer begins to perceive selectively certain features of his inner and/or outer environment with a view to writing about them—usually at the instigation of a stimulus—to the time when he first puts words or phrases on paper elucidating that perception" (39). Emig defined *planning* as "any oral and written establishment of elements and parameters before or during a discursive formulation" (39). Others, like Sondra Perl, used case studies to analyze the writing processes of unskilled writers; and still others proposed somewhat different conceptions of the writing process, such as writing as inquiry (e.g., Lauer, "Writing"; and Young, Becker, and Pike).

Later, a linear and reductive conception of the composing process emerged in classrooms as "prewrite-write-rewrite." Responding to this rigid view of the composing process, Linda Flower and John Hayes developed a cognitive model of writing based on protocol analyses of novice and experienced writers, positing distinctive writing features: (1) the task environment; (2) long-term memory; (3) planning; (4) translating; (5) reviewing; and (6) monitoring ("Cognitive"). They demonstrated that these features are hierarchical (one embedded in another), recursive, and goal-directed. Later, they also conducted research on the variety of ways writers record their planning ("Images"); the function of pauses in writing ("Pregnant"); the earliest act of composing ("Cognition"); and ways of working with constraints ("Dynamics"). In the 1980s, more studies were published on cognitive theories of writing, including Judith Langer and Arthur N. Applebee's *How Writing Shapes Thinking,* which reviewed research and included their own inquiry on how writing works to support learning; and Ronna Dillon and Robert Sternberg's edited collection *Cognition and Instruction,* which focused on cognition in different fields.

Features of Writing and Teaching Writing

The following section offers a closer look at significant writing features that became the focus of attention as the field grew throughout the final decades of the twentieth century: invention and audience; modes of discourse and genres; style, voice, ethos, ethics, and affect; responding to, revising, and evaluating texts; and literacy development, writing dysfunction, and writing diversity. Anyone interested in this field will find that current research and teaching continue to address these aspects, enlarging, building on, correcting, foregrounding, or, in some cases, even marginalizing them.

Invention and Audience

In the 1960s and 1970s, scholars argued for new theories of invention based on the classical topics and enthymemes (Corbett); adaptations of tagmemic linguistics that yielded an inventional guide of nine perspectives for students to deploy in the process of inquiry about their subjects (Young, Becker, and Pike); studies of heuristics—flexible discovery procedures (Lauer, "Heuristics"); and prewriting practices, including keeping a journal to help students discover their personal contexts and their points of urgency; engaging in meditation to transform an event into a personal experience; and creating analogies to generate and organize aspects of their subject (Rohman and Wlecke).[6] Later inventional pedagogies included freewriting (Elbow, *Writing*), the double notebook (Berthoff, *Forming*), and Kenneth Burke's pentad ("Questions").

In the 1960s, several scholars also published provocative essays on audience. Wayne Booth argued for the importance of considering audience, an aspect of writing that had been sidelined by the New Criticism. Walter Ong outlined a view of the writer's audience as a fiction, requiring specific skills on the part of the writer to invoke readers into particular roles ("Writer's"). Burke explained the notion of identification with readers (*Rhetoric*). Chaim Perelman elaborated on the centrality of audience for argumentation. In the 1970s, Young, Alton Becker, and Kenneth Pike developed a Rogerian audience theory that requires a negotiated middle ground for writers and readers. In the 1980s, Lisa Ede and Andrea Lunsford explained the notion of readers as addressed (present, right there) and invoked (constructed through the wording in a text) ("Audience"). Patricia Bizzell ("College") and James Porter ("Intertextuality") wrote about the discourse community as an audience for written discourse. In the 1990s, Phelps reviewed these audience theories and argued for Bakhtinian ideas of addressivity and heteroglossia as key concepts in a theory of readers ("Audience"). Finally, guides for analyzing audience and writing for readers began to appear in textbooks and scholarly monographs, including Porter's method of forum analysis (*Audience*) and Janice Lauer et al.'s "Writer/Reader Positioning Strategy."

Modes of Discourse and Genres

In the 1960s and 1970s, most composition courses and textbooks emphasized expository discourse, particularly critical essays on literature or other readings, and employed a category system that had originated earlier: the modes of discourse—exposition, description, narration, and argumentation. Early rhetoric and composition theorists criticized this modal system on several grounds, and they proposed new theories of discourse to supplant them. In 1968, James Moffett developed a structural model based on the evolving relations between writers, readers, and texts, arguing that the modes did not account for the developmental processes of children from K–12. In 1971, James Kinneavy proposed a set of four rhetorical aims (expressive, persuasive, literary, and referential) based on semiotics and the communication triangle, demonstrating that the current-traditional modes neglected expressive discourse and sidelined persuasion (*Theory*). In 1976, with John Cope and J. W. Campbell, Kinneavy argued for different modes (narration, description, classification, and evaluation) based on classical *status* and psychological notions of static and dynamic. James Britton and colleagues in England constructed a multidimensional model of mature written utterances to explain how children's writing becomes differentiated into diverse purposes and audiences. They based their model on the concept of participant/spectator and on a national survey of writing taught in the British schools from grades 5 to 12. All of these new classifications of discourse challenged the emphasis on teaching expository discourse throughout the grades and argued for the value of personal and persuasive discourse as well. In the 1980s, the International Association for Educational Achievement conducted a large study of composition instruction in seventeen countries, creating another model of types of writing (Gorman, Purves, and Degenhart). Alan Purves demonstrated that these countries also overemphasized expository writing and the teacher-examiner as audience. All of these new theories exposed the inadequacy of the reigning discourse model of exposition, description, narration, and argumentation, dubbed "EDNA" by Sharon Crowley (*Methodical*).

Studies also addressed the related concept of genre and its bearing on the teaching of writing. Here scholars argued that the reigning conception of genre was text-based: students learned only the formal features of genres like letters, résumés, and book reports. M. M. Bakhtin's influential work on "speech genres" offered a much richer view of genre, as did Carolyn Miller's new rhetorical theory of genre as social action, which defined genre as "typified rhetorical actions based in recurrent situations" (159). Miller maintained that the exigencies for writing genres are located in the social world and thus provide a social motive for action. Later, Anthony Paré and Graham Smart defined a genre as "a distinctive profile of regularities across four dimensions: a set of texts, the composing processes involved in creating these texts, the reading practices used to interpret them, and the social roles performed by writers and readers" (147). More recently, Anis Bawarshi has argued for the relationship between invention and genre. Although all of this work on theories of discourse and genres has influenced a number of textbooks and teaching practices, EDNA still governs many texts and classrooms. Why? The reasons for this intransigence are multiple. A huge percentage of composition teachers are unfamiliar with the above work on modes and genres because they have not been educated in the field of rhetoric and composition. Others wish to remain comfortable with a modal and form-based approach to teaching writing with which they are familiar. Textbook companies are also loath to go against this profitable grain. Further, teaching the modes of discourse with their emphasis on forms (however theoretically repudiated) fits with writing assignments that are still limited to classroom exercises or products.

Style, Voice, Ethos, Ethics, and Affect

Style was a prominent aspect of rhetoric in the Renaissance, and attention to formal style continued into the twentieth century in composition instruction. However, as rhetoric and composition emerged as a discipline in the 1960s, some scholars began to draw new attention to style, questioning dated doctrines like the hegemony of the periodic and balanced sentence and the preference for academic diction. Francis Christensen, for example, devised a generative rhetoric of the sentence and the paragraph, especially the cumulative sentence, based on his analysis of published contemporary writers. Louis Milic formulated a metaphysics of style and the practice of stylistics as a quantitative (later, computer-based) set of features of a writer's style that were less impressionistic than the then-current analyses of style. Richard Ohmann suggested the use of speech-act theory to analyze style and the nature of syntactic fluency. In the 1970s, Frank O'Hare and others conducted extensive studies on the pedagogy of sentence combining, proclaiming that sentence combining could not only improve syntactic skills throughout the grades but also teach grammar without formal terminology. Others, such as Richard Lanham, published textbooks emphasizing new ways of teaching style.[7]

The concept of voice has also been a staple of composition instruction over the years, although several meanings of the term *voice* have circulated. In the 1960s, new theories were postulated by scholars like Rohman and Wlecke, who suggested that students could reach self-actualization, their authentic voices, by using the journal, meditation, and analogy. Walker Gibson demonstrated how every writer's choices (of words, sentence structures, and other features) create a personality or voice. Ken Macrorie questioned the traditional advice about voice, condemning the artificial language in academic writing he called "Engfish." Others have associated voice with the classical concept of ethos, or a writer's character as it relates to a particular argument (Corder; Baumlin and Baumlin). Rhetoric and composition's notions of ethos have recently been complicated by postmodern views of subjectivity, or material and social identity (gender, race, class, etc.). Ethos has been related to ethics, and scholars such as Susan McLeod have proposed sophisticated roles for pathos in creating powerful written discourse of all kinds.[8]

Responding to, Revising, and Evaluating Texts

As rhetoric and composition grew into a full-fledged discipline, it turned its scholarly attention toward the matter of responding to students' texts. If writing is a process that cannot be codified into neat sequences (prewrite-write-rewrite), then teachers' interventions into those creative processes are critical to effective writing instruction. In contrast to the practice of giving students a single grade on a finished paper, scholars began to argue for alternative ways to respond. They conducted research on the kinds of responses that best facilitate deeper levels of revision than correcting surface errors and infelicities in vocabulary. In the 1980s, Nancy Sommers argued for the value of responding to student papers during the writing process to create a motive for revising and to offer revision tasks with different orders of complexity ("Responding"). Brooke Horvath differentiated formative from summative responses, describing formative responses as aimed at improving students' abilities and indicating what needs to be done, addressing large-scale problems, taking into account rhetorical processes, and offering comments with transfer value. Phelps characterized four types of attitudes toward reading students' texts: (1) a decontextual reading, cut off from the ongoing text and reader and often error-oriented; (2) a formative response that reacts to an evolving text and that treats writers and readers as "co-creators"; (3) a developmental attitude that incorporates the whole body of student work in a portfolio as extended text and analyzes work as stimulated by the class; and (4) a contextual attitude that reads a text as embedded in and interpenetrating many other discourses, a text with no determinate edges, and one in which development is analogous to the social construction of self ("Images"). Elizabeth Flynn described a feminist approach to reading student papers that entails oscillating between empathy and judgment; speaking about moral problems, especially conflicting responsibilities; offering solutions to problems through contextual and narrative means; receiving the language of the student with understanding, warmth, and concern; and allowing multiple revisions ("Learning").

During this time, scholars also became interested in the process of revision, conducting research and writing about its nature and pedagogy. In early composition classrooms, students received little advice about revision until after their papers had already been graded, assuming that this advice would carry over to the next papers. This lack of attention to revision as part of the composing process was another feature of the product-based pedagogy of the "current-traditional" paradigm. In 1978, Donald Murray stressed the value of revision as seeing again, not just correcting errors; Ellen Nold researched the difference between surface and meaning-based revision; and Sommers contrasted the revisions of first-year college students and experienced adult writers ("Revision"). In the 1980s and later, other research addressed the features of good revising: Lester Faigley and Stephen Witte, for instance, demonstrated that expert writers based their revision on situational variables like reasons for writing, genre, medium, and level of formality. Just as research on invention entailed a process conception of writing, so too did work on revision.

One of the thorniest issues in rhetoric and composition teaching has been the matter of grading. In the 1970s, two longstanding practices were critiqued: the teacher's use of single grades on class papers and the machine grading of multiple-choice answers on national tests. Consequently, new methods of evaluation were proposed. Charles Cooper described the practice of holistic grading of writing samples on national tests by several raters who had been carefully trained. Richard Lloyd-Jones developed primary-trait scoring for the National Assessment of Educational Progress, in which trained raters examined student writing for several different key factors. In these two cases, students submitted writing samples in response to prompts, a major step for testing institutions. Paul Diederich advocated analytic grading on student papers in which teachers both commented on and evaluated student work in several categories. In the 1980s, members of the field raised questions about validity and reliability (Huot) and the evaluation of other aspects of writing, such as students' abilities to invent and revise. Faigley, Roger Cherry, David Jolliffe, and Anna Skinner devised a way to test the development of writers' knowledge and processes of composing. Witte and Faigley constructed methods for evaluating writing programs, while Barbara Davis, Michael Scriven, and Susan Thomas elaborated on the evaluation of composition instruction. In 1997, contributors to a volume edited by Kathleen Yancey and Irwin Weiser described the recent widespread use of portfolios as a basis for assessment.

Literacy Development, Writing Dysfunction, and Writing Diversity

In the 1980s, scholars in rhetoric and composition began to draw on another body of scholarship—literacy studies. Stimulated by the work of Ong (*Orality*), Jack Goody and Ian Watt, and Sylvia Scribner, researchers such as Shirley Brice Heath, David Bartholomae, Deborah Brandt, and Cheryl Geisler addressed developmental issues, questions of orality and writing, and different kinds of literacy. One of the issues opened up by this body of research was the extent to which "natural" literacy (being immersed in community environments) or schooling can develop higher levels of literacy.[9]

With the introduction of open admissions policies at many universities, students brought a range of writing problems with them to college writing courses. Responding to these needs, scholars conducted research on writing dysfunction and other problems characteristic of underprepared students. Mina Shaughnessy examined the "errors" of students at an urban university. Mike Rose analyzed the cognitive dimension of writer's block. Tom Fox studied the difficulties of African American students. Glynda Hull and Mike Rose researched the sociocognitive implications of remediation. Other scholars analyzed the nature of error (Williams, "Phenomenology," and Bartholomae, "Study").[10] In addition, institutions across the country initiated writing labs or centers and basic writing courses, and founded publications to share these efforts. For example, Muriel Harris established a writing lab at Purdue University and started the *Writing Lab Newsletter*. Over the years, the area of basic writing has developed its own organization, conferences, and journals.[11]

In 1974, an important document was published by the Conference on College Composition and Communication, supporting the legitimate use of social dialects in students' writing: "Students' Right to Their Own Language." Based on linguistic scholarship on regional and social dialects (e.g., the work of Geneva Smitherman and William Labov), the document rejected the requirement for a single American Standard English in all student writing and affirmed "the students' right to their own patterns and varieties of language—the dialects of their nurture or whatever dialects in which they find their own identity and style" (2).

In addition to the differences in literacy development mentioned above, another kind of diversity has concerned the field—second-language writers and cross-cultural literacy. Scholars in ESL writing and contrastive rhetoric have produced a burgeoning literature on teaching writing to ESL students and on writing in different cultures. For example, Ulla Connor and Purves studied cross-cultural writing for first- and second-language writers, and Ilona Leki, Tony Silva, and Paul Kei Matsuda researched the nature of second-language writing and the relationship between composition studies and the field of ESL writing.[12]

The Social Turn

In the 1980s, a rhizomatic spread of theory, research, and new pedagogy occurred, called by some the "social turn." New theories of social construction and collaboration emerged. For example, Bizzell and Kenneth Bruffee argued against what they believed to be the field's individualist orientation. Bizzell dubbed theorists as either inner-directed (those concerned with how individuals construct meaning) or outer-directed (those studying how communities shape thinking). She also urged that teachers should involve students in learning the strategies of particular discourse communities ("Foundationalism"). Bruffee advanced the social construction of knowledge, claiming that while cognitive theorists held to an objective/subjective binary, believed in a view of knowledge as certainty, and viewed the individual self as the source of thought, he on the other hand considered thought as created by a community of peers. In 1986, Karen Burke LeFevre delineated rhetorical invention as a process in which the individual and the socioculture coexist and define each other; she argued for invention as collaboration between the writer and audience. LeFevre also asserted that there were several ways in which invention was social: when writers are influenced socially; when they employ language that is itself created and owned by discourse communities; when they use knowledge from earlier generations; when they conduct internal dialogues with others that grant premises; when they work with editors and evaluators; when they are shaped by social collectives; and when they rely on receivers and evaluators in the social context.

A corollary of social-construction theory that began to enter the classroom was the practice of collaboration. The first efforts involved students in writing groups responding and giving feedback and advice on their final drafts before revising. Later, groups collaborated throughout the composing process.[13] Another social theory was introduced in response to critiques of cognitive rhetoric, as Linda Flower outlined a theory of sociocognitive rhetoric arguing for a theory of interaction between cognition and context and advocating a grounded theory based on observation that would help teachers teach and enable the field to learn something new about how writers negotiate context and create goals (*Construction*).

Sites of Research and Teaching

During the early years of rhetoric and composition's development into a full-fledged discipline, the predominant site for inquiry was the introductory composition course. In the following decades, however, the field extended its research and teaching into multiple sites, including writing across the curriculum, writing program administration, professional writing, computers and composition, civic rhetoric, and issues related to writers' gender and race.

Writing Across the Curriculum (WAC) and Writing in the Disciplines (WID)

In the 1980s, scholars and teachers in rhetoric and composition began to devote attention to writing across the curriculum, with many universities starting WAC programs involving writing instructors from English and professors in other fields. The work in this area ranged from the development of new pedagogies to research and theory on the inquiry processes and the nature of knowledge in different fields. An early proponent of WAC, Elaine

Maimon, with several coauthors in different disciplines, published a textbook that provided examples of writing in a number of fields: literary-analytic papers, term papers in the social sciences, case studies, reports of empirical findings, and lab reports in the natural sciences (*Writing*). Toby Fulwiler and Art Young offered collections of essays that described WAC writing processes, such as the use of journals in different courses and effective research models, as well as surveys of classroom practices, a report on the effect of WAC on student writing apprehension, and the impact of peer critique on biology lab reports. Judy Kirscht, Rhonda Levine, and John Reiff argued that teaching a rhetoric of inquiry in the disciplines helps writers "learn how knowledge has been constructed as well as what that knowledge is" (374). A number of WAC textbooks have also been published, such as Christine Hult's *Researching and Writing Across the Curriculum*, which identifies a range of writing and inquiry processes in science, technology, social science, and the humanities, describing practices such as observation and hypothesis formulation; Donald Zimmerman and Dawn Rodrigues's *Research and Writing in the Disciplines*, which presents strategies for task analysis and generation of ideas about a topic using freewriting, brainstorming, patterned notes, and tree diagrams; and Katherine Gottschalk and Keith Hjortshoj's *Elements of Teaching Writing*, a text for instructors in all disciplines.

To complement this work on writing across the curriculum, scholars in rhetoric and composition began studying the writing practices of scientists, philosophers, historians, musicians, engineers, economists, and the like, initiating a corollary subfield called writing in the disciplines (WID). One purpose of this effort was to discover the kinds of discourses and writing processes that scholars used in their own academic publishing. Another goal was to show how writing helped these scholars create their own kinds of knowledge. For example, Rodney Farnsworth and Avon Crismore studied Darwin's use of the visual, showing how he employed drawings, diagrams, and maps to argue his theories. Surveying all of this work, David Russell produced a history of writing in the academic disciplines from 1870 to 1990.

Writing Program Administration (WPA)

Another site of theory and teaching in rhetoric and composition is writing program administration, which, according to James Slevin, is intellectual work that entails "pedagogical self-consciousness, curricular change, and institutional reform" (38). Collections of essays have recently featured accounts by writing program administrators on their research and program development. For instance, Shirley K. Rose and Irwin Weiser presented WPAs' research on various aspects of writing program administration, including evaluation; and Joseph Janangelo and Kristine Hansen's collection, *Resituating Writing*, offers advice on constructing and administering writing programs. Lastly, two professional organizations have issued statements to guide program administrators: the CCCC Executive Committee's "Statement of Principles and Standards for the Postsecondary Teaching of Writing" and the Council of Writing Program Administrators' "Evaluating the Intellectual Work of Writing Program Administrators" (WPA). This context of teaching and research is now a flourishing corollary field of rhetoric and composition.

Writing in the Workplace and Professional Writing

Another site of rhetoric and composition research is workplace and professional writing. Scholars such as Jean A. Lutz and C. Gilbert Storms have investigated the types of writing done in different corporations, nonprofit sites, and a range of other professional discourse areas. Some, like Patricia Sullivan and Porter, and the authors in a collection edited by Nancy Blyler and Charlotte Thralls, have developed a body of professional writing theory.[14] Professional writing has become a strong corollary field of rhetoric and composition with its own graduate programs, conferences, and journals.

Computers and Composition

Since rhetoric and composition's beginning, there has been a focus on writing as a technology (e.g., the work of Ong). As the computer emerged, and then the Internet, theorists and teachers investigated the relationship between composition and these technologies. The field has also introduced technology into composition classrooms, both in terms of planning, drafting, and revising online, and of participating in chatrooms. Work on technology has burgeoned into a large subfield of rhetoric and composition, with its own journals, such as *Computers and Composition*, and conferences, such as Computers and Writing, and an important related area for research and teaching is visual rhetoric.[15] For more discussions of these developments, see the CCCC statement on teaching writing in digital environments.

Civic Rhetoric

The field of rhetoric and composition has also maintained an abiding interest in another context—civic rhetoric, the original emphasis in classical rhetoric. In terms of pedagogy, students have more recently received instruction in writing texts for various communities to which they belong, including neighborhood groups, churches, state organizations, and public media, addressing issues of concern to members of these communities. Currently, this effort has been linked with service-learning projects. In terms of research, scholars have investigated all kinds of civic discourse, both in contemporary and historical settings. For example, Thomas Moriarty analyzed the role of public discourse in peacefully ending apartheid in South Africa. Ellen Cushman studied the rhetorician as an agent of social change. William Craig Rice examined the relationship between public discourse and academic inquiry. Sandra Stotsky and Barbara Beierl argued for connecting civic education and language education. Issues in this field continue to attract the attention of many rhetoric and composition theorists.

Writing, Gender, and Race

Since the 1980s, rhetoric and composition has investigated the relationship between gender and writing, drawing on feminist studies of various persuasions. Composition scholars including Flynn, Lillian Bridwell-Bowles, and Lynn Worsham have described women's ways of knowing and composing, including language play; using body language and personal and emotional discourse; composing personal narratives; and stressing the nonlinear, associative, and inchoate. Others have fashioned feminist pedagogies: for instance, Cinthia Gannett has advocated journal writing and Elisabeth Däumer and Sandra Runzo have promoted naming oneself instead of being defined by others. Joy Ritchie and Gesa Kirsch (*Women*) have critiqued some of this work as essentialist, i.e., hiding differences in race, class, sexual orientation, and ethnicity, and Susan Jarratt has criticized pedagogies that urge women to avoid conflict ("Feminism"). Another emphasis in this work can be seen in Susan Miller's arguments against the practice of hiring part-time instructors, primarily women, to teach composition without adequate benefits. A newer area of inquiry, queer studies, has emerged with the writings of people such as Harriet Malinowitz. In addition, feminist researchers have conducted studies in revisionary historiography, investigating women who were ignored in history (e.g., Lunsford; Donawerth).[16]

Others scholars have researched the connection between writing, race, and ethnic groups. Prominent in this area are Jacqueline Jones Royster, who has studied the writings of nineteenth- and early twentieth-century black women, and Shirley Wilson Logan, who has analyzed the persuasive discourse of nineteenth-century black women. Another example from this growing body of scholarship includes the work of Beverly J. Moss and Keith Walters, who have examined "difference" in the classroom. Victor Villanueva, David Chaille, Kay M. Losey, and Pedro Reyes and colleagues have described the challenges and successes of Chicanos and other Latinos inside and outside the classroom. Scholars like Jeanne Smith, Bea Medicine, and Malea Powell have provided insights into Native American rhetoric and the challenges of teaching Native American students. And recently Gary Olson and Worsham have edited a collection of essays dealing with race, rhetoric, and the postcolonial.

Concerns and Debates in the Field

As the above history chronicles, in both teaching and scholarship specialists in rhetoric and composition have engaged in a number of debates about important issues. As new ones arose, previous ones moved out of the limelight or were reconfigured. The sections below discuss some of the most prominent of these issues over the last forty years, including disciplinarity, writing processes and pedagogies, and writing ideologies.

Disciplinarity

As rhetoric and composition gained the status of a discipline, several conflicts arose. A good description of these conflicts is summarized by Phelps as "constitutive tensions":

> conflicts of method, and of their underlying epistemologies and values; the dichotomy of theory and practice; conflicting notions of the ideal relationship and the balance between the individual and culture or society, as mediated by language or literacy; language as knowing versus language as doing, as an epistemology or as symbolic action; and ethical conceptions of the disciplinary project as obligated primarily to individual students or to society. ("Composition" 131)

In the 1990s and the new millennium, the notion of disciplinarity itself has been challenged with arguments such as the limitations imposed by the narrowness of disciplinary methods of inquiry. Yet others have argued that because of its multimodality, rhetoric and composition does not have such disciplinary limitations. Slevin maintains that a discipline should deal with "the work of transmission and transformation, and its representation therefore incorporates all the agents, students as well as teachers, teachers as well as scholars, who engage in this activity" (41).[17]

Writing Processes and Pedagogies

In the 1970s, one of the field's first disagreements occurred between Ann Berthoff ("Problem") and Janice Lauer ("Heuristics" and "Response") over the value and nature of heuristics, initiating a continuing debate over the teaching of invention. In the following decades, critiques and rejoinders were published about the use of heuristics, including David Perkins's *The Mind's Best Work* and Worsham's "The Question Concerning Invention."

Theorists of social construction argued for new frameworks for invention beyond what they considered to be an excessive focus on individual inquiry. LeFevre outlined a theory of invention as a social act, and other composition theorists designed new heuristics to guide cultural critique, to analyze signifying practices, and to move invention into the civic sphere (e.g., James Berlin and Michael Vivion; Victor Vitanza, "From Heuristic"; and Bruce McComiskey, *Teaching Composition*).[18]

Another nettling issue that continues to plague the field is the superficial or even missing attention to audience or readers in teaching composition. Most composition courses still assume that the English teacher is the only reader for all papers in the course, thus failing to develop in students flexibility in writing for other readers—both academic and outside the academy. In grading papers, many teachers still do not take into account the suitability of the text for the intended reader. Even though a variety of new audience theories have been developed and implemented in pedagogy (as discussed above), many textbooks today continue to offer students minimal help in analyzing their rhetorical situations and writing for a range of readers. This issue is related to the continuing dominance of the modes of discourse—exposition, description, narration, and argumentation—which continues to place emphasis on the teacher as audience and on exposition and literary analysis as the types of writing assigned. Pedagogy still largely centers on the imitation of genres in collections of essays organized on these modal principles. This orientation persists even though scholars such as Moffett, Kinneavy, Frank D'Angelo, Britton et al., and Purves have exposed the inadequacy of this model and despite the fact that scholars like Bakhtin, Miller, Aviva Freedman and Peter Medway, Paré and Smart, and Bawarshi have developed more rhetorically based and relevant conceptions of genre.

One of the most controversial aspects of the work in rhetoric and composition in the eyes of the public is the field's teaching of grammar, spelling, and punctuation. Research and theory have discredited the full-frontal teaching of grammar: George Hillocks's meta-analysis demonstrated that direct grammar instruction has a negative effect on the use of "correct" grammar. However, this formalist pedagogy continues as students today face national assessments. The more effective approach—working with grammar and errors on a more individual basis in relation to the rest of the student's writing—has not yet been implemented in as many classrooms as the research warrants.

A newer issue is the challenge to process theories of composing by a postprocess theory of writing which claims that providing guidance to students during composing is not useful; instead, teachers are advised to return to the pedagogy of interpreting finished texts as classroom writing instruction (Kent). Among others, Debra Jacobs has responded to the postprocess critique, arguing that "dismissing process theories and pedagogies by identifying them with only certain versions of process can limit instructors' efforts to help students engage in critical inquiry and to develop ethically" (662). Some have contended that Thomas Kent is attacking a straw person—a rigid and limited version of "process"—and is ignoring the fact that the rich body of research on aspects of writing (described above) assumes a process conception of writing.

Writing Ideologies

By the end of the 1980s, several different ideologies were claiming the allegiances of different groups of scholars and teachers in rhetoric and composition. These conflicting ideologies have influenced not only the types of scholarship conducted but also the types of teaching practices used. In 1986, Faigley described three competing theories of process, informed by different ideologies: (1) the expressive, valuing integrity, spontaneity, and originality; (2) the cognitive, valuing heuristics and recursive processes; and (3) the social, valuing discourse communities and language development as a historical and cultural process. Faigley concluded that studies of writing should draw on the best of these theories ("Competing"). In 1988, Berlin situated composition theories within three ideologies he called the cognitive, expressivist, and social-epistemic, critiquing the first two by arguing that cognitive rhetoric centers on the individual mind whose structures are considered to be in perfect harmony with the structures of the rational, invariable, material world, and that expressive rhetoric stresses the power of the inherently good individual whose writing process seeks self-discovery ("Rhetoric"). Berlin privileged social-epistemic rhetoric, which, he contended, is a self-critical dialectical interaction between the writer, society, and language. Some theorists have concluded that these ideologies are not mutually exclusive, while others argue that only some features of these ideologies are compatible with those of other ideologies.

In the late 1980s, rhetoric and composition scholars began to use theories of deconstruction and poststructuralism in their theory building. Sharon Crowley described some of deconstruction's challenges to composition's primary beliefs, such as that (1) the writing process begins with the originating author; (2) writing repeats the student's knowledge; (3) language is a transparent medium; (4) the writer is the center of writing; and (5) the absence of readers is a necessary condition for composing (*Teacher's Introduction*). As Berlin explains, poststructuralism maintains that the subject (the writer) is constructed by various signifying practices and ways of using language in a given historical moment ("Poststructuralism"). A debate that has emerged from this influence concerns the apparent loss of the writer's agency.

In the 1980s and 1990s, some rhetoric and composition theorists and teachers started using cultural studies to inform their work. They envisioned composition classes as sites where students could examine their values and the views of other groups in society and prepare to be active citizens. For example, contributors to a volume edited by Ira Shor developed Freirean approaches to teaching composition that encouraged students to pose problems about their cultures and to engage with their teachers in dialogue. Bizzell also called on the work of Paulo Freire to help students develop a critical consciousness that is both deconstructive and constructive (*Academic*). Berlin devised and taught guides to help students analyze how their subjectivities of race, class, and gender are constructed by the codes in their cultures ("Composition").[19] This work in cultural studies provoked concerns from other composition instructors that students were only able to retain negative attitudes after critique as long as they were not given strategies for revisioning or changing their cultures.

By the twenty-first century, postmodernism had become influential in rhetoric and composition, although it also generated considerable debate. Faigley listed several postmodern tenets that the field should consider: (1) that consciousness is not primary; (2) that master narratives of human progress or human rights should be rejected and language should be considered the start of knowledge; (3) that the writer is written by the discourse; and (4) that there is no agency as in a conscious and directed view of invention (*Fragments*). Victor Vitanza described postmodern invention in terms of Lyotard's notion of paralogy as "'discontinuous, catastrophic, nonrectifiable, and paradoxical.' It (re)turns —that is, radically tropes" (*Negation* 147). Instead of consensus, Vitanza drew on Gilles Deleuze and Félix Guattari's focus on "'outsider thought,' 'nomad thought,' and 'schizo-dissensus.'" (148). Vitanza also probed the consequences of postmodernism for historical studies of rhetoric.

Contending with some of these postmodern tenets, Barbara Couture critiqued their "exclusion of truth from writing [. . .], their acceptance of philosophical relativism as the basis of all truth claims" (2–3); and their acceptance of "personal resistance as *the* method of securing a true and valued self-identity" (2–3). In contrast, she described a phenomenological rhetoric of writing that "considers writing [. . .] consonant with the view of people as purposeful beings" (3); that has three central premises: "(1) all essences or truths are located in subjective experience, (2) truth is an outcome of intersubjective understanding, and (3) intersubjective understanding progresses toward truth through writing" (4). Couture also maintained that the following standards could be used for evaluating the truth and rightness of discourse: congruence, consensus, and commensurability. This issue remains salient in the field today.

Methodology

Crucial to developing rhetoric and composition's identity as a discipline has been its incorporation of several methods of inquiry. In "Composition Studies: Dappled Discipline," Lauer argues for composition as a discipline that uses multiple modes of inquiry (theoretical, historical, and empirical) in studying the complex domain of written discourse. She also explains that the field has dual readerships for its work (i.e., scholars and teachers) and is largely motivated in its research by challenges in teaching composition. Lauer also described these features of the field's methodology as multimodal ("Rhetoric"). Prominent among these modes of inquiry have been historical studies; theory building; empirical research (from qualitative studies like ethnographies to quantitative studies like experiments and meta-analyses); discourse analysis and interpretive studies; feminist and teacher research; and postmodern investigations. In turn, multimodality has put pressure on the field, especially in terms of the responsibility it poses to graduate programs for preparing students to become literate in all of these modes. In addition, postmodernists have attacked empirical research, especially quantitative studies, as positivist. Some graduate programs have ignored historical inquiry. But the field as a whole continues to pursue these diverse types of scholarship.

Conclusion

Where is the discipline of rhetoric and composition now, in the first decade of the twenty-first century? Doctoral study in the field has increased from a small number of programs in the late seventies and early eighties to over seventy programs, as represented by the Consortium of Doctoral Programs in Rhetoric and Composition, while masters' programs and undergraduate majors and minors are appearing at increasing rates.

All of the above methodologies, theories, sites of research, and issues still circulate in rhetoric and composition, continuing to stimulate research and influence teaching. Some have been foregrounded in different periods of rhetoric and composition's development, exerting theoretical and ideological dominance at various times. Some have had more impact on teaching than others. Some modes of inquiry have flourished, like theory building, critical inquiry, and interpretive studies. Historical studies have continued steadily, with increased interest in later periods like the nineteenth century and in revisionist historiography of figures marginalized on the bases of race, gender, class, and sexual orientation, as well as neglected international cultures. Observation-based studies (empirical, especially quantitative studies) have declined, largely due to changes in dominant ideologies, such as postmodernism. As this chapter has attempted to chronicle, there has been a rhizomatic spread of different contexts of writing and levels of teaching in which research and study are being conducted. Significantly, the field has embraced and contributed to developments in technology and visual rhetoric. Finally, the emphasis and nature of different writing pedagogies has fluctuated, rising, declining, and recycling.

What have been the impacts of these expansions, shifts, and issues? I would maintain that each of the decades of work in rhetoric and composition has contributed to our understanding of written discourse and its teaching, opening hitherto unexplored aspects, building on previous work, critiquing or qualifying it, and sometimes challenging its underlying claims and arguments. This is the normal work of a healthy discipline. For example, the social turn helped the field to recognize important dimensions of previous work that had been neglected and also initiated fruitful new lines of inquiry. Occasionally that debate became unnecessarily dismissive of good prior work. While critiques of some aspects of empirical work (both qualitative and quantitative) have been a useful caution for the field, a negative result has been the exclusion of this mode of inquiry from some graduate programs, preventing students from becoming literate in part of the field's research. Another unfortunate consequence has been to limit the number of empirical studies conducted to determine the effectiveness of different pedagogies (e.g., Hillocks's meta-analysis), thus leaving the field without evidence to support pedagogical claims. Postprocess discussions have been helpful in debunking rigid and limited conceptions of the writing process. Unfortunately, however, some claims of postprocess are encouraging the same text-based approach to teaching writing favored by the current-traditional paradigm, propagating the notion that the *only* way to develop writers is to have students read and discuss other texts as a source for topics, information, ideas, and models of writing, denying that any process elements, particularly inventional arts, can be taught. Overall, though, rhetoric and composition has indeed become a dappled discipline, addressing the twenty-first century's need for deeper and richer understanding of texts and of their contexts and processes, the development of all levels of literacy, and the potential central role of that literacy in empowering people to shape contemporary world culture. Rhetoric and composition continues to be dynamic, fluid, and ever more complex, with practitioners increasing exponentially. What remains constant is a dedication to studying and teaching written discourse, motivating and inspiring new research and pedagogies. What also sustains the field is a commitment to helping students and others develop their powers of inquiry and communication in order to reenvision and enrich their everyday, civic, academic, and workplace lives.

Notes

1. For accounts of this history, see Atwill; Berlin and Inkster; Connors, *Composition-Rhetoric;* Crowley, *Methodical;* and Lauer, *Invention.*

2. For fuller accounts of these developments, see Goggin; Lauer, "Doctoral"; Phelps, *Composition;* and Roen, Brown, and Enos, *Living.*

3. On topics and *status,* see Gage; Lauer, "Issues." For a discussion of enthymemes and examples, see Raymond, "Enthymemes," and Walker. On *kairos,* see Kinneavy, *"Kairos."* For discussions of the Sophists, see Jarratt, *Rereading;* McComiskey, *Gorgias;* and Vitanza, *Negation.* On recovering the work of women and minorities, see Hobbs, *Nineteenth-Century;* Logan; Royster, "Perspectives" and *Traces.*

4. Some of these histories include Atwill; Berlin, *Rhetoric and Reality* and *Writing Instruction;* Crowley, *Methodical;* Richard Enos, *Literate Mode* and *Greek Rhetoric;* Hobbs, *Rhetoric;* Lunsford; Stewart and Stewart; Swearingen; and Welch.

5. Some of these organizations include the American Educational Research Association, the National Council of Teachers of English, the Rhetoric Society of America, the National Communication Association, the International Society for the History of Rhetoric, and the American Society for the History of Rhetoric.

6. For a variety of treatments of the role of heuristics in the composing process, see Lauer, *Invention.*

7. Later, researchers like Donald Rubin and Kathryn Greene studied the relationship between gender and style; Peter Elbow wrote on academic discourse style ("Reflections"); and Wendy Bishop edited a collection of essays on style. In terms of form, Winterowd explained the rhetorical consequences of form and forged a grammar of coherence ("Dispositio" and "Grammar"); and Phelps proposed a theory of writing coherence ("Dialectics").

8. In the 1990s, Porter discussed postmodern ethics ("Developing"), ethics and the Internet (*Rhetorical*), and ethics in corporate composing ("Role"); and Kirsch discussed the importance of ethics in qualitative research (*Ethical*).

9. For an overview of these subjects, see Phelps, *Composition*.

10. Others who have contributed to this body of research include Robert Connors, who published a history of grammar instruction in American colleges ("Grammar"); Patrick Hartwell, who distinguished four types of grammar; and Dennis Baron, who studied the relationship between grammar and gender.

11. Scholarship on basic writing and remediation includes Marilyn Sternglass's *Time to Know Them* and Bruce Horner and Min-Zhan Lu's *Representing the "Other."*

12. Also see the volume edited by Joan Carson and Leki. Haixia Wang and others have examined the role of rhetoric in the writings of other cultures.

13. Other publications on this pedagogy include Kris Bosworth and Sharon Hamilton's collection and James Leonard et al.'s collection of essays that addressed the issue of authority in collaborative writing. Ede and Lunsford researched the collaboration of professional writers (*Singular*). John Schilb examined the ethics of collaboration; and John Trimbur and others offered critiques of collaboration ("Consensus").

14. Other collections of essays have been published in this area including those edited by Patricia Sullivan and Jennie Dautermann and by Rachel Spilka.

15. For example, see Gail Hawisher and Patricia Sullivan's scholarship on writing and the internet, and Tharon Howard's work on the rhetoric of electronic communities. Other work includes collections of essays on technology, e.g., that edited by Stuart Selber; and, in 1999, a review of the work on technology and literacy provided by Cynthia Selfe.

16. See also collections of essays on gendered work in composition that have offered diverse perspectives, e.g., Phelps and Emig; Sutherland and Sutcliffe; and the "Special Cluster: Queer Theory" in *JAC*.

17. For a discussion of this disciplinary complexity, see Phelps, "Composition"; Enos and Brown; and Dale L. Sullivan.

18. In the late 1990s and the new millennium, several books on invention were published, including a reference guide to the field's work on invention since the 1960s, with a history of inventional issues since the classical period (Lauer, *Invention*); a collection of essays (Atwill and Lauer); and other books on invention, including Michael Carter's *Where Writing Begins: A Postmodern Reconstruction*; Janet Atwill's *Rhetoric Reclaimed*; and Bawarshi's *Genre and the Invention of the Writer*.

19. Trimbur (*Call*) and McComiskey (*Teaching*) developed pedagogies based on cultural studies.

Works Cited

Atwill, Janet M. *Rhetoric Reclaimed: Aristotle and the Liberal Tradition*. Ithaca, NY: Cornell UP, 1998.

Atwill, Janet M., and Janice M. Lauer, eds. *Perspectives on Rhetorical Invention*. Knoxville: U of Tennessee P, 2002.

Bakhtin, M. M. *Speech Genres and Other Essays*. Trans. Vern W. McGee. Ed. Caryl Emerson and Michael Holquist. Austin: U of Texas P, 1986.

Baron, Dennis E. *Grammar and Gender*. New Haven: Yale UP, 1986.

Bartholomae, David. "The Study of Error." *College Composition and Communication* 31 (1980): 253–69.

———. "Writing on the Margins: The Concept of Literacy in Higher Education." *A Sourcebook for Basic Writing Teachers*. Ed. Theresa Enos. New York: Random, 1987. 66–83.

Baumlin, James S., and Tita French Baumlin, eds. *Ethos: New Essays in Rhetorical and Critical Theory*. Dallas: Southern Methodist UP, 1994.

Bawarshi, Anis. *Genre and the Invention of the Writer: Reconsidering the Place of Invention in Composition*. Logan: Utah State UP, 2003.

Berlin, James A. "Composition and Cultural Studies." *Composition and Resistance*. Ed. C. Mark Hurlbert and Michael Blitz. Portsmouth, NH: Boynton, 1991. 47–55.

———. "Poststructuralism, Cultural Studies, and the Composition Classroom: Postmodern Theory in Practice." *Rhetoric Review* 11 (1992): 16–33.

———. "Rhetoric and Ideology in the Writing Class." *College English* 50 (1988): 477–94.

———. *Rhetoric and Reality: Writing Instruction in American Colleges, 1900–1985*. Studies in Writing and Rhetoric. Carbondale: Southern Illinois UP; Urbana, IL: CCCC/NCTE, 1987.

———. *Writing Instruction in Nineteenth-Century American Colleges*. Studies in Writing and Rhetoric. Carbondale: Southern Illinois UP; Urbana, IL: CCCC/NCTE, 1984.

Berlin, James A., and Robert P. Inkster. "Current-Traditional Rhetoric: Paradigm and Practice." *Freshman English News* 8 (1980): 1–4, 13–14.

Berlin, James A., and Michael J. Vivion, eds. *Cultural Studies in the English Classroom*. Portsmouth, NH: Boynton, 1992.

Berthoff, Ann. *Forming, Thinking, Writing: The Composing Imagination*. Rochelle Park, NJ: Hayden, 1978.

———. "The Problem of Problem Solving: Response to Janice Lauer." *Contemporary Rhetoric: A Conceptual Background with Readings*. Ed. W. Ross Winterowd. New York: Harcourt, 1975. 90–97.

Bishop, Wendy, ed. *Elements of Alternate Style: Essays on Writing and Revision*. Portsmouth, NH: Boynton, 1997.

Bizzell, Patricia. *Academic Discourse and Critical Consciousness*. Pittsburgh: U of Pittsburgh P, 1992.

———. "College Composition: Initiation into This Academic Discourse Community." *Curriculum Inquiry* 12 (1982): 191–207.

———. "Foundationalism and Anti-Foundationalism in Composition Studies." *Pre/Text* 7 (1986): 37–56.

Blyler, Nancy Roundy, and Charlotte Thralls, eds. *Professional Communication: The Social Perspective*. Newbury Park, CA: Sage, 1993.

Booth, Wayne C. "The Rhetorical Stance." *College Composition and Communication* 14 (1963): 139–45.

Bosworth, Kris, and Sharon J. Hamilton, eds. *Collaborative Learning: Underlying Processes and Effective Techniques.* San Francisco: Jossey, 1994.

Brandt, Deborah. *Literacy as Involvement: The Acts of Writers, Readers, and Texts.* Carbondale: Southern Illinois UP, 1990.

———. *Literacy in American Lives.* New York: Cambridge UP, 2001.

Bridwell-Bowles, Lillian. "Discourse and Diversity: Experimental Writing within the Academy." *Feminine Principles and Women's Experience in American Composition and Rhetoric.* Ed. Louise Wetherbee Phelps and Janet Emig. Pittsburgh: U of Pittsburgh P, 1995. 43–66.

Britton, James, et al. *The Development of Writing Abilities (11–18).* London: Macmillan, 1975.

Bruffee, Kenneth A. "Social Construction, Language, and the Authority of Knowledge: A Bibliographic Essay." *College English* 48 (1986): 773–90.

Burke, Kenneth. "Questions and Answers about the Pentad." *College Composition and Communication* 29 (1978): 330–35.

———. *A Rhetoric of Motives.* New York: Prentice, 1950.

Carson, Joan G., and Ilona Leki, eds. *Reading in the Composition Classroom: Second Language Perspectives.* Boston: Heinle, 1993.

Carter, Michael. *Where Writing Begins: A Postmodern Reconstruction.* Carbondale: Southern Illinois UP, 2003.

CCCC. "Students' Right to Their Own Language." *College English* 36 (1974): 709–26.

CCCC Committee on Assessment. "Writing Assessment: A Position Statement." *College Composition and Communication* 46 (1995): 430–37.

CCCC Executive Committee. *CCCC Position Statement on Teaching, Learning, and Assessing Writing in Digital Environments.* 2004. 15 May 2006 http://www.ncte.org/cccc/resources/positions/123773.htm.

———. *Statement of Principles and Standards for the Postsecondary Teaching of Writing.* 1989. 15 May 2006 http://www.ncte.org/cccc/resources/positions/123790.htm.

Chaille, David. *English as a Second Language: A Guide to Culture and Writing for Teachers of Hispanic Students.* Culture and Writing, Vol. 1. Beverly Hills: Easy Aids, 1978.

Christensen, Francis. *Notes toward a New Rhetoric: Six Essays for Teachers.* New York: Harper, 1967.

Connor, Ulla. *Contrastive Rhetoric: Cross-Cultural Aspects of Second-Language Writing.* New York: Cambridge UP, 1996.

Connors, Robert J. *Composition-Rhetoric: Backgrounds, Theory, and Pedagogy.* Pittsburgh: U of Pittsburgh P, 1997.

———. "Grammar in American College Composition: An Historical Overview." *The Territory of Language: Linguistics, Stylistics, and the Teaching of Composition.* Ed. Donald A. McQuade. Carbondale: Southern Illinois UP, 1986. 3–22.

Cooper, Charles R. "Holistic Evaluation of Writing." *Evaluating Writing: Describing, Measuring, Judging.* Ed. Charles R. Cooper and Lee Odell. Urbana, IL: NCTE, 1977. 3–31.

Corbett, Edward P. J. *Classical Rhetoric for the Modern Student.* New York: Oxford UP, 1965.

Corder, Jim. "Hunting Lieutenant Chadbourne: A Search for Ethos Whether Real or Pretended." *Ethos: New Essays in Rhetorical and Critical Theory.* Ed. James S. Baumlin and Tita French Baumlin. Dallas: Southern Methodist UP, 1994. 343–65.

Couture, Barbara. *Toward a Phenomenological Rhetoric: Writing, Profession, and Altruism.* Carbondale: Southern Illinois UP, 1998.

Crowley, Sharon. *The Methodical Memory: Invention in Current-Traditional Rhetoric.* Carbondale: Southern Illinois UP, 1990.

———. *A Teacher's Introduction to Deconstruction.* Urbana, IL: NCTE, 1989.

Cushman, Ellen. "The Rhetorician as an Agent of Social Change." *College Composition and Communication* 47 (1996): 7–28.

D'Angelo, Frank J. *A Conceptual Theory of Rhetoric.* Cambridge, MA: Winthrop,1975.

Däumer, Elisabeth, and Sandra Runzo. "Transforming the Composition Classroom." *Teaching Writing: Pedagogy, Gender, and Equity.* Ed. Cynthia L. Caywood and Gillian R. Overing. Albany: SUNY P, 1987.

Davis, Barbara Gross, Michael Scriven, and Susan Thomas. *The Evaluation of Composition Instruction*. Inverness, CA: Edgepress, 1981.

Diederich, Paul B. *Measuring Growth in English*. Urbana, IL: NCTE, 1974.

Dillon, Ronna F., and Robert J. Sternberg, eds. *Cognition and Instruction*. Orlando: Academic, 1986.

Donawerth, Jane, ed. *Rhetorical Theory by Women before 1900*. Lanham, MD: Rowman, 2002.

Ede, Lisa, and Andrea Lunsford. "Audience Addressed/Audience Invoked: The Role of Audience in Composition Theory and Pedagogy." *College Composition and Communication* 35 (1984): 155–71.

———. *Singular Texts/Plural Authors: Perspectives on Collaborative Writing*. Carbondale: Southern Illinois UP, 1990.

Elbow, Peter. "Reflections on Academic Discourse: How It Relates to Freshmen and Colleagues." *College English* 53 (1991): 135–55.

———. *Writing without Teachers*. New York: Oxford UP, 1973.

Emig, Janet. *The Composing Processes of Twelfth Graders*. NCTE Research Report 13. Urbana, IL: NCTE, 1971.

Enos, Richard Leo. *Greek Rhetoric before Aristotle*. Prospect Heights, IL: Waveland, 1993.

———. *The Literate Mode of Cicero's Legal Rhetoric*. Carbondale: Southern Illinois UP, 1988.

Enos, Theresa, and Stuart C. Brown, eds. *Defining the New Rhetoric*. Newbury Park, CA: Sage, 1993.

Faigley, Lester. "Competing Theories of Process: A Critique and a Proposal." *College English* 48 (1986): 527–42.

———. *Fragments of Rationality: Postmodernity and the Subject of Composition*. Pittsburgh: U of Pittsburgh P, 1992.

Faigley, Lester, Roger Cherry, David Jolliffe, and Anna Skinner. *Assessing Writers' Knowledge and Processes of Composing*. Norwood, NJ: Ablex, 1985.

Faigley, Lester, and Stephen Witte. "Analyzing Revision." *College Composition and Communication* 32 (1981): 400–14.

Farnsworth, Rodney, and Avon Crismore. "On the Reefs: The Verbal and Visual Rhetoric of Darwin's Other Big Theory." *Rhetoric Society Quarterly* 21 (1991): 11–25.

Flower, Linda. *The Construction of Negotiated Meaning: A Social Cognitive Theory of Writing*. Carbondale: Southern Illinois UP, 1994.

Flower, Linda, and John R. Hayes. "The Cognition of Discovery: Defining a Rhetorical Problem." *College Composition and Communication* 31 (1980): 21–32.

———. "A Cognitive Process Theory of Writing." *College Composition and Communication* 32 (1981): 365–87.

———. "The Dynamics of Composing: Making Plans and Juggling Constraints." *Cognitive Processes in Writing*. Ed. Lee W. Gregg and Erwin R. Steinberg. Hillsdale, NJ: Erlbaum, 1980. 31–50.

———. "Images, Plans, and Prose: The Representation of Meaning in Writing." *Written Communication* 1 (1984): 120–60.

———. "The Pregnant Pause: An Inquiry into the Nature of Planning." *Research in the Teaching of English* 15 (1981): 229–44.

Flynn, Elizabeth A. "Composing as a Woman." *College Composition and Communication* 39 (1988): 423–35.

———. "Learning to Read Student Papers from a Feminine Perspective, I." *Encountering Student Texts: Interpretive Issues in Reading Student Writing*. Ed. Bruce Lawson, Susan Sterr Ryan, and W. Ross Winterowd. Urbana, IL: NCTE, 1989. 49–58.

Fox, Thomas. "Repositioning the Profession: Teaching Writing to African American Students." *Journal of Advanced Composition* 12 (1992): 291–303.

Freedman, Aviva, and Peter Medway, eds. *Learning and Teaching Genre*. Portsmouth, NH: Boynton, 1994.

Fulwiler, Toby, and Art Young, eds. *Language Connections: Writing and Reading across the Curriculum*. Urbana, IL: NCTE, 1982.

———, eds. *Programs That Work: Models and Methods for Writing Across the Curriculum*. Portsmouth, NH: Boynton, 1990.

Gage, John T. "An Adequate Epistemology for Composition: Classical and Modern Perspectives." *Essays on Classical Rhetoric and Modern Discourse*. Ed. Robert J. Connors, Lisa S. Ede, and Andrea A. Lunsford. Carbondale: Southern Illinois UP, 1984. 152–73.

Gannett, Cinthia. "Academic Journals: Panacea or Problem." *Gender and the Journal: Diaries and Academic Discourse.* Albany: SUNY P, 1992. 19–42.

Geisler, Cheryl. *Academic Literacy and the Nature of Expertise: Reading, Writing, and Knowing in Academic Philosophy.* Hillsdale, NJ: Erlbaum, 1994.

Gibson, W. Walker. *Tough Sweet and Stuffy: An Essay on Modern American Prose Styles.* Bloomington: Indiana UP, 1966.

Goggin, Maureen Daly, ed. *Inventing a Discipline: Rhetoric Scholarship in Honor of Richard E. Young.* Urbana, IL: NCTE, 2000.

Goody, Jack, and Ian Watt. "The Consequences of Literacy." *Literacy in Traditional Societies.* Ed. Goody. Cambridge: Cambridge UP, 1968. 27–68.

Gorman, T. P., A. C. Purves, and R. E. Degenhart. *The IEA Study of Written Composition I: The International Writing Tasks and Scoring Scales.* New York: Pergamon, 1988.

Gorrell, Robert M. "Very Like a Whale—A Report on Rhetoric." *College Composition and Communication* 16 (1965): 138–43.

Gottschalk, Katherine, and Keith Hjortshoj. *The Elements of Teaching Writing: A Resource for Instructors in All Disciplines.* Boston: Bedford, 2004.

Hartwell, Patrick. "Grammar, Grammars, and the Teaching of Grammar." *College English* 47 (1985): 105–27.

Hawisher, Gail E., and Patricia Sullivan. "Women on the Networks: Searching for E-Spaces of Their Own." *Feminism and Composition Studies: In Other Words.* Ed. Susan C. Jarratt and Lynn Worsham. New York: MLA, 1998. 172–97.

Heath, Shirley Brice. *Ways with Words: Language, Life, and Work in Communities and Classrooms.* New York: Cambridge UP, 1983.

Hillocks, George. "What Works in Teaching Composition: A Meta-analysis of Experimental Treatment Studies." *American Journal of Education* 93 (1984): 133–70.

Hobbs, Catherine, ed. *Nineteenth-Century Women Learn to Write.* Charlottesville: UP of Virginia, 1995.

———. *Rhetoric on the Margins of Modernity: Vico, Condillac, Monboddo.* Carbondale: Southern Illinois UP, 2002.

Horner, Bruce, and Min-Zhan Lu. *Representing the "Other": Basic Writers and the Teaching of Basic Writing.* Urbana, IL: NCTE, 1999.

Horner, Winifred Bryan, ed. *Historical Rhetoric: An Annotated Bibliography of Selected Sources in English.* Boston: Hall, 1980.

——, ed. *The Present State of Scholarship in Historical and Contemporary Rhetoric.* 2nd ed. Columbia: U of Missouri P, 1990.

Horvath, Brooke. "The Components of Written Response: A Practical Synthesis of Current Views." *Rhetoric Review* 2 (1984): 136–56.

Howard, Tharon W. *A Rhetoric of Electronic Communities.* Greenwich, CT: Ablex, 1997.

Hull, Glynda, and Mike Rose. "Rethinking Remediation: Toward a Social-Cognitive Understanding of Problematic Reading and Writing." *Written Communication* 6 (1989): 139–54.

Hult, Christine A. *Researching and Writing Across the Curriculum.* Boston: Allyn, 1996.

Huot, Brian. "Reliability, Validity, and Holistic Scoring: What We Know and What We Need to Know." *College Composition and Communication* 41 (1990): 201–13.

Jacobs, Debra. "Disrupting Understanding: The Critique of Writing as a Process." *Journal of Advanced Composition* 21 (2001): 662–74.

Janangelo, Joseph, and Kristine Hansen, eds. *Resituating Writing: Constructing and Administering Writing Programs.* Portsmouth, NH: Boynton, 1995.

Jarratt, Susan C. "Feminism and Composition: The Case for Conflict." *Contending with Words: Composition and Rhetoric in a Postmodern Age.* Ed. Patricia Harkin and John Schilb. New York: MLA, 1991. 105–23.

——. *Rereading the Sophists: Classical Rhetoric Refigured.* Carbondale: Southern Illinois UP, 1991.

Kent, Thomas, ed. *Post-Process Theory: Beyond the Writing-Process Paradigm.* Carbondale: Southern Illinois UP, 1999.

Kinneavy, James L. "*Kairos*: A Neglected Concept in Classical Rhetoric." *Rhetoric and Praxis: The Contribution of Classical Rhetoric to Practical Reasoning.* Ed. Jean Dietz Moss. Washington, DC: Catholic U of America P, 1986. 79–105.

————. *A Theory of Discourse: The Aims of Discourse.* New York: Norton, 1971.

Kinneavy, James L., John Q. Cope, and J. W. Campbell. *Writing—Basic Modes of Organization.* Dubuque: Kendall, 1976.

Kirsch, Gesa E. *Ethical Dilemmas in Feminist Research: The Politics of Location, Interpretation, and Publication.* Albany: SUNY P, 1999.

————. *Women Writing in the Academy: Audience, Authority, and Transformation.* Carbondale: Southern Illinois UP; Urbana, IL: CCCC/NCTE, 1993.

Kirscht, Judy, Rhonda Levine, and John Reiff. "Evolving Paradigms: WAC and the Rhetoric of Inquiry." *College Composition and Communication* 45 (1994): 369–80.

Labov, William. *The Study of Nonstandard English.* Rev. ed. Champaign, IL: NCTE, 1970.

Langer, Judith A., and Arthur N. Applebee. *How Writing Shapes Thinking: A Study of Teaching and Learning.* NCTE Research Report 20. Urbana, IL: NCTE, 1987.

Lanham, Richard A. *Revising Prose.* 2nd ed. New York: Macmillan, 1987.

Lauer, Janice. "Composition Studies: Dappled Discipline." *Rhetoric Review* 3 (1984): 20–29.

————. "Disciplinary Formation: The Summer Rhetoric Seminar." *Journal of Advanced Composition* 18.3 (1998): 503–08.

————. "Doctoral Programs in Rhetoric." *Rhetoric Society Quarterly* 10 (1980): 190–94.

————. "Getting to Know Rhetorica." *Living Rhetoric and Composition: Stories of the Discipline.* Ed. Duane H. Roen, Stuart C. Brown, and Theresa Enos. Mahwah, NJ: Erlbaum, 1999. 7–14.

————. "Heuristics and Composition." *Contemporary Rhetoric: A Conceptual Background with Readings.* Ed. W. Ross Winterowd. New York: Harcourt, 1975. 79–89.

————. *Invention in Rhetoric and Composition.* West Lafayette, IN: Parlor, 2004.

————. "Issues in Rhetorical Invention." *Essays on Classical Rhetoric and Modern Discourse.* Ed. Robert J. Connors, Lisa S. Ede, and

Andrea A. Lunsford. Carbondale: Southern Illinois UP, 1984. 127–39.

———. "Response to Ann E. Berthoff." *College Composition and Communication* 23 (1972): 208–10.

———. "Rhetoric and Composition Studies: A Multimodal Discipline." Enos and Brown 44–54.

———. "Writing as Inquiry: Some Questions for Teachers." *College Composition and Communication* 33 (1982): 89–93.

Lauer, Janice M., et al. "Writer/Reader Positioning Strategy." *Four Worlds of Writing: Inquiry and Action in Context*. 4th edition. New York: Pearson, 2000. 280–87.

LeFevre, Karen Burke. *Invention as a Social Act*. Studies in Writing and Rhetoric. Carbondale: Southern Illinois UP; Urbana, IL: CCCC/NCTE, 1987.

Leki, Ilona. *Understanding ESL Writers: A Guide for Teachers*. Portsmouth, NH: Boynton, 1992.

Leonard, James S., Christine E. Wharton, Robert Murray Davis, and Jeanette Harris, eds. *Author-ity and Textuality: Current Views of Collaborative Writing*. West Cornwall, CT: Locust Hill, 1994.

Lindemann, Erika, ed. *CCCC Bibliography of Composition and Rhetoric*. Carbondale: Southern Illinois UP; Urbana, IL: CCCC/NCTE, 1990–92.

———. *Longman Bibliography of Composition and Rhetoric*. White Plains, NY: Longman, 1987–88.

Lloyd-Jones, Richard. "Primary Trait Scoring." *Evaluating Writing: Describing, Measuring, Judging*. Ed. Charles R. Cooper and Lee Odell. Urbana, IL: NCTE, 1977. 33–66.

Logan, Shirley Wilson. *"We Are Coming": The Persuasive Discourse of Nineteenth-Century Black Women*. Carbondale: Southern Illinois UP, 1999.

Losey, Kay M. *Listen to the Silences: Mexican American Interaction in the Composition Classroom and Community*. Norwood, NJ: Ablex, 1997.

Lunsford, Andrea A., ed. *Reclaiming Rhetorica: Women in the Rhetorical Tradition*. Pittsburgh: U of Pittsburgh P, 1995.

Lutz, Jean A., and C. Gilbert Storms, eds. *The Practice of Technical and Scientific Communication: Writing in Professional Contexts.* Stamford, CT: Ablex, 1998.

Macrorie, Ken. *Writing to Be Read.* New York: Hayden, 1968.

Maimon, Elaine, Gerald Belcher, Gail Hearn, Barbara Nodine, and Finbarr O'Connor. *Writing in the Arts and Sciences.* Cambridge, MA: Winthrop, 1981.

Maimon, Elaine, Barbara F. Nodine, and Finbarr W. O'Connor, eds. *Thinking, Reasoning, and Writing.* New York: Longman, 1989.

Malinowitz, Harriet. *Textual Orientations: Lesbian and Gay Students and the Making of Discourse Communities.* Portsmouth, NH: Boynton, 1995.

Matsuda, Paul Kei. "Composition Studies and ESL Writing: A Disciplinary Division of Labor." *College Composition and Communication* 50 (1999): 699–721.

McComiskey, Bruce. *Gorgias and the New Sophistic Rhetoric.* Carbondale: Southern Illinois UP, 2002.

———. *Teaching Composition as a Social Process.* Logan: Utah State UP, 2000.

McLeod, Susan H. *Notes on the Heart: Affective Issues in the Writing Classroom.* Carbondale: Southern Illinois UP, 1997.

Medicine, Bea. "The Role of American Indian Women in Cultural Continuity and Transition." *Women and Language in Transition.* Ed. Joyce Penfield. Albany: SUNY P, 1987. 159–66.

Milic, Louis T. "Metaphysics in the Criticism of Style." *College Composition and Communication* 17 (1966): 124–29.

———. "The Problem of Style." *Contemporary Rhetoric: A Conceptual Background with Readings.* Ed. W. Ross Winterowd. New York: Harcourt, 1975. 271–95.

Miller, Carolyn R. "Genre as Social Action." *Quarterly Journal of Speech* 70 (1984): 151–67.

Miller, Susan. "The Feminization of Composition." *The Politics of Writing Instruction: Postsecondary.* Ed. Richard H. Bullock and John Trimbur. Portsmouth, NH: Boynton, 1991. 39–53.

Moffett, James. *Teaching the Universe of Discourse.* Boston: Houghton, 1968.

Moriarty, Thomas A. *Finding the Words: A Rhetorical History of South Africa's Transition from Apartheid to Democracy.* Westport, CT: Praeger, 2003.

Moss, Beverly J., and Keith Walters. "Rethinking Diversity: Axes of Difference in the Writing Classroom." *Theory and Practice in the Teaching of Writing: Rethinking the Discipline.* Ed. Lee Odell. Carbondale: Southern Illinois UP, 1993. 132–85.

Murray, Donald M. "Internal Revision: A Process of Discovery." *Research on Composing: Points of Departure.* Ed. Charles R. Cooper and Lee Odell. Urbana, IL: NCTE, 1978. 85–103.

Nold, Ellen W. "Revising." *Writing: Process, Development and Communication.* Ed. Carl H. Frederiksen and Joseph F. Dominic. Vol. 2 of *Writing: The Nature, Development, and Teaching of Written Communication.* Hillsdale, NJ: Erlbaum, 1981. 67–80.

O'Hare, Frank. "Syntactic Maturity and Sentence Combining." *Sentence Combining: Improving Student Writing without Formal Grammar Instruction.* Urbana, IL: NCTE, 1973. 19–34.

Ohmann, Richard. "Speech, Action, and Style." *Literary Style: A Symposium.* Ed. Seymour Chatman. London: Oxford UP, 1971. 241–54.

Olson, Gary A., and Lynn Worsham, eds. *Race, Rhetoric, and the Postcolonial.* Albany: SUNY P, 1999.

Ong, Walter J. *Orality and Literacy: The Technologizing of the Word.* London: Methuen, 1982.

———. "The Writer's Audience Is Always a Fiction." *PMLA* 90 (1975): 9–21.

Paré, Anthony, and Graham Smart. "Observing Genres in Action: Towards a Research Methodology." *Genre and the New Rhetoric.* Ed. Aviva Freedman and Peter Medway. London: Taylor, 1994. 146–54.

Perelman, Chaim. *The Realm of Rhetoric.* Trans. William Kluback. Notre Dame, IN: U of Notre Dame P, 1982.

Perkins, D. N. *The Mind's Best Work.* Cambridge, MA: Harvard UP, 1981.

Perl, Sondra. "The Composing Processes of Unskilled College Writers." *Research in the Teaching of English* 13 (1979): 317–36.

Phelps, Louise Wetherbee. "Audience and Authorship: The Disappearing Boundary." *A Sense of Audience in Written Communication* Ed. Gesa Kirsch and Duane H. Roen. Newbury Park, CA: Sage, 1990. 153–74.

———. *Composition as a Human Science: Contributions to the Self-Understanding of a Discipline.* New York: Oxford UP, 1988.

———. "Composition Studies." *Encyclopedia of Rhetoric and Composition: Communication from Ancient Times to the Information Age.* Ed. Theresa Enos. New York: Garland, 1996. 123–34.

———. "Dialectics of Coherence: Toward an Integrated Theory." *College English* 47 (1985): 12–29.

———. "Images of Student Writing: The Deep Structure of Teacher Response." *Writing and Response: Theory, Practice, and Research.* Ed. Chris M. Anson. Urbana, IL: NCTE, 1989. 37–67.

Phelps, Louise Wetherbee, and Janet Emig, eds. *Feminine Principles and Women's Experience in American Composition and Rhetoric.* Pittsburgh: U of Pittsburgh P, 1995.

Porter, James E. *Audience and Rhetoric: An Archaeological Composition of the Discourse Community.* Englewood Cliffs, NJ: Prentice, 1992.

———. "Developing a Postmodern Ethics of Rhetoric and Composition." Enos and Brown 207–26.

———. "Intertextuality and the Discourse Community." *Rhetoric Review* 5 (1986): 34–47.

———. *Rhetorical Ethics and Internetworked Writing.* Greenwich, CT: Ablex, 1998.

———. "The Role of Law, Policy, and Ethics in Corporate Composing: Toward a Practical Ethics for Professional Writing." *Professional Communication: The Social Perspective.* Ed. Nancy Roundy Blyler and Charlotte Thralls. Newbury Park, CA: Sage, 1993. 128–43.

Powell, Malea. "Rhetorics of Survivance: How American Indians *Use* Writing." *College Composition and Communication* 53 (2002): 396–434.

Purves, Alan C., ed. *Writing across Languages and Cultures.* Newbury Park, CA: Sage, 1988.

Raymond, James C. "Enthymemes, Examples, and Rhetorical Method." *Essays on Classical Rhetoric and Modern Discourse.* Ed. Robert J. Connors, Lisa S. Ede, and Andrea A. Lunsford. Carbondale: Southern Illinois UP, 1984. 140–51.

Reyes, Pedro, Jay D. Scribner, and Alicia Paredes Scribner, eds. *Lessons from High-Performing Hispanic Schools: Creating Learning Communities.* New York: Teachers College P, 1999.

Rice, William Craig. *Public Discourse and Academic Inquiry.* New York: Garland, 1996.

Ritchie, Joy S. "Confronting the 'Essential' Problem: Reconnecting Feminist Theory and Pedagogy." *Journal of Advanced Composition* 10 (1990): 249–73.

Roen, Duane H., Stuart C. Brown, and Theresa Enos, eds. *Living Rhetoric and Composition: Stories of the Discipline.* Mahwah, NJ: Erlbaum, 1999.

Rohman, D. Gordon, and Albert O. Wlecke. *Pre-writing: The Construction and Application of Models for Concept Formation in Writing.* Cooperative Research Project 2174. Cooperative Research Project of the Office of Education. Washington, DC: U. S. Dept. of Health, Education, and Welfare, 1964. ERIC, ED 001 273.

Rose, Mike. *Writer's Block: The Cognitive Dimension.* Studies in Writing and Rhetoric. Carbondale: Southern Illinois UP; Urbana, IL: CCCC/NCTE, 1984.

Rose, Shirley K., and Irwin Weiser, eds. *The Writing Program Administrator as Researcher: Inquiry in Action and Reflection.* Portsmouth, NH: Boynton, 1999.

Royster, Jacqueline Jones. "Perspectives on the Intellectual Tradition of Black Women Writers." *The Right to Literacy.* Ed. Andrea A. Lunsford, Helene Moglen, and James Slevin. New York: MLA, 1990. 103–12.

———. *Traces of a Stream: Literacy and Social Change among African American Women Writers.* Pittsburgh: U of Pittsburgh P, 2000.

Rubin, Donald L., and Kathryn Greene. "Gender-Typical Style in Written Language." *Research in the Teaching of English* 26 (1992): 7–40.

Russell, David R. *Writing in the Academic Disciplines, 1870–1990: A Curricular History.* Carbondale: Southern Illinois UP, 1991.

Schilb, John. "The Sociological Imagination and the Ethics of Collabo-ration." *New Visions of Collaborative Writing*. Ed. Janis Forman. Portsmouth, NH: Boynton, 1992. 105–19.

Scribner, Sylvia. "Knowledge at Work." *Anthropology and Education Quarterly* 16 (1985): 199–206.

Selber, Stuart A., ed. *Computers and Technical Communication: Peda-gogical and Programmatic Perspectives*. ATTW Contemporary Stud-ies in Technical Communication 3. Greenwich, CT: Ablex, 1997.

Selfe, Cynthia L. *Technology and Literacy in the Twenty-First Century: The Importance of Paying Attention*. Studies in Writing and Rheto-ric. Carbondale: Southern Illinois UP; Urbana, IL: CCCC/NCTE, 1999.

Shaughnessy, Mina P. *Errors and Expectations: A Guide for the Teacher of Basic Writing*. New York: Oxford UP, 1977.

Shor, Ira, ed. *Freire for the Classroom: A Sourcebook for Liberatory Teaching*. Portsmouth, NH: Boynton, 1987.

Silva, Tony. "Toward an Understanding of the Distinct Nature of L2 Writing: The ESL Research and Its Implications." *TESOL Quar-terly* 27 (1993): 657–77.

Slevin, James F. "Inventing and Reinventing the Discipline of Composi-tion." *Introducing English: Essays in the Intellectual Work of Com-position*. Pittsburgh: U of Pittsburgh P, 2001. 37–56.

Smith, Jeanne A. "Native American Composition and School Language Curriculum." *Encyclopedia of English Studies and Language Arts: A Project of the National Council of Teachers of English*. Ed. Alan C. Purves. 2 vols. New York: Scholastic, 1994. 862–65.

Smitherman, Geneva. *Talkin and Testifyin: The Language of Black America*. Boston: Houghton, 1977.

Sommers, Nancy. "Responding to Student Writing." *College Composi-tion and Communication* 33 (1982): 148–56.

———. "Revision Strategies of Student Writers and Experienced Adult Writers." *College Composition and Communication* 31 (1980): 378–88.

"Special Cluster: Queer Theory." Ed. Michelle Gibson and Jonathan Alexander. *Journal of Advanced Composition* 24.1 (2004): 1–111.

Spilka, Rachel, ed. *Writing in the Workplace: New Research Perspectives.* Carbondale: Southern Illinois UP, 1993.

Sternglass, Marilyn S. *Time to Know Them: A Longitudinal Study of Writing and Learning at the College Level.* Mahwah, NJ: Erlbaum, 1997.

Stewart, Donald C., and Patricia L. Stewart. *The Life and Legacy of Fred Newton Scott.* Pittsburgh: U of Pittsburgh P, 1997.

Stotsky, Sandra, and Barbara Hardy Beierl, eds. *Connecting Civic Education and Language Education: The Contemporary Challenge.* New York: Teachers College P, 1991.

Sullivan, Dale L. "Displaying Disciplinarity." *Written Communication* 13 (1996): 221–50.

Sullivan, Patricia, and Jennie Dautermann, eds. *Electronic Literacies in the Workplace: Technologies of Writing.* Urbana, IL: NCTE, 1996.

Sullivan, Patricia, and James E. Porter. *Opening Spaces: Writing Technologies and Critical Research Practices.* Greenwich, CT: Ablex, 1997.

Sutherland, Christine Mason, and Rebecca Sutcliffe, eds. *The Changing Tradition: Women in the History of Rhetoric.* Calgary: U of Calgary P, 1999.

Swearingen, C. Jan. *Rhetoric and Irony: Western Literacy and Western Lies.* New York: Oxford UP, 1991.

Trimbur, John. *The Call to Write.* New York: Longman, 1999.

———. "Consensus and Difference in Collaborative Learning." *College English* 51 (1989): 602–16.

Villanueva, Victor, Jr. *Bootstraps: From an American Academic of Color.* Urbana, IL: NCTE, 1993.

———. "Hispanic/Latino Writing." *Encyclopedia of English Studies and Language Arts: A Project of the National Council of Teachers of English.* Ed. Alan C. Purves. 2 vols. New York: Scholastic, 1994. 573–75.

Vitanza, Victor J. "From Heuristic to Aleatory Procedures; or, toward 'Writing the Accident.'" Goggin 185–206.

———. *Negation, Subjectivity, and the History of Rhetoric.* Albany: SUNY P, 1997.

Walker, Jeffrey. "The Body of Persuasion: A Theory of the Enthymeme." *College English* 56 (1994): 46–65.

Wang, Haixia. "Inventing Chinese Rhetorical Culture: Zhuang Zi's Teaching." *Perspectives on Rhetorical Invention.* Ed. Janet M. Atwill and Janice M. Lauer. Knoxville: U of Tennessee P, 2002. 163–75.

Welch, Kathleen E. *The Contemporary Reception of Classical Rhetoric: Appropriations of Ancient Discourse.* Hillsdale, NJ: Erlbaum, 1990.

Williams, Joseph M. "The Phenomenology of Error." *College Composition and Communication* 32 (1981): 152–68.

Winterowd, W. Ross. "Dispositio: The Concept of Form in Discourse." *College Composition and Communication* 22 (1971): 39–45.

———. "The Grammar of Coherence." *College English* 31 (1970): 828–35.

———. "The Prospect (and the Future) of Rhetoric." *Newsletter: Rhetoric Society of America* 2 (1972): 4–5.

Witte, Stephen P., and Lester Faigley. *Evaluating College Writing Programs.* Carbondale: Southern Illinois UP, 1983.

Worsham, Lynn. "The Question Concerning Invention: Hermeneutics and the Genesis of Writing." *Pre/Text* 8 (1987): 197–244.

———. "Writing against Writing: The Predicament of Écriture Féminine in Composition Studies." *Contending with Words: Composition and Rhetoric in a Postmodern Age.* Ed. Patricia Harkin and John Schilb. New York: MLA, 1991. 82–104.

WPA Executive Committee. "Evaluating the Intellectual Work of Writing Program Administrators: A Draft." *Writing Program Administration* 20 (1996): 92–103.

Yancey, Kathleen Blake, and Irwin Weiser, eds. *Situating Portfolios: Four Perspectives.* Logan: Utah State UP, 1997.

Young, Richard E. "Paradigms and Problems: Needed Research in Rhetorical Invention." *Research on Composing: Points of Departure.* Ed. Charles R. Cooper and Lee Odell. Urbana, IL: NCTE, 1978. 29–47.

Young, Richard E., Alton L. Becker, and Kenneth L. Pike. *Rhetoric: Discovery and Change.* New York: Harcourt, 1970.

Zimmerman, Donald, and Dawn Rodrigues. *Research and Writing in the Disciplines.* Fort Worth: Harcourt, 1992.

CHAPTER THREE

Creative Writing

KATHARINE HAAKE

California State University, Northridge

When I first started working on this chapter, another scene of writing lay among the random clutter of my desk. It was a poor-quality Xerox reproduction of a photograph in which three grinning and casually dressed men looked back at the photographer with amiable self-consciousness. One, half his body cut off by the left edge of the frame, held a plastic cup of what was, presumably, coffee. Another, puffy in a loose down jacket, cocked his head at an awkward angle and covered his mouth with his left hand, as if to smother a giggle. The third, in a mirror image of the first, had one hand jammed deep into a rumpled jeans pocket and gestured broadly with the other, in which he was clasping his own white cup of—what, coffee?

The photograph was here because I had recently brought it back with me from a memorial service for my friend Wendy Bishop. Trained in photography in her undergraduate major, Wendy took this picture in July 1978, at the first Santa Cruz writer's conference, where our long friendship began. The three men were Raymond Carver, James B. Houston, and Carter Wilson. Remembering it now, I imagine Wendy taking it and cannot help being struck, as I was at the time, by how neatly the difficulties I face in this attempt to define creative writing as an academic discipline are somehow contained in, or by, this image: the history of the years between then and now, Wendy—the full scholarship poet—snapping the picture, me—not shown, but watching somewhere from the periphery, hanging out on a token half tuition reduction and, too poor to pay for a dorm room, sleeping in the literary magazine office—half a life later, trying to resolve the discrepancy between what that image intimated for our futures, all that promise, and the rich and surprising paths those futures somehow traced. I imagine a form of triangulation, among the three men themselves; and another, among them and Wendy and me; and yet a third among points in time, marking the moments when those men started out, the moment of the photograph itself, and now. All three triangles embrace, in one way or another, not just the recent history of creative writing, but the principles, issues, and assumptions by which we know ourselves inside that history and within the current context of who we are today.

I love this photograph, not just because it takes me to the time when Wendy and I met and began the conversation that would go on until she died, but also because it reminds me of the blissful time when I knew nothing and, knowing nothing, needed to do nothing more, within my discipline at least, than I had ever done, that is, to write. And writing, in that time, was somehow simple too, a natural activity I'd practiced from when I was small, and, however lacking my writing might have been in those days, it was a pleasing practice, and not at all vexed.

Before that time, the time when I was small, and before even that, throughout the whole twentieth century, creative writing was evolving, at least in the academy, as a stable model, defined by a highly consistent method and uniform purpose. But this stability would not last. Today, I sit in Wendy's beach house, reflecting on the end of dreams we spun out as young women primed to enter a discipline we thought lay open before us. And it's beautiful and sad and confusing, because the world we thought we were entering is—in part because of Wendy—no longer what it was when we first imagined it, and remains, at this point, entirely elusive.

Things We Expected

I don't know what I expected. Looking back, I find myself curiously fixed on that moment. I'd published a couple of stories by then. I expected to publish a couple more. Wendy expected to publish a book of poems, probably within the year. I know she did expect that because she told me that that's what one of her teachers had told her to expect. If we'd let ourselves be conscious of our expectations, we might have expected (anyone would have) that if we worked hard and if our writing were good, as the years passed, we'd begin to resemble the men in the photo, with small lists of books, and maybe teaching jobs of our own, and summer workshop stints, carrying the camaraderie of writers around with us wherever we went. I think we did expect that. Both of us, at the time, already had MAs in creative writing and did not expect that more graduate school lay in our futures. My own PhD, some five years later, was a last-ditch effort to sort out the years of writing that had come before it. I arrived as a writer and intended to make writing—not teaching—my future, but in the meantime I was teaching. Besides, it was a job, and more money than I'd made in all the years since I had finished school. Wendy's PhD, in rhetoric and composition, came a few years after mine and followed years of varied teaching stints all over the world. It seemed an odd choice to me at the time. Despite my own graduate studies, I was only vaguely aware that rhetoric and composition existed as a separate field. But as Wendy writes in *Teaching Lives: Essays and Stories,* one of more than twenty books she published on writing and teaching, "Writing captured me and composition helped me understand that captivation" (219). In my own case, it was "theory" that helped me understand that captivation, but our experiences were remarkably similar and would work, in important ways, to define our thinking about writing, teaching, and the parallel disciplines in which we would find ourselves for many years. And yet, it's also true that many prominent creative writing teachers inside the academy—writers of commercially successful novels who hold academic appointments—know nothing of Bishop or her dual career path, her lifelong commitment not just to writing but to the teaching of writing, and the rich intersections between composition and creative writing that take us back, as a discipline, to where we began.

This peculiar oblivion in which she worked, in the eyes of a substantial part of what might count as the discipline of creative writing, marks perhaps the most telling schism of the discipline itself. Between those who've been captivated by writing, and those who seek, through intradisciplinary investigation, to understand that captivation in order—and this is important—to teach it, lies the line that divides creative writers inside the academy and tells us how to know ourselves. Practitioners of the craft of writing who make their living as dedicated teachers of that craft have, for many years, dominated the discipline of creative writing. But a sizeable portion of others have sought more systematically to move beyond the lore and craft-based vision of their work, and in so doing to find ways to understand the captivation of writing, especially in ways that might be empowering for students. This essay will attempt to trace that shift and to suggest what it might mean for creative writers, both inside and outside the university. Although I might at one point, in the heat of the activist moment—as Wendy said, "I'm hoping for nothing less than to change our profession" (*Teaching* 245)—have presented this trajectory in hierarchical terms, I no longer think of this split as an either/or kind of problem, but rather as a failure throughout the discipline to sustain effective dialogue with colleagues equally engaged in the problems, challenges, and pleasures of linking our working lives as writers to our working lives as teachers.

If the goal of this book is, as Bruce McComiskey argues in the introduction, at least in part to find a common language through which all of the disciplines comprised by English studies can speak to one another, creative writing will have to begin by developing such a language internal to itself. And while Richard C. Taylor may be right when he suggests that a discipline in conflict is more interesting than one that is static and unified, I can't but hope for a future in which creative writers—inside and outside the academy—will see themselves joined in a more common purpose, at least in their lives as teachers and promoters of writing. For, at least as far as our academic posts are concerned, the form of patronage writers have managed to secure for ourselves is dependent on the services we provide for our students. To the extent that creative writing can begin to be defined as an academic discipline, we must begin—and end—by examining our own classroom practices.

Two Caveats

1. Don't ask a writer to define creative writing: everything goes into everything else.

2. I don't know how to do this without telling a story. The story is my story, but I am not alone in it. It is also the story of my discipline itself.

But First

As we try to imagine what we may look like from the outside, it may be useful to admit that part of the essential neurosis of our discipline (for almost unobserved by the rest of English studies, creative writing has traced an increasingly acrimonious path, fractious and divided through the last quarter-century) derives from the name we have given ourselves, replete with the descriptor that sets us apart, not as "other," perhaps, but as "different," our cherished, defining trait. But what, it may be asked—we have asked it ourselves—distinguishes one form of writing as "creative" from other forms that are not, if not the generalized parsimoniousness with which the culture manages what counts as "creativity," and who gets to have it, and who does not.

Thus, we hold the discipline together with a name that is mildly provocative to begin with, a name that works both for and against us, as it marks and foregrounds our essential alienation and conflicted nature, both inside the larger discipline and among ourselves.

During a recent root canal, my endodontist reflected on how much he looked up to creative writers and on how he wasn't good at writing at all. My mouth was full of stuff so I couldn't really answer, but for nearly two hours, this man bent over me, excavating the roots of a tooth that had plagued me and mystified a series of dental professionals over a period of years. He had met and solved the problem of a root anomaly. He had tenderly delivered me from pain. At the end of the procedure, as he was removing the bib from my neck, he paused to remark, "But isn't all writing creative?"

The endodontist was intuiting an essential element of our own historical genesis, one with which we've long since lost touch ourselves. For in the beginning, it was not so much our "creativity" that set us apart, as the desire to reconnect with literary study more from a writer's point of view. In his seminal history of creative writing, *The Elephants Teach*, D. G. Myers locates the earliest use of "creative writing" in Harvard composition classes where the important distinction was not the kind of writing that might be produced, but its differentiation from English scholarship. "English composition," Myers writes, "cleared the road for creative writing not in accepting poems and stories as academic work but in showing that literature could be used in the university for some other purpose than scholarly research" (41). The idea, at least initially, was not so much to provide a venue in which students could produce their own literary texts, but instead to come to a fuller and deeper understanding of literature itself by approaching it from the inside.

Of all the disciplines in English studies, creative writing moves through the world in complex and multidimensional ways, with increasingly as vital and large a presence outside the academy as inside. Undergraduate students of literature and theory may find their way into a variety of real-world professions, but if they remain in the discipline itself they have few other options outside of teaching, where scholarship is viewed among the highest achievements and required for successful tenure and promotion. But writers live dual lives, inside and outside of academia, and their life paths are neither direct nor clear.

Years ago, in an unemployment office, the job seeker beside me helpfully directed me to listings under "T" where, he said, "there are lots of jobs for writers." But when I told him, "not that kind of writing," he looked confused; then he brightened. "Oh, I get it," he said, glad to have things cleared up, "you're a Shakespeare."

It's not that long ago that Oprah decided who, in this culture, was a real writer, and who was not, that Jonathan Franzen politely turned her down, and that she gave up on the idea altogether and reverted to resurrecting canonical texts. Our students come to make the best-seller list, and our parents—not to mention our spouses—want to know when we're going to start earning a real income. As a young teacher, I remember feeling impatient with basic-skills students who enrolled in my undergraduate creative writing classes dreaming of best-seller lists, but that's how the concept is packaged for them, and they need to learn to recognize the packaging. Some years ago, Linda Brodkey described the modernist writer as a male author writing literature alone by the thin gray light of a candle; these days, the scene our students might envision is Stephen King accepting the National Book Award. Either way, it hardly makes a difference, because what Brodkey asserted was that the scene she describes is so monumental we can't write without it, but it's also a scene upon which very few of us can easily project ourselves.

Meanwhile, in our own lives, things are no more transparent, as one of our first clear and early lessons was, "Those who can't, teach." In supermarket lines, if we tell the stranger next to us (who is just, after all, making friendly conversation) that we teach "creative writing," we receive bland stares and awkward responses. But if we admit that we are writers, the first question is what our books are, or, if you live in L.A., as I do, where they've been reviewed or if they've been made into movies. Even my own husband wonders why I work for "nothing."

And yet, the very concept of writing for its own sake lies at the heart of our discipline and history. The rub is that most of us can't help wanting more.

As Trinh T. Minh-ha observes, "Accumulated unpublished writings do stink" (8). But in the fiercely competitive world of contemporary creative writing, most of us entering the discipline accumulate a lot of such stink. How are we to mediate this stinkiness for our students, even as we must prepare them for their own?

A Brief History Lesson

In "Theory, Creative Writing, and the Impertinence of History," R. M. Berry traces two divergent views of the origins of creative writing. The first, also explored by D. G. Myers, locates the earliest instances of creative writing as an educational experiment embarked upon in Harvard composition classes. Fully invested in the "creative expressionist wing of the progressive education movement," with roots in New England transcendentalism and popular journalism (Berry 63), the primary motivation behind this experiment was to restore "literary and education value to the teaching of rhetoric" (D. G. Myers 37). The second view, Berry explains, was developed in Stephen Wilber's history of the Iowa Writers' Workshop, that is, that creative writing emerged from a vigorous Midwestern regionalism and investment in the work of apprentice writers.

Either way, Iowa's program, headed by Norman Foerster, himself a former student of Irving Babbitt at Harvard and widely acknowledged as the architect of creative writing inside the academy, was the first to institutionalize the study of writing as a separate enterprise, one designed to combine in a single, unified model both the study and the practice of literature. Conceived as a reaction against the increasing influence of scholarship and science on the humanities, Foerster's "new humanist" curriculum envisioned a multidiscursive study of letters that would include, along with creative writing, linguistics and literary history as complementary and interdependent strands.

For many years, this paradigm would serve as the functional center for creative writing as it was beginning to emerge as one of the fastest-growing and most vital branches in the whole constellation of English studies. Fueled by returning veterans and funded, in large part, by the GI Bill, creative writing thrived in the academy almost from its very inception. In the immediate years after the end of the Second World War and up to the end of the twentieth century, creative writing programs proliferated and flourished as writers began to shift from day jobs in journalism to teaching. And the programs they entered then looked very much the same as the one Foerster founded—studio-based workshops where apprentice writers with strong vocational commitments to writing would gather together to submit their poetry, prose, and other texts to peers and the master writer for commentary and criticism. In such workshops, writers could bring the reading strategies they developed in the study of literature to bear on their own creative texts, and they could do so with the explicit aim of creating new literature themselves. They were artists who, like artists throughout history, aimed to steep themselves in the long tradition of the art they aspired to practice and to do so in the company of like-minded peers. As new programs quickly emerged, they adopted this essential model, for the model was inarguably attractive—at Johns Hopkins, Stanford, the University of Denver, and Cornell.

These would be just the first in a vast expansion of such programs that would develop over time and evolve according to what has been described as a kind of academic pyramid scheme: the more writers there were who received a writing education, the more there were who needed day jobs in an academy that had already taken them in once. For a while, everything seemed to be working in a kind of steady state, as the interests of the academy were initially well matched to the interests of its graduates and a wide range of new students who were beginning to seek out their classes. But as creative writing teachers need not only students to teach, but programs to teach them in, new programs started springing up all over, producing more students who went on to graduate school, who then got their own jobs in English departments, where new creative writing programs were formed—and, increasingly, these programs were to include undergraduate as well as graduate options. In a single generation—the generation of the three men in the photo on my desk—creative writing was to be transformed from a primarily graduate concentration, with competitive admission, into a handful of homogenous programs, to a widely available undergraduate major developed in response to high student demand.

For more than thirty years, this process of development continued, and by 1967—nearly one hundred years after the founding of the Modern Language Association and twenty years after that of the Conference on College Composition and Communication—creative writing had become a prominent enough presence in higher education that fifteen writers from thirteen programs joined together to form the Associated Writing Programs (AWP), and the professionalization of creative writing had significantly begun. The early goals of the AWP were to coordinate and provide professional services for creative writing programs and their graduates and to support "the growing presence of writers in higher education, thereby fostering new generations of writers and new audiences for literature" (Fenza, "Brief"), though within another twenty years it would expand its reach to include other venues beyond those of higher education that served the needs of writers and of the literary community in general. But at the time, a kind of generalized enthusiasm for writing existed that was entirely contagious, and Wendy and I were to enter the field not long after that, when just wanting to write was somehow enough.

Today we have reached a point of saturation, though the ever-rising number of applicants to my own small program in the California State University system makes it hard to imagine there will ever be an end to the demand. In little more than a quarter-century, the AWP has grown from its original and arguably insular group of 13 chummy programs to a highly professionalized organization that counts among its membership some 292 graduate and 361 undergraduate creative writing programs. Degrees conferred by such programs include the BA, MA, MFA, DA, and PhD with creative dissertation, and all certify years devoted to the sustained investigation of both writing and reading.

The numbers alone can sometimes seem staggering. Dana Gioia estimates that these programs will produce some twenty-five thousand graduate-degree-certified creative writers every decade in this country ("Can" 95). Add that to the seventy-five thousand writers John Barth once predicted we'd have trained by 1984 (Berry 57), and it's easy to think that maybe my father was right when he worried in advance of sending me off to my first writing program in 1974 that perhaps we were training too many creative writers in this country. And these estimations don't even begin to include participants in the vast array of available private workshops, or extension or community-based creative writing classes, or creative writing classes taught in hospitals and jails, never mind the recent emergence of creative writing in the international arena, with programs now being offered in England, Germany, and Australia.

What, we might wonder, are we training these writers to *do?*

Some Preoccupations

The men who were our teachers, mine and Wendy's—the men in the photograph—were among the first wave of creative writers to fan out from Iowa and other like programs, working their way into academia, where they began to make a place for themselves, and, later, us. They settled easily into lives that must have seemed miraculous at times—lives devoted to writing, to thinking about writing, and to teaching other writers much of what they thought about writing. And soon, the early reliance on literature—the commingling of reading and writing in the context of long literary traditions—began curiously to shift, as the literature brought into creative writing classrooms was either nonexistent or, increasingly, that of other contemporary writers—the friends and peers of the teachers themselves.

Not that these workshops didn't have rules. They had rules: the texts were read out loud, without printed copies, and treated as autonomous artifacts, unrelated to the author; the student author could not speak but listened closely; and the teacher would wait until everyone had commented before saying anything at all. Sometimes, the teacher never said anything, or only mumbled some closing commentary, some final, sometimes seemingly unrelated advice. Most often, the teacher did not offer written commentary of any kind. These first-generation master writer-teachers were products of writing programs themselves, and taught what they'd learned in their programs and from the practice of writing itself—a kind of hands-on, seat-of-the-pants pedagogy in which they dispensed bits of wisdom with a natural ease and charm that was often as disarming as it was, at least sometimes, impoverished.

Lore: All it takes to be a writer is to sit at your desk four hours a day, and pretty soon you'll be so bored that you'll produce *something*. Also—be sure to let your wife know not to disturb you.

Lore: The writers who "make it" are not necessarily the most talented and not even the ones who work the hardest, but those who take rejection the best.

Lore: Don't drink from a straw when you give a reading because you might slurp something up your nose.

And, of course, looking up to our teachers, it must have seemed that if we wanted to be writers we should be like them, but the match was not always easy. Our teachers were almost always men. And many of them were hard living—it was not unusual, in those days, for creative writing classes to take place in bars, for writing teachers to take up with their students, for publishing careers to be arranged over late-night assignations. Promises were made and kept and broken, and writers were forged in contexts that today already seem strangely anachronistic.

These first-wave, master writer-teachers were generally well-intentioned, but they were writers first and teachers second. And surely it must have seemed, as we moved into the 1980s, that English departments everywhere were making way for one or two of them. They were maybe the department eccentrics, or they were maybe the department stars, but it was hard to take their work very seriously, since really, they did little more in their classes than chat about their own work and that of their students.

For myself, it was never my intention to join these burgeoning ranks, for I, too, saw myself as a writer first and had gone to PhD school on a whim, believing, somewhat superstitiously (*Don't go back to school*, I'd been warned at an artist's retreat) that it was bad for writing, but lured by what seemed like the generous teaching stipend—more money than I had made in five years as a writer—and the prospect of security for four long years. I went to PhD school fully intending to write my heart out, and instead, almost despite myself, I ended up with an education. In the unexpected career that followed, I began, almost at once, to wish, like Wendy, for things to be different, to accommodate in more comprehensive ways our status as both writers and teachers in the university. Though we followed different paths in our attempts to understand and, now, *teach* the way in which writing had first *captivated,* and then *held* us, we would both discover that the path was not easy. As Bishop writes in *Teaching Lives*:

A graduate student came to my office recently and said, "I want to do what you do, combine two fields." I said, "Faith, it's not that easy and it's not exactly what you see." Meaning, my teaching life has been one of searching, bumping up against problems, and writing my way out of them into more celebratory stances. And the fields of composition and creative writing certainly don't yet comfortably align themselves. I had to tell her: "I see creative writing as a very competitive profession where each student is grooming him- or herself to be the *best* writer, thinking in terms of *service for* (oneself). I find the field of composition to be more collegial (although certainly there *is* competition), filled with colleagues who are trying to solve problems in writing classrooms; these are people who tend to think in terms of *service toward*. I find a better home in the latter," I told her, though I want to and try to do both—serve the writer in me and serve communities of writers. (viii)

As for me, my own course of study in graduate school had led me to be interested in the interrelations between critical theory and writing, which I set out to explore.

The field I entered, at the time we entered it, was only just beginning to make its first tentative steps toward self-definition, steps motivated as much by our failures as by any coherent sense of who we were or what we were about. The years when we were starting out were those years of critique, and as we began to examine our own experience as students—the way we had come into being as writers—we found it terribly inadequate and wanting. It had not served us well, as writers, to base our writing aspirations and aesthetics on those of other writers (our teachers) whose experiences of life and writing, too, had had little in common with our own. And it did not serve us well as teachers, for if the master-writer-mentor model of a creative writing education had been inadequate for us, what good was it going to be for our students?

We did not, at that time, have anything more with which to conceive of our teaching—and of our discipline—than the models we received from our own teachers. We did not have a language to talk about writing very well—though, in this, poets are historically better equipped than fiction writers. If we had a methodology at all, it was one of emulation, and those of us who managed to persist did so largely by virtue of stubbornness or luck.

Wendy's story was not exactly my story—Wendy was a poet, and her teachers liked her, while I was a gawky prose-writer, who had already stopped writing once, when, at sixteen, I read *Moby Dick* and determined I was neither smart enough nor talented enough to be a writer. I had found my way back to writing clumsily, and spent the better part of my MA program diffident and mute, attempting to write like the "good" writers around me in a lifelong habit of self-effacing mimicry at which I developed considerable proficiency. It would take me years—first writing alone, then in the company of others as I pursued my PhD, then as a teacher—before I began to sort out who I was as a writer and, after that, who I was as a teacher. But the short version is that what we learned about writing—both Wendy and I—from our long, formal educations in it, had to be pieced together, bricoleur-fashion, and then adapted, as if by sleight-of-hand, to our own experience and need, and then to that of our students.

But it's that very story—and not just the story, but the *telling* of it, for how long had others like us lived such stories in silence—that has enabled creative writing to grow out of inchoate beginnings as a discipline and construct itself as it is today. In my own view, creative writing, like other strands of English studies, can be organized conceptually around the three fundamental questions David H. Richter poses in *Falling into Theory*. Though Richter's subject is literature and the question is reading, the essential critical framework he poses—asking what we do, why we do it, and how we do it—applies as elegantly, and as productively, to writing as it does to reading. In turn, this framework can be used to illuminate what has emerged, since the time when Wendy and I were starting out together, as the enduring triptych of our field—product, process, writing—which can be said to define and organize us.

One way of imagining these preoccupations—what they mean to us and how we conceive them—is in relation to the different categories of advanced degrees we offer and about which our students are both endlessly interested and confused. What is the nature, they ask, of the MFA degree, and how can it be distinguished from the PhD or the MA? What separate functions do these degrees serve? How are their graduates differently perceived?

Any cursory review of academic job lists in English demonstrates an uneasy equivalence between the MFA and the PhD with creative dissertation. Both are terminal degrees; both provide academic preparation for college-level teaching of creative writing; both require scholarship and writing; both are widely accepted. But in creative writing, there are roughly ten times as many MFA programs as there are programs that offer PhDs, and the time spent in earning the latter can be three times the time spent in earning the former. In my own department, half the creative writing faculty have earned the MFA and half have earned the PhD, and the edgy alliances that form and shift between and among us and our colleagues in other English studies disciplines are sometimes—not always—marked by the nature of our training in writing.

One conventional way of distinguishing the degrees is that the MFA is, first and foremost, a studio arts degree. Harking back to its beginnings at Iowa, the MFA is modeled on the education of a painter, who produces work based on models for scrutiny and comment. The goal in such a model is almost exclusively the finely wrought thing—the publishable literary artifact (in commercial or professional terms), or, more generously, art. Although this distinction may seem imprecise or arbitrary, it runs as surely through the discipline as does the distinction between poetry and fiction—and indeed, the two sets of categories are closely linked.

Maybe it's a small thing, but the question my father posed these many years ago—what are we training these writers to *do?*—critically informs this division, and, in theory, the studio arts degree—that is, the MFA—has, as its purpose, preparing students not just to teach, but also to publish. But if creative writing has anything to learn from theory, we should begin with the question Michel Foucault poses in "What Is an Author?" which seeks to examine the modes of existence of a discourse, where it has been used, how it might circulate, and who might appropriate it. And here, creative writing splits, and splits again, for if success is going to be determined by publishability alone, then the criterion by which we agree to judge ourselves is already tacitly being shifted from artistic to market concerns.

And though I don't like to say so, fiction writers tend to be more comfortable with commercial aspiration than poets, which suggests that the apparently superficial division among genres in creative writing programs defines a fundamental difference that goes straight to the heart of our ideologies and practices. But while genre distinctions remain, like many others, conventionally constructed, the attraction of programs in fiction, on the whole, remains the lure of publication, while those in poetry sometimes seem to focus more exclusively on the pursuit of art—of writing for its own sake (though plenty of fiction writers will make this claim, too). And creative nonfiction, which I discuss later, is adding its own new elements to the mix. All three genres, each in its own way, remains subject to the fetish of the book—whether commercial or small press, commercial or literary—having a book in print is the ultimate goal.

And isn't that an odd thing, when the 2004 National Endowment for the Arts report, *Reading at Risk*, finds that less than half of American adults, 47 percent, read literature in 2002, and of those, most calculated that they'd read approximately six books that year. Some 7 percent admitted to having done some creative writing during the year, and some 13 percent to having taken a creative writing class at some point in their lives. Of these, only 1 percent had gotten a work published (4). Increasingly, we are becoming a nation of writers who do not read, and as creative writing teachers face this paradox in their classrooms every day, the discipline is struggling to respond.

If the MFA degree is principally a studio arts degree, the PhD (and, though to a lesser degree, the MA) is a scholarly or academic degree, which may be said to concentrate as much on the why and the how of the work as on what it aspires to be. As a consequence, the critical inquiry that takes place in such programs returns in important ways to the intradisciplinary roots of creative writing, attempting to ground the work of the practicing writer in the context of both its literary and its critical traditions, and so to frame it in relation to the broader conversation that is writing. I do not mean to suggest that such inquiry does not take place in the MFA workshop—how could it not? But the focus, the proportions, the affiliations are perpetually shifting, and in the more academic setting of the PhD, writers are trained not just to act and think as writers, but also as scholars, and to value scholarly activity as primary—as equivalent, in important ways, to creative writing—and to examine what the two activities might share in common as systematically and rigorously as what might set them apart.

Beyond the production of primary texts, creative writing, in every kind of institutional setting and context, has begun to concern itself with self-reflexive thinking about where writing comes from—both our own, and that of others—and why and how it may inform and enrich both our private lives and the culture in general. If, as Helen Vendler has asserted, "[W]hat we have loved, others will love" (qtd. in Richter 27), then creative writing will inevitably reflect a little bit of our original passion for writing. But it is also true that, paraphrasing Gerald Graff, to a large extent "our ability to [write] well depends more than we think on our ability to *talk well* about what we [write]" (Richter 40). Creative writing, then, must also commit itself to the rigorous study of both text and theory, an innocuous enough proposition it seems, but no easy transition for the writing world.

I had been teaching full-time for two years and was already beginning to find myself lacking (my best students were turning into very good writers, but what was going on with the rest?) when the first edited volume on creative writing in the academy, *Creative Writing in America*, was published in 1989, with some fanfare, by the National Council of Teachers of English (Moxley). Conceived in anticipation of the paradigm shift that was evolving to reframe creative writing—our theory and our practice— this volume was an early attempt to engage in just that kind of self-reflexive thinking. Marking a new area of interest for NCTE, and a certain coming of age for creative writing, the book assembled some twenty-odd writer-teachers to reflect on problems in the discipline, issues of craft, and professional concerns, such as editing and publishing. For me, as for the discipline in general, everything about it was exciting, and for the first time, in one place, twenty or so writer-teachers reflected on the practice of their teaching as thoughtfully and as articulately as they might have reflected on the practice of their writing.

In this way, creative writers had begun a slow, tentative movement toward inclusion in the broader discipline that did not depend exclusively on what we ourselves made—presumably "literature," the stuff that our colleagues in English sought to study, though of course they never studied us. Looking beyond ourselves to our practice in our classrooms, and as practitioners of writing, we sought in this publication, for the first time, to frame a larger purpose and praxis, something beyond the formidable navel-gazing for which we were by then renowned.

In the years that immediately followed, a series of new publications gave rise to optimism that things might be changing. Among them, Wendy's first composition-influenced study of creative writing, *Released into Language*, would come out two years later, followed, in another four years, by *Colors of a Different Horse* (which Wendy coedited with Hans Ostrom). Each new volume made important contributions to rethinking the nature of creative writing, especially as an academic discipline closely linked to other strands of English studies, and as it was making its uneasy transition from graduate to undergraduate instruction. By the early 1990s, it was common enough for creative writers to entertain the possibility that our work, both in writing and teaching, might be strengthened and deepened by intertextual explorations that went beyond the traditional fusion of reading and writing to include the scholarship of both composition and theory. Looking back, it seems now that we were, at least in part, tired of being the department eccentrics or drunks and looking for legitimacy. We were writers, yes. We were maybe arty, and we maybe wore strange clothes. But this did not make us special. And we were academics, too—critics, scholars, teachers—colleagues in departments that were rapidly evolving into places that the men who had hired us no longer recognized.

"What department?" I overheard a revered senior colleague remark one day after the earthquake that leveled my campus in 1994. I was sitting in the rubble of my office, wearing a hardhat and sorting through what remained of half a decade of work. He was picking his way through the debris in the hallway, talking to someone who did not respond. "It's not," he said, with some bitterness, "my department anymore."

The tone in his voice was familiar, unnerving. There was something, I don't know, bereft about it. Then it struck me, and, momentarily, I too felt a kind of trenchant loss as I recognized the same forlorn sound I'd heard not long before in the voice of a man at an AWP meeting, who, in the question period following a session on theory, had lamented, "But how can I even teach if I can't nurture my students with the same great writers who nurtured me in my own development as a writer?"

But Is It Art?

To paraphrase Virginia Woolf, somewhere around the year 1986 creative writing changed, and, twenty years behind the rest of English studies, creative writing began a period of self-assessment that would include our early attempts to articulate who we were and what we were about. So it is fair to say that Wendy and I came of writing age on the cusp of this change, and the world we had naively entered not that long before was about to look very different.

Since that time, three debates have largely framed the discourse that defines creative writing. One has been prominently played out in the popular press, testy and rancorous, for everyone to see, not unlike the public skewering of deconstruction, though in plainer terms that people understand. In it, we were being accused and roundly chastised for killing poetry, which should, we were told, be cherished and revered as the most elevated of all verbal arts, and we have come, with some alacrity, to our own defense. The second and third debates have been somewhat more private affairs, more self-contained, but not less passionate. In one, we've taken on the pros and cons of theory, and in the other, we've at least tried to develop some systematic framework for our teaching and to resolve the schisms that had begun to separate us. In each of these three debates, we have directly engaged, with varying degrees of ease and success, another strand of English studies, and we begin with art.

For in 1989, even as we were beginning our own internal, somewhat tentative moves toward a newly emerging sense of creative writing as an academic discipline, we found ourselves suddenly blindsided by the national press. Appearing first in *Commentary*, and subsequently republished in what was then called the *AWP Newsletter* (once was not enough), Joseph Epstein's "Who Killed Poetry?" was a blistering attack on American letters—mostly us—and a rousing wake-up call. For most of us, Epstein's critique was a little like having one's dirty laundry aired out in public—or worse, like being accused of wearing nothing at all—for in it, he claimed that the democratization of poetry—as in the proliferation of creative writing programs and their graduates (maybe my father was right)—constituted little more than its demise. A whole country of poets—for by then, it was beginning to seem that this was precisely what we were producing—was, according to Epstein, the worst thing that could happen to the art of poetry, and among the literally thousands of academically trained writers, it would be a miracle of substantial proportions for even one of them to produce a single real poem. We'd reduced ourselves, in Epstein's view, to the petty bourgeoisie of poetry, incapable of little more than self-indulgent blather—small-minded, mediocre, and, perhaps worst of all, professional. And so was ushered in the era of "McPoetry" (and soon the "MFA story"), and a kind of open season was declared on poetry—and by extension, all academic writers—such that, for a while in the 1990s, almost everybody seemed to know that what was wrong with American letters began in creative writing programs themselves.

But this was a kind of internal critique and, ironically, when the popular press finally got around to being interested in savaging fiction (see B. R. Myers, "A Reader's Manifesto"), what came under attack was not our slavish submission to convention and commerce nor our reduced reach, but what Myers characterized as the growing pretentiousness of literary prose. If the primary failure of poetry was that it had lost touch with its highest aspirations to "surprise and delight," to achieve the sublime, to be art, fiction failed when it saw itself as anything more than a good story and popular entertainment.

In the 1990s, nonetheless, we were still reeling from Epstein and beginning to take note of what suddenly did seem like a nation of poets where a thousand or more books of poetry were being published every year. A forum framed in response to Epstein, for example, filled two full issues of what was then called the *AWP Chronicle,* with writers, on the whole, coming to the passionate defense of their work and art. Did this proliferation of poetry and poets, which could now be found in every school and on every corner, really mark a general decline of literary arts, or might it not be seen as a state of unprecedented health? If, as Donald Hall would lament in *Death to the Death of Poetry*, "[N]obody reads poetry anymore, except, perhaps, poets themselves" (1), then that still might constitute a wider—or, calculated by sheer numbers—larger audience for poetry than had ever existed before.

Then, in 1991, Gioia's influential "Can Poetry Matter?" appeared in the *Atlantic Monthly,* and the terms of the argument shifted. Gioia's complaint was familiar by now, as he again lodged the criticism that American poetry, in general, had been reduced to an inwardly focused, solipsistic subculture, severed from the mainstream of artistic and intellectual life and lacking the ability—or will—to make itself a form of public speech. Either way, things looked bad for us, and the academy—the very existence of creative writing as an academic discipline—was indisputably at fault. Incapable of producing serious art, we couldn't speak for the people either, and Gioia's subsequent challenge—"whether the arts will continue to exist in isolation and decline into subsidized academic specialties or whether some possibility of rapprochement with the educated public remains" (*Disappearing* 18)—is one that continues to resonate today.

The Theory Wars

Meanwhile, another, more sibling-like squabble was also taking shape in what are seen now as the creative writing "theory wars." A full year before Epstein, the opening round of these "wars" took place in what was then called the *AWP Newsletter* (now the *Writer's Chronicle*) as a mild-mannered and friendly enough exchange between Peter Stitt and Marjorie Perloff on the relative value of theory to writing, a topic in which I was keenly interested. Less visible to the public eye, more internecine, and in some sense, far more influential on our actual practice, these were the earliest beginnings of a discussion that would indelibly mark us, nudging us ever so slowly away from our own naiveté and abiding faith in our romantic origins. Today, it may seem hard to even imagine the passions this exchange was about to unleash, but at the time it seemed heady enough. As the first to raise the alarm about the increasingly stultifying influence of theory on creative writing, Stitt took a commonsense approach, attempting to pull us back from the dangerous edge of our own worst academic impulses. Like Oliver Wendell Holmes, the genial armchair critic whose virtues he extolled, Stitt wanted the experience of literature returned to the purview of the ordinary reader, and as he exhorted us to "fight mysticism" (i.e., theory) wherever it might be encountered (4), he waxed nostalgic for the plainspoken critic who said what was on his mind and gave "perfectly balanced and good-natured commentary on the books that came his way" (5). But Perloff wasn't having it, arguing in her companion article, "'Theory' and/in the Creative Writing Classroom," that any recent theorist worth her salt would know that "'what is in [the poet's] mind or heart' is not *his* to begin with; it has been planted there by the language he/she uses, the dominant ideology of the culture, the moment in history in which he/she writes" ("'Theory'" 2).

So began the argument, pro and con, back and forth: were we the makers of the songs we sang, or did they come from somewhere else, somewhere outside our own romantic poet souls, somewhere in the culture and its polyphony of discourse, as artificially constructed tissues of quotation and convention, like identity itself? Stitt didn't like the way that theorists had begun to strut, to act like "special people, possessed of a special and difficult body of knowledge" who read "weird texts" and "rode on hobby horses of their own devising" (5); and Perloff countered, yes, but "they also *write* weird texts of their own devising" (3); and even then, it was hard not to blush. For poets, too, are sometimes seen to strut, to act like special people, possessed of special talent, to write weird texts, and to ride on hobbyhorses of their own self-promotion. Much of what followed in the theory wars would echo this initial exchange, especially as they concerned the problem of the author—who he or she is and what he or she does, and what that might tell us about where what we do comes from and why. In "The Writer in the University," for example, Scott Russell Sanders deplores the way that theory turns artists into puppets whose "strings are jerked by some higher power—by ideology or the unconscious, by genetics, by ethnic allegiance, by sexual proclivities, by gender, by language itself" (11) when, he argues, "language is not a prison house [. . . but] the means of our freedom" (13). Sanders goes on to exhort creative writers to focus more exclusively on "artistic criteria" as the only things over which they might have any "control." But, of course, the very thing that theory helps us see is that this control is also somehow a construct, strictly regulated by the culture and its guardians of literary discourse, and therein lies the paradox by which what may imprison us may also set us free.

Throughout the next decade, this theory debate, and its auxiliary discussions, like creative writing itself, has continued to proliferate as the discipline, already half a century old, begins finally to sort itself out. And the pro- and antitheory camps will become much more clearly defined and aligned. As theory-influenced writer-teachers take on the institutions that trained them and second-generation writing program graduates begin to establish themselves professionally, the creative writing world will increasingly divide over questions of language, identity, and power. Thus, it is striking that when the polemic was revisited in 1999, not much seems to have changed. In "Creative Writing in the Academy," David Radavich argued that the teaching of creative writing had come to an important crossroads, with the "collapse of traditional literary publishing and the globalization of popular culture and the Internet" (106); and in "Creative Writing and Its Discontents," David Fenza (then AWP director) accused Radavich of paradoxical thinking (encouraging students to "duplicate solipsistic work," even as they strive to write "commercially, for publishing glory") that belies the real goal of undergraduate writing instruction, which is, or should be, Fenza argues, "exaltation"—an experience unlikely to be nurtured in any classroom "tempered by recent literary theories." For, as Fenza goes on to argue,

> The professors of theory remind us that words, after all, are not the things they represent and so are hopelessly inexact and distorted by social powers. Such demotions of authors and language, especially among undergraduates, does not cultivate a keen appreciation of literature. In contrast, creative writing classes have always esteemed, not texts, but literary works, which writers willed into being because they needed to name an experience or idea their culture had not yet named. When they do succeed in

> naming something new, we are all the richer for having yet an-
> other image, story, song, or character by which we can know our
> pleasures and predicaments. The teaching of creative writing is
> the teaching of these appreciations. (Par. 56)

So there it is. Despite Fenza's own brief flirtation with theory in the early 1990s, he's brought us back again, at last, to our own beginnings, and this attempt to resurrect the romantic notion of the writer as special being and creator would seem anachronistic if it did not represent official sanction. And while it's difficult to imagine how, exactly, these appreciations may be conceived in the absence of a critical understanding of the cultural contexts that engender them in the first place—or to teach them—that, I suppose, is the mystique of art.

But Fenza's did not turn out to be the last word, and in 2002 a provocative Internet cluster on creative writing and its peda-gogies appeared in the *Electronic Book Review*. Anchored by Joe Amato and H. Kassia Fleisher's wide-ranging and exhaustive manifesto, "Reforming Creative Writing Pedagogy: History as Knowledge, Knowledge as Activism," this forum exhorted us, once again, to seek a stronger sense of self-awareness, a broader knowledge base and greater intellectual rigor in our classrooms, which should be designed not just to foster writing, but to engage both us and our students in a "constant, thoughtful, practical confrontation with issues: of classroom authority, of community, of critical engagement, of social responsibility, of education as such, of poiesis, of content and form." It is theory that enables us to conceive of such a classroom, so much richer, with so much more to yield—and so much more open to its participants—than Fenza's archaic model of "appreciations."

Among the respondents, both Perloff and Sandy Huss be-lieve that this reformation is already underway, that creative writ-ing, on the whole, is doing better than Amato and Fleisher suggest. "I want to believe," Huss writes, "that a lot of us who emerged from first generation writing programs [. . . went] on to chal-lenge the top-down, genius-reverent, pronouncement-preponder-ant, phallogocentric pedagogy of the bad old days." And Perloff, as if to complete the circle she started long ago, weighs back in with a correction, suggesting that in fact creative writing has come to fill the vacuum critics and theorists left in English departments with the abdication of "literary passion and the pleasure of the text" ("Amato/Fleisher"). That creative writers may still provide this passion and pleasure is cause—it really is—for celebration.

As for myself, I wish I knew. Like Huss and Perloff, I want to believe that things are evolving. But if Patrick Bizarro can observe in 2004 that "the mere mention of theory or praxis sets off alarms in the brains of most creative writers" (295), it's pretty clear that no resolution of these issues is in sight. And as Perloff rues her own failure to effect change in her home department, but looks across the bay to the hiring of Lynn Hejinian ("one of the most theoretically-informed and critically astute poets writing today" ["Amato/Fleisher"]) at Berkeley as a sign of positive change, it's hard not to reflect that Berkeley doesn't even have a creative writing program.

Teaching What We Do

But there is another ongoing debate that I like to think of as no less central to the discipline and equally engaging, and that has to do with what counts as creative writing teaching. More than perhaps any other strand of English studies, except composition and rhetoric, creative writing frames the principles that organize the discipline as parallel to those that organize our teaching. And this goes back to the complex identity issues introduced at the start of this chapter. The writer in the university is not the same as the critic or scholar, and without claiming any special status (there's been far too much of that already), it is important to imagine the haven that the university provided writers, back when we were starting out, just after the second great war. Prior to this moment, the day job of choice for the American writer—though of course, you took what you could get—had been journalism, which, after all, was writing, too. But I once heard William Manchester describe writing five novels, after dinner, as a family man, having spent the day at his journalism job, and it didn't sound at all enviable. As writers began their steady, postwar move into teaching positions, it must have been with some relief, if not a sense of marvel.

Theorists and literary scholars, composition teachers, linguists, English education specialists—all the disciplines represented in this volume—have their own "callings," but I don't imagine they expect to live by them outside the academy either. And it isn't really that writers expect to live by their writing—we may be eccentric, but we're not delusional. But in our hearts we always also know that teaching really is a good gig, that it enables us—it *supports* us—in our other work, the work that makes us who we are and helps us make sense of the world.

Thus, writers in the university have always been split, and the discipline itself is similarly split between its private and public personae. In the paradoxical logic of both/and thinking, it is possible to say, and to believe, that there is nothing special about writing, but that there also is. And I also know that all the other people in my department—all the linguists, all the theorists, all the literary critics, and all the composition teachers—are deeply passionate about their work. But at some level, creative writers, on the whole, may be temperamentally inclined to suspect that Foerster was right and that there is something in the nature not just of literature but the practice of it that lies at the core of what brings us to a life of language in the first place.

But that's our private self, and in our public self—our institutional self—we are teachers. It took us a while to work this out, but as we moved from the days of elite graduate workshops to those of populist undergraduate programs, our concept of what the creative writing teacher does or who she or he even is has undergone radical change.

Perhaps the most familiar icon of creative writing, both within academia and in the larger culture, is the writing workshop, a classroom model so closely affiliated with creative writing as to be very nearly indistinguishable from it. People who have never set foot in such a classroom (although there seem to be fewer and fewer of these)—from those you stand in line with at the grocery store to your theory colleague down the hall—will feel familiar, almost intimate, with it, as if what we do in the privacy of our own classrooms were everybody's business, a cultural cliché as nonsensical to the average person as the idea of deconstruction or the college professor herself. The writing workshop strikes an uneasy chord in almost all of us. You recognize the moment: A dark and brooding student anxiously approaches a daunting circle of student critics to present his work; there's a strained and awkward moment; then he opens his mouth and begins to read. And as the words spill out—self-conscious, pretentious, and devastatingly vapid, we are publicly skewered all over again.

Part of the story Wendy and I were to tell, over and over, when we first started had to do with how and why the workshop failed us, both when we were students and as teachers in our own classrooms. As students, we were never really trained to think about our work, nor were we provided with any useful way to talk about it, although for me this was to change when I became a doctoral student. For the men who were our teachers, however well-intentioned, were always writers first, and many were ill-prepared even to listen, never mind respond, to the work of young women writers. As teachers, we went out into the world, equipped, like most other second-generation creative writing teachers, with little more than a vague sense of how we had been taught shored up by our lifelong practice of imitation, of trying to write the way we thought we were supposed to write, and now to teach the way we thought we were supposed to teach.

Today, what we missed at the time seems self-evident—that the homogenous groups of highly motivated, self-identified writers with clear aspirations toward literary achievement that assemble in our MFA and PhD programs have little in common with the rich mix of students who often show up in undergraduate classes. Enrolled for such diverse reasons as the need for self-expression, an easy A, a general education course fulfillment in the humanities or fine arts, or a lifelong desire to write, these students display widely varying levels of preparation, and levels of commitment that vary just as widely. Today, it is easy to see that these differences between graduate and undergraduate students must be reflected in our pedagogies. Teachers can't, for example, simply assign three stories or ten poems to students who may not know what a story or a poem looks like or is, or even have a very strong desire to write one. But we did not always know this. And for those of us who stumbled into our own undergraduate workshops expecting to proceed as we had been taught, the experience was chastening.

In my own early critique of the workshop, first presented at the 1993 Conference on College Composition and Communication (and later revised and reprinted in *What Our Speech Disrupts*), I struggled to come to terms with what still seemed to prevail as its fundamental assumptions:

> We assume, for example, that such workshops will be composed of homogeneous groups of talented students with strong vocational commitments to writing. We agree that the appropriate product of the class will be a publishable literary text in a conventional genre. We assess "publishability" in terms of poorly articulated, but nonetheless prevalent standards of "good writing." We promote the idea that these standards reflect universal and enduring aesthetic values that exist somehow outside of their cultural construction. We regard publishing in more elevated terms than other forms of writing achievement. We proceed as if writing is somehow a "natural" activity, firmly rooted in talent, which cannot really be taught, but only nurtured. We assure the credibility of the writer as an "inspired," often tormented genius, who presents a special case in the academy. We imagine that creative writing is somehow different from other kinds of writing, and that this difference could be described, though not defined, by its resistance to articulation. (*What* 45–46)

In the time since I wrote this, we have grown more self-aware, more deliberate about this model, which has worked, after all, to provide stability and coherence throughout the discipline since its inception. The unexamined workshop can still exert a hostile influence on students whose experience of life and view of what writing is, as well as what they may desire or expect from it, can differ profoundly from our own. But in its more self-reflexive modes, there is something endearing about the way it has endured, and it's certain to continue in ever-evolving forms. Despite the countless hours of grief it may have caused (and believe me, they *are* countless), I do love the workshop in the same way I love all finely made things, things with a past. The workshop is a kind of private space for creative writers where we find as much of a home as we are likely ever to get in the academy.

But what does it do?

What the Workshop Does

One way to understand the current thinking in the discipline—or rather, the schisms that continue to inform the current thinking—is in relation to the various functions we can now see for the workshop, along with the different ways we have begun to conceive of its product or products, especially in relation to the other strands of English studies. Looked at this way, it is possible to say that creative writing is, at its core, inextricably interdisciplinary, and that inside the university it has hardly ever had a discrete identity of its own—or if it has, it is not one that is very much in favor anymore. For while that identity, the one in which our main goal is to produce writers who publish, may have been our earliest and most familiar incarnation—may still be what draws students to us in prodigious numbers—it is also the incarnation that has led to the charges of mediocrity and homogenization discussed above and earned us our vexed reputations. Some few elite programs will continue to network students directly into publishing contracts and teaching positions, but this does not begin to account for the thousands of other creative writing students who just want to write, or for the value writing may have in their lives.

In the first, most familiar model of the workshop, novice writers continue to gather around their writer-teachers, hoping to improve their writing and, ultimately, to publish it. The teachers of these workshops will be successful writers themselves who hold academic appointments and are valued in their universities for the prestige their own achievements bring. Committed to producing the very "best" writing they can, these teachers may view their primary object as culling "real writers" from the rest, and they construct their classroom practice around the nuts and bolts of craft. To the extent that their pedagogy is systematic, its primary affiliation will be with other writers and the expectation that students will commit themselves not just to sustained practice in writing, but also to exhaustive reading in the genres and canons to which the students aspire and in which the teacher is him- or herself accomplished. They'll work with models, focusing on contemporary writing of the sort they may want their students to produce, whether from small-press literary publishing, mainstream commercial presses, or more experimental venues. In their efforts to produce the "best" writing possible, they'll see their way toward that largely by offering advice on how to improve student drafts. The standard for the work will continue to be the hugely imprecise notion of "publishability," still somewhat vaguely conceived as whatever looks most like whatever model is provided for the class, work favored by the writer-professor and resulting in what Bizarro has described as a "vertical" workshop production of "sameness" (305). These are star-centered classes where the teacher is the final arbiter of success and where people know "good writing" when they see it. These workshops may also concern themselves with pragmatic, real-world writing problems—how to break into the literary marketplace, publish, get an agent, write reviews, find a job.

Today this model of the workshop still powerfully persists, but there are also, increasingly, other kinds of creative writing classrooms, richly informed by critical and composition theories. These may be process-driven classes that look a lot like composition classes and employ a wide range of classroom procedures —small groups and collaborative activities, directed writing exercises, writing rubrics, writing about writing, self-reflection— and any other practice that might work to develop a metadiscursive self-consciousness about what it is we think we are doing when we are writing, and why, and what value that might have to ourselves, privately, or to the culture at large. Whether based on weird theoretical texts or straightforward treatments of genre or process, what distinguishes these classrooms from more traditional creative writing classrooms is that, in them, not just the practice but also the subject is writing. And while it is commonly held that an auxiliary function of the traditional creative writing classroom is to produce readers of serious writing, in the "new" kind of class, the auxiliary goal might be to produce lifelong writers as well—people for whom writing continues to exist as an organizing principle and a mechanism of agency and meaning in daily life.

If things are changing, it would have to be because a growing number of us in the academy have come to embrace the idea that effective pedagogies and curricula depend upon sustained, intensive, and rigorous interdisciplinary work that embraces the whole constellation of English studies. This work imagines that creative writing students be expected not just to write in their classes, but also to locate their writing within a wide variety of literary, cultural, historical, critical, and creative traditions. And it does so in the context not just of an evolving discipline, but of a student population vastly different from the one the discipline imagined when it was starting out. In this, we are all a little bit bricoleurs.

Or, as Radavich puts it in the *Electronic Book Review* forum:

1) Very few creative writing students will ever achieve worldly success, let alone stardom, with their writing.

2) Therefore, my goal as a teacher of *all* my students, to the best of my (and their) ability, is to nurture, educate, enlighten, and stimulate the whole person—mind, body, and spirit—through the practice of writing and being together.

3) Creative writing cannot stop at expressing the individual self. While individual awareness is good, the arts succeed only when they build and nurture and operate within community.

4) Given our desire to educate the whole person, we need to encourage our students to also explore science, history, art and music, politics, sociology, religion, and other fields, in order to enrich their awareness and their writing.

5) As a professor at a regional comprehensive university, I seek to educate my creative writing students to be active participants in community who can communicate meaningfully to and about themselves and the larger world.

A Few Words about Craft and Genre

Craft. What is it? Craft is nuts and bolts. Craft is the ordinary wisdom of writers at work, readily available wherever writers reflect on their work—notably, in *Poets and Writers Magazine*, in *The AWP Chronicle*, and, for more than fifty years, in the three-hundred-plus *Paris Review* interviews, now being fully archived online with the generous support of an NEA grant, an astonishing resource for writers. Craft is writing habits, rules of thumb, helpful tips. But it's also architecture—plot, character, setting, conflict. It's how to build a shapely story and where to find a form. Craft is founded in the beloved books of writers, like Richard Hugo's *The Triggering Town* and William Stafford's *Writing the Australian Crawl*. It's John Gardner's *Art of Fiction* and Annie Dillard's *Living by Fiction*.

It's what to do and what not to do and how to do it or not to do it. It's how to write, as exhaustively explored in a seemingly endless stream of handbooks and textbooks that include *Writing Fiction* by Janet Burroway, *Poetry Writing: Theme and Variations* by David Starkey, *The Fourth Genre* by Robert Root and Michael Steinberg, *Three Genres* by Stephen Minot, and *The College Handbook of Creative Writing* by Robert DeMaria. There are thousands more such books (a Google book search on "the writer's craft" just turned up 5,630), and they reflect the dynamic landscape of creative writing. To a large extent, craft can be seen as synonymous with what we do or are perceived to do.

But as much as craft is rules and purpose and clarity, it is double-edged. Clarity, linked to mastery, provides the kind of certainty that works to shut down any other possibility. Craft is not prescriptive, but it can feel that way. In *Break Every Rule*, Carole Maso writes,

> If writing is language and language is desire and longing and suffering, and it is capable of great passion and also great nuances of passion [. . .] and if the syntax reflects states of desire, is hope, is love, is sadness, is fury, and if the motions of the sentences and paragraphs and chapters are this as well, if the motion of line is about desire and longing and want; then why when we write, when we make shapes on paper, why then does it so often look like the tradition, straight models, why does our longing look for example like John Updike's longing? (155)

Or, from Trinh, "Shake syntax, smash the myth, and if you lose, slide on, *unearth* some new linguistic paths. Do you surprise? Do you shock? Do you have a choice?" (20).

Between the two notions of what the writer does lie entirely different concepts of writing itself. Craft proceeds, albeit in indirect ways, from the notion that writing somehow exists as "idea" before it is put into words, that the process of writing is having the idea and then trying very hard to find the right words to express it, that it is primarily wrought. The other notion is that writing is somehow something else, something other, something that really only knows itself in the moment of its coming into being.

Genre. Another way creative writing works to fix and stabilize itself inside its classroom practice is through the concentration on fixed genres, especially the three classroom genres: poetry, fiction, drama. Genres provide clear categories, descriptions, and knowable conventions that can be understood and practiced, and creative writing inside the academy has long organized itself around generic distinctions and the groups they inherently promote. For many years, creative writing was an essentially binary world, split almost evenly between fiction writers and poets, with fiction writers being perceived to hold a kind of edge in their potential—however minute—to have successful commercial publishing careers. Playwriting has held a small corner of the creative writing market, but it also has long been seen as an essential part of the project.

In recent years, the emerging genre of creative nonfiction has become a fourth genre, which turns out not to be so recent after all, harking back to the origins of creative writing in Harvard's composition courses. Initially a source of some contention within the discipline, creative nonfiction is now more or less accepted as a mainstay of creative writing programs and, increasingly, as a possible bridge between creative writing and composition, a development recently examined in a special January 2003 issue of *College English*.

In many respects, it really is remarkable how quickly and pervasively the idea of creative nonfiction caught on, especially in the culture beyond the university, which, hungry for certainty and fact, has turned increasingly away from imaginative genres toward writing it takes to be true. Thus, the term *creative nonfiction* can be said to highlight not just a generic but an ideological difference, held together by the common thread of writing. Some people might argue that the term *creative nonfiction* is so hopelessly broad as either to be meaningless or to include almost any writing that purports to represent the world. But the pervasive popularity of the genre suggests that the desire for certainty trumps its improbability, and creative nonfiction—as a separate genre and an area of creative writing specialization—is clearly here to stay. In 1995, at the AWP Annual Conference in Pittsburgh, Lee Gutkind, editor of the magazine *Creative Nonfiction*, and affectionately known as godfather of the genre, described creative nonfiction to me as less "personal" than the essay and more fully engaged in some kind of "sustained investigation of the world." That same year, he described the five Rs of creative nonfiction as "real life," "reflection," "research," "reading," and "riting" (qtd. in Starkey 65). That said, I might add that creative nonfiction writers believe we can know—and have an obligation to describe—the difference between what we believe to be true and what we're convinced we make up.

In other respects, the emergence of creative nonfiction as a separate strand of creative writing studies, with its cottage industry of publications and newsletters and conferences and degrees, underscores a move toward increasing specialization and differentiation at a time when what holds us together might be argued to exert a more compelling logic than what sets us apart.

What Counts as Scholarship

It is possible to say that creative writing, as a field, is largely anecdotal, as creative writers tend not to cite each other or maintain scholarly habits. This can at least in part be attributed to what Bizarro describes as the "resistance of a powerful and conservative throng of poets, novelists, and dramatists" who still dominate the discipline (295). But it's also, at least in part, because of that private self I discussed above, and it strikes even me, from time to time, that there is something so intensely private about what the writer does that this very effort to stabilize the discipline by definition *is* counterintuitive. We're not really special beings possessed of special talents, but neither are we trained academics and, for more than half a century, we've done our best to demonstrate a deep-seated reluctance to become so.

A cursory glance at any recent issue of the *Writer's Chronicle* shows it to be dominated by interviews with writers, personal insight-driven discussions of some aspect of creative writing as identified by creative writers, craft-based how-to articles, and advertisements for writing programs and publishing venues. Of two issues I have on my desk, one (February 2004) contains thirty-six (out of sixty-six) full pages of "news," announcements, and advertisements, with only five devoted exclusively to text, and two of those, in the standard recent format of the journal, are long interviews with contemporary writers. In another (October/November 2003), Tracy Daugherty pronounces that "many of us have reached [where we are] because of failure" (49), opposite an advertisement for an MFA program that declares, "Our graduates don't just write. They publish."

But even the AWP, perhaps sensitized to longstanding charges of anti-intellectualism and chumminess, has made considerable effort to change, working to develop a more comprehensive sense of its institutional mission and past and indexing at least part of the *Writer's Chronicle* online. If the mechanisms by which work is archived remain mysterious, if not arbitrary, the record they produce is nonetheless instructive. Also available online are a calendar of submission deadlines and selected pedagogy papers from the conference forum.

In 1990, Wendy, Sandra Alcosser, and I collaborated to lead the first (and last) preconference pedagogy workshop at the annual AWP meeting, where some twenty or more participants joined together for a half-day workshop focused on new models for creative writing teaching—a workshop that was, by all reports, a success. Thirteen years later at another AWP, chatting with a board member at the elevator, I was surprised to hear her suddenly come up with the "new" idea that AWP should host preconference workshops, as at CCCC.

That sense of institutional amnesia is a frustration shared by two of my new creative writing colleagues, Brian Leung and Leilani Hall, as they edit this year's pedagogy papers for the AWP conference. Hardworking and ambitious, they've been reading submissions for months, and it's with an almost poignant sense of déjà vu that I watch them struggle to get submitters to cite sources or reframe their proposals in conversation with others.

In creative writing, it seems, the ideas themselves are always new, always waiting to be rediscovered again.

Some years ago, I sat on a panel that addressed the question: *Is creative writing scholarship?* My co-presenter, a poet, spoke with eloquence about what happens when poets read other poets, bringing to their readings the specialized discourse and insights they share, how different it is from a scholarly reading, how much it adds to the discourse at large. It is easy to see the virtue in this logic—that writers need to bring their own reading, their own interests and concerns, to the reading of the writers whom they love. Such a practice can clearly be conceived as scholarship, involving sustained close reading and being informed by both literary and textual competence. And much of the time, this is precisely what counts as scholarship in creative writing, which largely moves through the world in the form of long book reviews.

But there are other promising developments, notably in the work of scholars like Bizarro, Starkey, Kelly Ritter, Anna Leahy, and others, who seek to move us beyond our preoccupation with the figure of the writer or the text to the role of creative writing as an academic discipline inside a profession that includes, but is not limited to, the production and teaching of imaginative writing. In "Research and Reflection in English Studies," Bizarro presents a compelling argument that the emergence of creative writing as a separate discipline inside English studies is dependent on the evolution of sustained academic inquiry sufficiently distinguished from the kind of inquiry the others in this volume have described. To do so, we need to train graduate students not just to teach creative writing—which, as Ritter demonstrates, still does not happen—but also to reflect systematically on that teaching and to conduct research on creative writing as a teachable and researchable subject. Bizarro identifies six skills he describes as being "equally useful in writing creatively and in reflecting upon what we do when we teach creative writing" (301). These skills range from the observation that we are readers who understand people and the importance of history, to our belief in the writing process and ability to employ various genres. In claiming that these skills differ at an epistemological level for writers,

Bizarro lays the groundwork for developing what Ritter calls "markers of professional difference" (205), and he argues that as we move toward disciplinary status, we need to be looking toward developing new kinds of creative writing classes. Such classes should move beyond what Bizarro sees as the now-standard "Literature: The Writer's Perspective" to "Professional Issues in Creative Writing," "Research in Creative Writing," and "Teaching Creative Writing: Theory and Practice" (308). Increasingly, when we plan for such courses, there is more work to choose from.

Textbooks and handbooks, once scarce commodities in creative writing—a discipline notoriously resistant to the notion of textbooks at all—now abound, and are painstakingly documented in the forty-page Appendix B, "Teaching Creative Writing: A Bibliography," of the second edition of Bishop's *Released into Language*. As Wendy herself notes in the preface, the sheer number of available texts that had appeared since the first edition of the book was heartening, if not overwhelming. What she'd expected to be a "weekend's review turned into a monthlong bibliographic project" (viii). Divided into five systematic categories—Classroom Texts; Anthologies/Reading Resources; Writing on Writing: Conversations, Interviews, Photographic Essays; (Writing) Teachers and (Writing) Researchers to (Writing) Teacher Classroom/Curricular Ideas—Pre–K and Across the Curriculum; References, Resources, and/or Additional Class Texts—this bibliography is an exhaustive, invaluable resource for books about writing, or teaching, or writing about teaching, or any combination of the above.

Leahy's *Power and Identity in the Creative Writing Classroom* was just published by Multilingual Matters. Tim Mayer's *(R)eWriting Craft: Composition, Creative Writing, and the Future of English Studies* was just released by the University of Pittsburgh Press. D. G. Myers's *The Elephants Teach* is being reissued by the University of Chicago Press. And Bishop and Starkey's newly released volume, *Keywords in Creative Writing*, promises to be an important new resource, designed to provide a comprehensive framework and lens through which to see the multiple facets of this profession, from agents and intellectual property rights, to university programs, teaching jobs, and submission guidelines.

Creative Writing outside the Academy

Unlike other strands of English studies, creative writing can be said to have a far greater presence outside the academy, and increasingly, it seems, creative writers have taken the strategy of secession and done it one better, leaving not just their English departments but the university in general. Gioia's recent examination of poetry beyond print culture, originally published in the *Hudson Review* and subsequently reprinted in a book-length collection of essays, *Disappearing Ink: Poetry at the End of Print Culture*, provides a provocative analysis of what writing is beginning to look like as it moves off the page and out into the world. In it, Gioia argues that while creative writing has been concentrated, in a literary sense, inside the university, on the outside a major revolution has been occurring that is restoring the primacy of poetry as a form of popular culture. From rap, to cowboy poetry, to slam poetry fests, Gioia examines the difference between popular and literary forms of poetry and what the resurgence of the former portends for the latter. Gioia agues that these new popular poetries share certain common traits: that they are predominantly oral, that they emerged outside of the dominant literary establishment and were initially the product of marginalized groups, that all such forms are overwhelmingly formal, and that they can be differentiated from literary poetry by their ability to draw a large and paying public. And he sees similar developments in literary poetry, from increasing emphasis on oral forms to nonprint means of circulation to a progressive movement of poetry beyond the scope of the university, which throughout the latter part of the twentieth century had provided literary artists with a secure place to be in the world. Based on Gioia's estimation, with some twenty-five thousand new MFA's being credentialed every decade, it seems clear that only a small percentage of those will be able to—or will choose to—stay in the site in which they were trained. Though I am not in the habit of ranking my students, one of the best I've seen in years is currently trying to decide whether or not to finish his MA in creative writing. In a recent e-mail, Kevin writes:

I am never going to teach full time. I will probably never go on to a PhD or MFA program. I am really good at my nonacademic job (I hate to think of things in economic terms, but I am in the low-to-mid six figures, and I can't really afford to quit my day job to enter the academic world). I really enjoyed the writing class I took this semester, but it did not change the way I write. The last class that fundamentally changed the way I write was my first class with you—the 308 where I stopped writing linear fiction.

I am not suggesting that I have nothing left to learn. Every class I take with you improves my writing (the class I took with Brian this semester improved my writing as well). I know I have a lot to learn, but I am not sure that the academic environment is going to teach me what I need to learn. I don't write MFA stories. I am starting to think that I would be better served spending my time writing.

And somewhat surprisingly, I'm no longer sure how to advise him. A quarter-century ago, when I went back to PhD school, I, too, thought I had nothing to learn. The writing education I received transformed my thinking and my practice forever, but Kevin already knows what I learned at that time and is right to intuit that the world he seeks to enter is a changed landscape from the one I entered all those years ago.

At the time, we had no way of imagining the world Gioia so optimistically describes—one rich with literary culture that is taking place outside the university, one that might have trained its participants but could not sustain them. Gioia locates this new bohemia in independent nonprofit literary presses, like Graywolf and Milkweed, McSweeney's and Copper Canyon; in the emergence of electronic networks and desktop publishing technologies; in the "transformation of bookstores, libraries, galleries, museums, and community centers into venues for literary education and performance" ("Can" 96); and in nonacademic literary organizations, like Poets and Writers, and activist movements, like Poets against the War. Further, Gioia argues that literary bookstores, like Cody's in Berkeley and Powell's in Portland, have somehow managed to survive and even thrive despite the exigencies of big-money publishing and their big-box bookstore affiliates by essentially transforming themselves into small community centers that link the needs of the literary culture with their own commercial interests. Couple this with the long-extant network of writing retreats and colonies, from MacDowell's and Yaddo to Hedgebrook (for women) and Ucross (in Wyoming); the small industry of summer conferences and workshops, like Breadloaf and Squaw Valley and Writers at Work; and a wide range of other writing festivals and book fairs, and it is abundantly clear that the expansion of the creative writing world beyond the realm of the academy that spawned it works to enrich not just the literary culture but the culture at large.

In the End

What Wendy loved about this place where I am writing now, at least in part, was light, and as I've sat here working I've watched the sun move steadily across the water in a dazzling display of its refracted rays. When we first met, back when she snapped the photograph of three writers drinking coffee, we lived in the West and both loved the desert. Both here and there, it is and was the endlessly receding expanse of space that never quite came to an end that enthralled her and me. In such a space, everything seemed always possible, just as it did when we entered our professional lives as writers and teachers, with everything spread out and open before us.

But it's only in telling this story that I've begun to realize that it is impossible to have told it. There are too many threads to hold together, too many points of view, too many directions it might have gone, too many years since it started even just for us.

What did I hope for back then, I wonder. I hoped for an intellectually engaged discipline that, in its multiple investigations of literature and language and writing and teaching and theory, could invite and support and challenge and nurture the individual writing writer, whoever she or he might be. I hoped for an academic rigor and intertextual delight, along with strong doses of humility. I hoped that creative writing would evolve into a discipline that would enable us to bring the best of everything we knew into our classrooms. I hoped that we'd be able to let go of the tyranny of fame and publication—the crapshoot that kept getting crappier as the years rolled along, so that students—and us with them—could learn how to appreciate writing as a primary experience that distinguishes what Trinh calls the difference between "writing about the self and writing the self" (28). And I wanted all of this because I believed that it would work to enrich and sustain writing for us all.

And yet, saying so, it's hard not to reflect, with Perloff, on my own frustration at my failure to effect meaningful change in the English department where I've taught for nearly two decades, and where last year I convened the creative writing faculty to revise our curriculum and draft a new English major, the first attempt to do so since its inception in 1976. Our goal was to create an undergraduate model where all the different strands of English studies would intersect and work together. To this end, we conceived a sequence of creative writing workshops linked to concurrent, intensive subject-matter labs. We hoped that by linking creative writing with a focused subject area—literature, theory, performance, composition—student writing, reading, research, and performance would be integrated in a more sustained, coherent, and *writerly* way throughout the undergraduate experience. Not surprisingly, the department turned us down. What change we did mange to effect was small, but substantial, and out of lengthy discussions last year we were able to develop a new selected-topics course in creative writing to supplement and enrich the existing core of workshop courses.

In a January 2003 issue of the *New York Review of Books*, Joan Didion reflected on the prior year and a half, musing on how completely the national conversation sparked by the day that our world changed had been extinguished in a matter of months. Despite the risk of saying so, I suspect there has been some kind of connection between the coming down of silence in a culture and the way creative writing, and perhaps the discipline at large, reacts to vexed or complex questions about the way we see ourselves, who we are, and what we do—the way, despite a quarter-century of guarded conversation, we keep circling the same old issues, we keep splitting along the same lines.

In "Epic and Novel," M. M. Bakhtin defines the novel as the "only ever developing genre that takes place in a zone of contact with the open-ended present" (48). If creative writing as a discipline has a genre, let it be the novel. Of course, that zone of contact is a vexed one, since we cannot control or contain what happens in it. But the coming down of silence, however reassuring, is not an option either, for things will move forward without us.

I, for one, am tired of the conversation we have been starting and stopping for twenty years now. And after all of that, it may prove that Stitt was right, and that we should, indeed, fight mysticism wherever we find it, if by mysticism he means that which obscures by privileging some modes of received thinking over others.

Several years ago, I attended a showing of *Diary of a Midlife Crisis*, Judy Fiskin's award-winning video—her first. At one point, the narrator says, "After twenty years, I find I am no longer interested in making photographs." Toward the end of the film, the same narrator describes a dream that presents itself to her as a blank screen. When she wakes, she thinks, "Yes, but how can I represent that?"

Before us lies that screen, and all around it lie its complications. Whether or not we choose to shake loose from the reiterations of this long conversation to try, however clumsily, to acknowledge—even embrace—whatever in the world may be coming next, the one sure thing we know about the future is that it will not stop coming. But in it, it is possible to imagine creative writing as the logical site of a completely integrated English studies. Creative writing needs rhetoric and composition, as Janice M. Lauer's essay makes clear, to help us frame and understand not just our own composing processes but also how better to study and teach them. We need linguistics, as Ellen Barton demonstrates, to help us complicate our understanding of our medium. We need theory, as Amy J. Elias's work suggests, to help us understand not just the way our writing comes into being and why, but also how it moves through the world, by what mechanisms it is constrained, and how we may mediate them. We need literary study, as Richard C. Taylor might argue, to help us understand our origins and better conceive our futures. And given the findings of *Reading at Risk*, we need English education to better serve this population and do more of the talking to others that Robert P. Yagelski would have us do.

More, perhaps, than any other discipline, creative writing is held together at its center by the matrix that constitutes the intersection of every strand of English studies. And yet it does still sometimes seem that, paradoxically, creative writing remains among the most anachronistic of the strands, clinging to romantic notions of the artist and outdated workshop practices even as we seek to justify our practice by aspiring more and more to either professional or academic prestige, when what we have to teach our students is perhaps the greatest gift of all—writing as a way of being in the world, an organizing practice and structure, and, although I know I'm not supposed to say so, a method, too, to mediate the madness and the magic of what makes us human, after all. Maybe we can't really know what a completely integrated model of English studies will look like because the future into which it is evolving will not stop changing either, any more than it will stop coming. But if the conversations we've been having now for years, both inside our own disciplines and between and among those of others, have taught us anything, it would have to be what Wendy knew all along.

The three men in the photograph were all large and friendly men—generous men—full of writing wisdom to impart. Wendy and I were small women. She was a poet and I wrote fiction. And as she took their photograph, they showed a strange ambivalence—half posing, half as if unaware that the photo was being taken. Their link to one another was clear and strong, and mine and Wendy's was just beginning, but already we were starting to figure out what in the future we were getting ready to claim: if creative writing were a blank screen—or a novel—it would not look—not quite—like what we'd seen or already knew about it anymore than it does today.

Works Cited

Amato, Joe, and H. Kassia Fleisher. "Reforming Creative Writing Pedagogy: History as Knowledge, Knowledge as Activism." 2002. Creative Writing Pedagogy Cluster. *Electronic Book Review*. 2002. 11 May 2006 http://www.altx.com/ebr/riposte/rip2/rip2ped/amato.htm.

Bakhtin, M. M. "Epic and Novel." *Essentials of the Theory of Fiction.* Ed. Michael J. Hoffman and Patrick D. Murphy. Durham, NC: Duke UP, 1988. 48–69.

Berry, R. M. "Theory, Creative Writing, and the Impertinence of History." Bishop and Ostrom 57–76.

Bishop, Wendy. *Released into Language: Options for Teaching Creative Writing.* 2nd ed. Portland, ME: Calendar Island, 1998.

———. *Teaching Lives: Essays and Stories.* Logan: Utah State UP, 1997.

Bishop, Wendy, and Hans Ostrom, eds. *Colors of a Different Horse: Rethinking Creative Writing Theory and Pedagogy.* Urbana, IL: NCTE, 1994.

Bishop, Wendy, and David Starkey. *Keywords in Creative Writing.* Logan: Utah State UP, 2006.

Bizarro, Patrick. "Research and Reflection in English Studies: The Special Case of Creative Writing." *College English* 66 (2004): 294–309.

Brodkey, Linda. "Modernism and the Scene(s) of Writing." *College English* 49 (1987): 396–418.

Burroway, Janet. *Writing Fiction: A Guide to Narrative Craft.* 6th ed. New York: Longman, 2002.

Daugherty, Tracy. "Letter to a Prospective Writing Student." *The Writer's Chronicle: A Publication of the Association of Writers and Writing Programs* 36.2 (2003): 49–50.

DeMaria, Robert. *The College Handbook of Creative Writing.* 3rd ed. Florence, KY: Heinle, 1997.

Diary of a Midlife Crisis. Dir. Judy Fiskin. Independent, 1997.

Didion, Joan. "Fixed Opinions, or The Hinge of History." *New York Review of Books* 16 Jan. 2003. 11 May 2006 http://www.nybooks.com/articles/article-preview?article_id=15984.

Dillard, Annie. *Living by Fiction.* New York: Harper, 1982.

Epstein, Joseph. "Who Killed Poetry?" *Commentary* 86 (1988): 13–20.

Fenza, David. "A Brief History of AWP." Association of Writers and Writing Programs Web site. 2001. May 11 2006 http://www.awpwriter.org/aboutawp/index.htm.

———. "Creative Writing and Its Discontents." Association of Writers and Writing Programs Web site. 2002. http:///awpwriter.org/magazine/writers/fenza01.htm.

Foucault, Michel. "What Is an Author?" Trans. Donald F. Bouchard and Sherry Simon. *Language, Counter-Memory, Practice: Selected Essays and Interviews*. Ed. Bouchard. Ithaca: Cornell UP, 1977. 124–27.

Gardner, John. *The Art of Fiction: Notes on Craft for Young Writers*. New York: Vintage, 1991.

Gioia, Dana. "Can Poetry Matter?" *Atlantic Monthly* May 1991: 94–106.

———. *Disappearing Ink: Poetry at the End of Print Culture*. St. Paul, MN: Graywolf, 2004.

Haake, Katharine. *What Our Speech Disrupts: Feminism and Creative Writing Studies*. Urbana, IL: NCTE, 2000.

Hall, Donald. *Death to the Death of Poetry: Essays, Reviews, Notes, Interviews*. Ann Arbor: U of Michigan P, 1994.

Hugo, Richard. *The Triggering Town: Lectures and Essays on Poetry and Writing*. New York: Norton, 1982.

Huss, Sandy. "Reformation under Way." Response to Amato and Fleisher. Creative Writing Pedagogy Cluster. *Electronic Book Review*. 2002. 11 May 2006 http://www.electronicbookreview.com/thread/endconstruction/rhizomal.

Leahy, Anna. *Power and Identity in the Creative Writing Classroom: The Authority Project*. Clevedon, Eng.: Multilingual Matters, 2005.

Maso, Carole. *Break Every Rule: Essays on Language, Longing, and Moments of Desire*. Washington, DC: Counterpoint, 2000.

Mayer, Tim. *(Re)Writing Craft: Composition, Creative Writing, and the Future of English Studies*. Pittsburgh: U of Pittsburgh P, 2005.

Minot, Stephen. *Three Genres: The Writing of Poetry, Fiction, and Drama*. 7th ed. Upper Saddle River, NJ: Prentice, 2002.

Moxley, Joseph M., ed. *Creative Writing in America: Theory and Pedagogy*. Urbana, IL: NCTE, 1989.

Myers, B. R. "A Reader's Manifesto." *Atlantic Monthly* July/Aug. 2001: 104–22.

Myers, D. G. *The Elephants Teach: Creative Writing since 1880.* Englewood Cliffs, NJ: Prentice, 1996.

National Endowment for the Arts. *Reading at Risk: A Survey of Literary Reading in America.* Research Division Report 46. Washington, DC: NEA, 2004.

Perloff, Marjorie. "Amato/Fleisher Too Pessimistic." Response to Amato and Fleisher Creative Writing Pedagogy Cluster. *Electronic Book Review.* 2002. 11 May 2006 http://www.electronicbookreview.com/thread/endconstruction/carnets.

———. "'Theory' and/in the Creative Writing Classroom." *AWP Newsletter* Nov./Dec. 1987: 1–4.

Radavich, David. "Creative Writing in the Academy." *Profession* (1999): 106–12.

———. "CW and the Art of Living." Response to Amato and Fleisher. Creative Writing Pedagogy Cluster. *Electronic Book Review.* 2002. 11 May 2006 http://www.electronicbookreview.com/thread/endconstruction/pedagogic.

Richter, David H. *Falling into Theory: Conflicting Views on Reading Literature.* Boston: Bedford, 1994.

Ritter, Kelly. "Professional Writers/Writing Professionals: Revamping Teacher Training in Creative Writing Ph.D. Programs." *College English* 64 (2001): 205–27.

Root, Robert L., Jr., and Michael Steinberg. *The Fourth Genre: Contemporary Writers of/on Creative Non-Fiction.* 3rd ed. New York: Longman, 2004.

Sanders, Scott Russell. "The Writer in the University." *AWP Chronicle* 25 (Sept. 1992): 1, 9–13.

Solondz, Todd. *Storytelling.* London: Faber, 2002.

Stafford, William. *Writing the Australian Crawl: Views on the Writer's Vocation.* Ann Arbor: U of Michigan P, 1978.

Starkey, David. *Poetry Writing: Theme and Variations.* Lincolnwood, IL: NTC/Contemporary, 1999.

Stitt, Peter. "Writers, Theorists, and the Department of English." *AWP Newsletter* Sept./Oct. 1987: 1–3.

Trinh T. Minh-ha. *Woman, Native, Other: Writing Postcoloniality and Feminism.* Bloomington: Indiana UP, 1989.

CHAPTER FOUR

Literature and Literary Criticism

RICHARD C. TAYLOR
East Carolina University

In his review of the year's scholarship on eighteenth-century British literature, Michael McKeon uses the term *division of knowledge* to signify the central challenge that students of literature face, and to identify the source of much scholarly debate ("Recent" 707). The conventional boundaries of literary study have almost all been called into question. McKeon himself, in his influential book *The Origins of the English Novel, 1600–1740*, scrutinized the long-maintained figure of a "rising" genre, perhaps best associated with Ian Watt, and in attempting to historicize the concept of genre argued for a destabilization of traditionally defined generic categories. For example, defining the related and sometimes interchangeable terms *novel* and *romance* must be done in the ever-shifting contexts in which these forms emerged— fraught with evanescent ideological debate and never truly fixed, as the definitions in glossaries of literary terms might lead us to believe. In other words, genre is one traditional division of literary knowledge; yet that division itself is unsettled, a contested site.

In search of a solution, we might well turn to a standard reference work, James L. Harner's *Literary Research Guide*, for advice on identifying the divisions of knowledge in the field of literary studies. But this bibliographic resource, intended to be an introduction to the field, is massive and represents an area of research in flux, in which the genres of scholarship, like the genres of literature, are contested and uncertain. The term *literary studies*, to which some professors of literature object, implies plurality, interdisciplinarity, and transition. It is a term that implicitly acknowledges instability in the categories of knowledge and practice. *Literature*, on the other hand, seems somehow more fixed: a group of selected texts, belletristic rather than popular, approached critically from a variety of enlightening perspectives and conveyed reverentially from generation to generation. To some, the idea of diversity is threatening; to others it is inviting.

Students of literature—or literary studies—must confront this baffling set of contested definitions at the outset and, in a sense, imagine the discipline for themselves. According to Gertrude Stein, "Any one of us and anyway those of us that have always had the habit of reading have our own history of English literature inside us, the history as by reading we have come to know it" (32). Stein is suggesting that students have to construct the subject of literature as they study it, just as their professors did. The subject is, at once, the reading and the reader, as revealed and imagined in the pages to be read and discussed. Each reader, in turn, is simultaneously an island, with an isolated and unique perspective, and a member of what reader-response criticism calls an interpretive community, collaborating in the process of responding to texts and making meaning.

Literature and literary criticism are contested subjects, in part, because each reader must engage in the same process, along the way incorporating or rejecting the myths of origin that others have woven. To borrow from "Dover Beach" by Matthew Arnold, an important purveyor of one of those myths, each reader is a pebble "which the waves suck back, and fling, / At their return, up the high strand" (11–12) in an endless reiteration of interpretation and the making of meaning. Many literary scholars experience anxiety at the impossibility of a clear line of "critical progress"—of the certain accretion of knowledge, discovery built on discovery, that would render the most recent work more sophisticated and informed than all previous criticism on which it would rest. Others, however, would reject the idea that critical practice is purely cyclical, every idea flung up on the beach merely a reincarnation of an earlier one. Literary study is not a free-for-all; its own history, its arguments, and the rhetoric of its ongoing scholarly conversation circumscribe to some extent what can be said and what is heard.

The subject of literature rests on a series of complex dialogues. The present, embodied by living students and newly edited textbooks, stands in dialogue with the "mind of the past," as Ralph Waldo Emerson put it, and with crumbling manuscripts. Authors and works appear in dialogue: every anthology's table of contents is simultaneously a complex literary-historical narrative, an argument, a museum, a hypothetical "history of you" offered to students as a starting point. Juxtaposed in a single volume, the works are an exercise in intertextuality: how one writer responds to another, alludes to those who came before, rejects or embraces the past. National literatures stand in contrast with one another; centuries or more loosely defined literary epochs line up as separate contrasting entities. Genres vie with one another for popular attention and critical respectability. Critical schools form and evolve in dialogue with one another.

Literature? It is an infinitely fluid cultural record. Criticism, then, is an attempt to respond to that record, to contextualize it, narrativize it, argue about it. The texts that form that record are a reflection, once again, of a dialogue between present and past, of our living subjectivities and the fossil remains of all verbal expressions that have preceded us, Elizabethan sonnets and barbaric yawps alike. In the interstices of that dialogue concerning the selection and interpretation of the record can be found most of the professional debates that engage and divide literary scholars. To an extent, the debates can be viewed through the lens of our contesting narratives of professional origin.

Narratives of Origin

Where did *literature* as an academic subject come from? There is a remarkable number of different answers to that question, each providing some insight into the ideology, methodological preference, and sense of professional identity of the respondent. Clearly the study of Greek and Latin literature and the study of classical rhetoric long anticipated the formation of British and American literature as recognizable disciplines in the United Kingdom and in the United States. The idea that British and American literature should be integral parts of a humanistic education is a development of the past century or so. Undertaking an extensive study of the development of the profession of literature and its departmentalization, Gerald Graff encounters a common myth of origin: that literary study emerged as a broad, idealistic, and unified project to convey humanism and the belletristic tradition. The problem is the *unified* part of that myth. Graff writes, "What I discovered, however, was that although the transmission of humanism and cultural tradition in the Matthew Arnold sense was indeed the official goal of the literature department, there was from the outset fundamental disagreement about how that goal should be pursued" (3). One might argue that at this point, consensus regarding the goal itself and the meaning of that goal in "the Matthew Arnold sense" is as much in doubt as the means of pursuing departmental objectives, whatever they might be. For many critics, humanism has become a bête noire, and the idea of a cultural tradition is one that should be challenged rather than uncritically conveyed.

Certainly the profession of literature, as it is now constituted, owes its development to a growing nationalism and cultural angst, particularly in America but also discernible in the early British press. Students of the eighteenth-century periodical have identified a movement that gained momentum throughout the nineteenth century: a trend toward assessing and preserving works of national literature and their authors. What poems, plays, and novels ought to be preserved and studied, rescued from dusty corners of the British Museum and fed to young people for their cultural nourishment and patriotic appreciation? The magazine as a vehicle for cultural propagation is an important element in my own myth of disciplinary origins. But there are many others, more and less obscure.

Another frequently overlooked myth of origin lies in the field of hermeneutics, as created by Enlightenment scholars called exegetes, who developed methods and principles of textual analysis, predominantly in the area of biblical scholarship, that led to some astounding conclusions: for example, that the Gospel of Mark anticipated and served as a source for Matthew and Luke and that a hypothecated oral source labeled *Quelle* or *Q* must have been a common source for all three "synoptic" gospels. *The Quest of the Historical Jesus* by Albert Schweitzer, which provides a critical response to this research, is a landmark in religious studies, but it can also be read allegorically as an account of the hopes and frustrations of the textual scholar. Sensitive reading and the careful application of critical tools seemed to hold the promise of unveiling the most nearly impenetrable of secrets, even without reference to "external" evidence. More recently, the famous literary critic Harold Bloom follows in this tradition with his stunning work on *The Book of J*, a fragment of the Hebrew Bible identified by textual scholarship. Ongoing scholarship on attribution of authorship, including the celebrated and controversial work of Donald Foster on Shakespeare, owes much of its methodological origins to eighteenth-century German scholars, such as Hermann Samuel Reimarus, who attempted to write an accurate biography of Jesus, one that separates history and myth, with the aid of almost no documentary testimony. Literary research in the area of source study, textual analysis, and literary history generally are clearly indebted to the field of exegesis.

Many of the historically prestigious journals in literature identify themselves with *philology*, a term associated with linguistics but also applied broadly, especially in the early twentieth century, to the study of literature. The term evokes the work of these early textual critics and later "neo-Aristotelian" approaches like that of Ronald S. Crane at the University of Chicago, who like many literary scholars to follow adapted the language and methods of Aristotle to help make textual inquiries. Further, Crane differentiated between history, which had dominated much of what fell under the heading of philology, and criticism, by which he meant literary theory and textual explication. Perhaps the most enduring work of the "Chicago School" is Wayne Booth's *Rhetoric of Fiction*, which helped to bring Aristotelian perspectives on audience and purpose to the study of literary narrative.

For generations of literary scholars coming of age in the aftermath of World War II, "close reading" has been associated with the rise of the New Criticism as a method of interpretation and a philosophy of literary study. Disciples of critics such as John Crowe Ransom, Cleanth Brooks, and Robert Penn Warren proclaimed "the text itself" as a manifesto. For them, careful attention to the language of the work of literature yielded linguistic subtlety and artistic richness likely to be overlooked by more casual reading. Adherents to the New Criticism cast themselves in opposition to generations of historical and biographical scholars who, at least in the mythmaking, lost sight of literature in favor of the lives of the writers and the times in which they lived. New Critics taught—and continue to teach—*explication de texte:* a fairly rigid and methodical approach to literary interpretation that, at least for classroom purposes, seems to work best with short and linguistically complex works of poetry. Students patiently identify connotations and denotations, check etymologies, and search texts for *objective correlatives,* a term used by T. S. Eliot, who helped inaugurate a preference for poetry that is intellectually wrought, metaphysical, and heavily allusive. For some New Critics, recent movements away from the "text itself" represent a failure to teach students to read carefully and to value the intellectual rigor of close textual analysis.

Hermeneutics framed itself as a corrective to the superstitious approaches of the past, and the New Critics saw themselves initially as rebelling against the myopic historical focus of their forebears; but many contemporary critics and literary scholars see themselves in contradistinction to predecessors who ignored questions of race, gender, class, ethnicity—and, more broadly, questions of identity in literature. What the philosopher Jacques Derrida represented for many was a fundamental challenge to the tidy objectivity of formalist criticism, of the very possibility of "shared meaning." Also, as Alexander Pope's *Essay on Criticism* (written in 1711) makes dramatically clear, poetry (or what has come to be called creative writing) and criticism have long been considered separate enterprises, and the debate has centered on their proper relationship. Now, however, criticism is no longer the "handmaid" of poetry but, for many, it is a creative genre in itself, potentially separable from and independent of any other work of literature. This myth of liberation, then, casts itself as loosing the critic from a servile role, freeing criticism from its tethers to a tradition of "dead white male" European writers, abolishing the "canon." The resulting view of literature is one that is inclusive, healing, egalitarian—clearly of social benefit.

In his famous 1864 essay "The Function of Criticism at the Present Time," Arnold defines criticism as "a disinterested endeavor to learn and propagate the best that is known and thought in the world" (595). Perhaps all students of literature and literary criticism, no matter their chosen myth of origin, must respond to Arnold. One of the fundamental observations of recent literary theory is that all readers are historically and culturally situated, influenced by socially constructed identities and shaped by their class, race, gender, culture, ethnicity, and other factors. None of us is disinterested, and the claim of critical objectivity has become, for most, a red flag. The second part of Arnold's assertion provides a possible answer to the question, What is literature? Literature is "the best that is known and thought." Immediately, voices protest, "Thought to be the best by whom?" and "Best by what standard of measurement?" Surely literature remains in the academic curriculum because of the social perception that it is somehow good for our students. Good in what way? Have professors of literature, by virtue of their degrees and years of study, earned the right to choose "the best that is known and thought?" On what basis? These questions remain at the heart of professional debates. For critics who see literature primarily as an aesthetic phenomenon, as many of those who conceived and wrote about "belles-lettres" throughout the early modern period clearly did, the challenge must be not simply to convey an appreciation of what is "best" but to articulate and defend their principles of judgment. Few are accepting proclamations of transcendent greatness anymore, and even Shakespeare's place in the "canon" can no longer be considered self-evident. It is no longer an article of faith that there are critical standards that transcend the historical moment and subjectivity of the scholar. What exactly makes Shakespeare or any author great?

The term *belletristic* itself has become suspect, like *literature,* fraught with the prejudices and exclusivity of the past. Belletristic works have been screened in a sense: selected for their capacity to illuminate a historical moment, for their ability to delight and instruct. By definition, they are exclusive, a tightly monitored list. In response, the recent evolution of the term *text* offers, perhaps, an alternative to the initial question and some insight into current critical argument. A text is a sort of specimen chosen for critical analysis. The term avoids aesthetic or qualitative judgment. To study a text is to sample a cultural fragment, a bit of communication that may have emanated from "low" or "high" culture, a man or woman, a rich or poor person, a famous author or "Anon." Its creator may have intended it as an indestructible monument or as ephemeral jotting. It might be an epic or an advertisement. It is chosen because it contributes to the process through which someone is narrativizing—about literature, about culture, about self. If literature is to be a "history of you," then the movement from *belles-lettres* to *text* represents, at least, a great expansion in the types of stories that can be constructed and the varieties of histories written, especially if "you" were unrepresented in the stories historically conveyed.

Literary Periodicity

New literary histories are emerging, ones that are more culturally diverse and inclusive, and the reach of literary study is becoming progressively more interdisciplinary. These challenges to traditional myths of origin lead inevitably to a related question: how is literary study organized? As recently as two decades ago, when I began doctoral study in English, that question seemed to have a simple answer: one chose British or American literature (American literature being the relative upstart and for many of its practitioners morphing into the interdisciplinary field of American studies) and then a historical period within one of the two national literatures as an area of specialization. World literature, or the burgeoning field of multicultural studies, was at that time exclusively the province of comparative literature, a separate field, at least in my experience. Literary theory was a new curricular choice, not yet a developed area of study and certainly not a choice for specialization or professional identification. A few declared their expertise via genre: poetry, history of the novel, or theatre, for example. A few embraced one of the handful of single authors with their own cottage industries: Shakespeare, Milton, Chaucer, Joyce. But most identified themselves as specialists in nineteenth-century American literature, the medieval period, or—in my case—eighteenth-century British literature.

At that time, the system seemed so obvious as not to need justification, and the term *periodicity* is a neologism that implicitly recognizes that arranging literary study by nationality and time period is only one approach—and possibly not the best one. And yet I think the choice remains defensible, even when a new array of appealing options has emerged. Chronology has the virtue of an illusory orderliness that provides a sort of access. The year 1660 has a potentially rich textuality—in the cozy neighborhoods of Samuel Pepys's London, for example, as they spring from his diaries. The word *Restoration* certainly does not encapsulate all of British experience in that year and certainly not for the entire late-seventeenth-century period. But it is a handle, a powerful ideological expression that opens a window on a particular historical and cultural shift. If the *Age of Reason* is a misapplication, its use is nonetheless a teachable moment: Why would this term have been used? What insight does it try to convey? What social segment or ideology does it target? What can we learn from the way the term misreads the period?

The literary periods are convenient linguistic and cultural neighborhoods. Though they may seem fairly arbitrary, they do nevertheless provide a template to help map the past. Within the confines of the literary periods readers locate shared intellectual currency, a relatively defined list of players and famous works on which to build. Periodicity offers a model of expertise: a time in which to plant one's scholarly flag, to explore that moment in depth, and to work outward in expanding knowledge. While anything like true expertise in a literary period is impossible, the system at least allows for a process that can happily sustain a productive career.

Period designations themselves change in response to new theoretical models, such as the new historicism, which has transformed the study of *early modern* literature, the term supplanting *Renaissance* in the critical lexicon. Theoretical realignments have drawn scholars away from strict period identification and toward interdisciplinary scholarship. Those of us who have focused on women's literature, for example, feel a shared alliance with women's studies. I would guess that most specialists in eighteenth-century literature would now identify themselves more broadly with eighteenth-century studies, encouraging work that brings together a variety of traditional disciplines and new cross-cultural and theoretical perspectives. The shift from a discrete focus on literature to interdisciplinary studies is one that has occurred throughout the traditionally defined periods and has anticipated a shift in the English department itself. Neither shift has been seamless, but both have represented a great deal of scholarly opportunity and innovation.

Traditional organization by period and national literature differentiates specialists in literature from others in English studies in another important sense. Baseball commentators confirm there are actually very few "baseball fans" per se, but rather fans of particular teams. One of the reasons that the Modern Language Association, which has tried to serve as a sort of governing body for the study of language and literature, has had limited appeal for many literature specialists is that—to continue the analogy—it is an organization for fans of the whole sport, whereas each fan is interested almost exclusively in a single team. My own experience is probably not unique: my professional identification is with eighteenth-century studies, primarily British literature. I feel a degree of academic kinship with specialists in seventeenth-century and nineteenth-century British literature, and a considerably more distant connection with the earlier periods and contemporary literature. The same applies to publication and other professional activity: the university expects me to focus on my own period, although I have done some work in the centuries preceding and following my own focus. The American Society for Eighteenth-Century Studies is a much more relevant organization for me than the MLA, except in its capacities of helping to organize departmental job searches and publishing an annual bibliography and directory of periodicals. The research most central to my own is more likely to appear in an eighteenth-century specialist periodical, rather than in a journal with a more general focus.

Across national literatures, I suspect that the degree of professional kinship varies from department to department and scholar to scholar. Many eighteenth-century specialists now include both British and American literature in their research agendas. On the other hand, some consider British and American literature separate fields, with credentialing processes and bodies of knowledge sufficiently discrete to consider them separate disciplines. Similarly, specialists in world literature or multicultural literature have developed their own conferences and specialist journals, and scholars in those areas, at least at my university, seem to be moving rapidly in the direction of organizational independence from the "traditional" areas of literary study. In other words, professors of literature, at least in my experience, do not constitute a recognizable "team," a group unified by shared assumptions about method, ideology, or professional values generally. While in traditional departments the sheer numbers of literature professors would seem to confer on them a degree of institutional power, they are typically a less cohesive unit than specialists in, say, linguistics or rhetoric and composition.

In the aftermath of postcolonial theory and the explosion in interest generated by courses and programs in multicultural literature, placing British and/or American literature at the core of literary studies has come under critical scrutiny. In public-school education, in which civic awareness is both central and explicit, knowledge of culturally celebrated literature is a part of knowing "one's own heritage." The problem, of course, especially for universities, is that this "one" comes from all parts of the world and from an infinite variety of cultural traditions, many of them oppressed by the dominant cultures that produced the celebrated literature. The global university must train its sights on producing citizens of the world, rather than parochially well-informed patriots. To justify the study of traditionally defined periods, in the context of literary history, the instructor casts them as "social constructs," to use Paul Lauter's phrase, subject to critical scrutiny as meaningful templates, significant by virtue of their traditional authority. For the doctoral student now choosing the identity of, say, a seventeenth-century British literature specialist, there is the same risk that surprised the practitioners of the New Criticism: that a focal expertise organized around periodicity might not coordinate well with an evolving curriculum and profession.

Canon (De)Formation

More than any other factor, the breakdown of traditional unifying structures of knowledge has led to profound disagreement in the profession of literature. Perhaps the most obvious of those structures is the so-called literary canon, a hypothecated gallery of works and writers collectively constituting a fairly circumscribed literary core. To replicate this structure, graduate programs culminate in "area" examinations organized around the established periods of British and American literature. My own doctoral menu consisted of five areas: seventeenth-, eighteenth-, and nineteenth-century British literature, and nineteenth- and twentieth-century American literature. For passing those exams and defending a dissertation, I was awarded a PhD in *English* (not literature or eighteenth century literature, but English). Everyone so honored was certified as having read *Billy Budd*, *Light in August*, *Paradise Lost*, *Tristram Shandy*, and *Middlemarch*, along with an implicit promise to publish exclusively (or nearly so) in one area of specialization and to teach, in a pinch, any of the areas of literature at any level.

One of the most dramatic and tangible products of the challenge to this traditional structure was the *Heath Anthology of American Literature*, edited by Paul Lauter. While scholarly argument and political persuasion slowly resulted in the gender and ethnic diversification of literature course syllabi, the work of the Reconstructing American Literature Project and the economic success of the Heath anthology represented institutional acceptance of the challenge to the canon and were visible reminders that the profession was changing. Almost overnight, it seemed, conservative canon-bound journals like *College Literature* and *American Literature* were transformed into venues for new theory and studies of authors and works that had been neglected. Even those of us steeped in eighteenth-century British culture were required to read *Their Eyes Were Watching God* and *The Color Purple*. Professors of American literature who ordered "The Heath" were teaching very different courses from professors who were using the older anthologies. Advocates of canonical inclusiveness among the British literature specialists waited impatiently for a challenge to the doggedly resistant Norton series, a challenge met successfully, if belatedly, by the publishers of *The Longman Anthology of British Literature* (Damrosch). The business of choosing an anthology for a survey course, once a matter of noting fine and few distinctions among the options, suddenly became a hotly ideological issue. For Lauter, "The literary canon does not, after all, spring from the brow of the master critics; rather it is a social construct" (*Canons* 36). The ideas of timelessness and aesthetic greatness that had served as unifying ideals were revealed as illusory, and the consequence of a "canon as social construct" is that what is taught must reflect the social reality of the moment and the experiences and identities of an interpretive community. The canon is and always has been in flux and responsive to social contexts. Lauter uses the "core" concept to reflect on the professors themselves, the core being "a small cadre of professors of literature, mainly critics in style, at elite graduate and a few undergraduate institutions" (12). The rest of us are teaching on the margins: with concerns about the dizzying culture wars and theoretical conflicts in the academic stratosphere, but even more concerned with rejection slips and students who refuse to read.

The dust has not fully settled on the "canon debate" nor on the culture wars generally, so retrospect is still particularly difficult. Certainly the idea of the literary canon as a straw figure for attacking the hegemony of one sort of academic humanism is a product of ideological distortion, in the same way the defensive appropriation of the canon as a last bastion of Western civilization is an equally facile maneuver. In reality, there has never been a fixed literary canon, as any diachronic examination of literature textbooks reveals—or a search of the contents pages of literary journals over the decades. The use of a single hypothesized course syllabus, in this debate, creates the illusion of a finite group of approved texts or authors and the terrible prospect of a modern "squeezing out" an ancient, or a popular work forcing a "classic" to the margins, or "multicultural" works replacing those which are somehow timeless and transcendent of any particular cultural milieu. Fortunately, there are a lot of syllabi, a lot of courses and professors, a lot of room for the study of works and writers of all stripes; and metaphors of constraint, like the single and exclusive course syllabus, serve more as a battle cry than as a representation of the conditions of literary study. On the other hand, the battle has been productive in many respects: students are reminded that works are not "great" simply because their forebears declared them so; the limitations and biases of many who saw themselves as conveyors of cultural traditions have been exposed; and the work of recovery—bringing to light for critical scrutiny literary works that have been overlooked, ignored, or lost—has gained a great deal of momentum.

Reading Closely

Another destabilized structure in literary study is the model of classroom instruction, which, in my undergraduate years, was dedicated almost exclusively to *explication de texte,* to close readings of privileged works of literature. The successful student could penetrate the metaphysical conceits of Donne and tease out verbal connotations and half-concealed etymological intimations in Yeats. The work of the critic, it appeared, was methodical and in some sense finite—ending when all language was accounted for, all linguistic possibility exhausted. And students were assured, by virtue of the "intentional fallacy," warned of by W. K. Wimsatt and Monroe C. Beardsley, that authorial intention was unknowable and irrelevant, and reassured by the comforting prospect of an objective criticism. The method of textual explication was easily replicable, produced a lot of steamy intellection in the classroom, and taught a useful critical discipline. With the advent of the new historicism, the emergence of literary theory as a dominant mode in English, and the rise of competing models of pedagogy, many of the practitioners of the New Criticism felt swept aside, their brilliant and original textual readings rejected by scholarly journals now proscribing "untheorized" studies of single authors or works. No single model has approached the classroom hegemony of the New Criticism, and the profession is, again, profoundly divided in its beliefs about teaching and interpreting literature.

In what ways, then, does the literary critic approach a text? Attentive students of Matthew Arnold's poetry might have detected something amiss in the passage from "Dover Beach" cited in the fourth paragraph of this chapter: "Of pebbles which the waves *suck* [emphasis mine] back, and fling." *Suck?* The source, as noted below, is Oxford's 1930 edition of Arnold's poetry. Most contemporary teaching editions, however, record, without comment, the following textual variant: "Of pebbles which the waves

draw [emphasis mine] back, and fling." Editions of the poem peppered throughout cyberspace seem indiscriminately divided, albeit silently, about whether to record *suck* or *draw*. Readers of the poem planning to explicate it, tease out possible meanings from its language, are foiled from the beginning by the apparent instability of the text. Indeed, the problems and debates associated with textual editing are one of the most fascinating and most often neglected areas of literary criticism, but they have been central to the study of authors such as Theodore Dreiser, Emily Dickinson, Herman Melville, William Wordsworth—to list just a few celebrated instances.

Made aware of the two textual variants, the critic might see an invitation to choose, and so consults the *Oxford English Dictionary*, that historically rich and prestigious arbiter that serves as a kind of common critical coinage. One definition of *suck* appropriate to the Victorian era (as illustrated by sample usage) is as follows: "The sucking action of eddying or swirling water; the sound caused by this." One might also consider a second usage: "The backward suction of air following an explosion"— and the *OED* exemplifies this usage in the language of coal mining. The word *draw*, on the other hand, has so many recorded usages that reference to the *OED* is, at least, less convenient. The typical student trained in the New Criticism, in trying to maintain a focus on the language of the poem itself, has advanced the cause but has also opened up a host of questions normally considered outside the purview of explication. The biographical critic might ask if there is some evidence in Arnold's life or career that would tell us if he might have ultimately preferred one word choice or the other. A historical or sociological critic might ask if the lewd modern connotations attached to the word *suck* have led to a kind of bowdlerizing of Arnold's text—a substitution of an imprecise word for one that perfectly conveyed the poet's meaning. Reader-response critics or reception theorists might, similarly, ask how these words would have been understood by different reading communities, how they act upon their manifold readers, how time has fundamentally altered the poem, as it is re-created in the reader's imagination. A myth critic might argue that the word *draw*, used in the context of Arnold's invocation of the archetypal power of the sea, personifies the waves as

a creative force using the pebbles as a kind of interminable artistic medium. The psychological critic might wonder if the presence of these apparently unresolved variants reveals an ambivalence in the poet himself.

The tool of close reading remains a powerful one, particularly as a beginning point for critical analysis. Ironically, its effectiveness in suggesting the richness and ambiguities embedded in texts contributed to its repudiation—as scholars trained in this method started insisting on the sorts of questions and possibilities illustrated above. At the strategic vortex of deconstruction, for example, is the brilliantly careful and imaginative consideration of texts leading to the arguably inescapable conclusion that the sought-for *meaning* of any text is infinitely irresolute, that any proposed meaning can come unraveled merely by the prodding of the same basic intellectual tools of analysis and questioning. Perhaps, as some despairing opponents of recent critical theory might maintain, we are "as on a darkling plain" without "certitude, nor peace, nor help for pain" ("Dover Beach," 34–35.) Others might argue, though, that encouraging students to reject the illusion of objective analysis—an ill-founded intellectual clarity—and of certainty in meaning might be a valuable service in itself: to complicate the all-too-tidy notions of truth to which many students stubbornly cling.

The Challenge of Interdisciplinarity

For many, there has been a subtle shift in focus from examining what works of literature might mean to considering what "work" they do—how they have been formed by and contribute to various cultural moments, how they "work on" their readers by invoking and subverting their assumptions and values, how they must be reinvented and revalued by each subsequent generation of readers. The lack of "certitude" is an opening for exploration and challenge, rather than an invitation to chaos, as many New Critics might have feared. In a review of the state of comparative literature, an area related to English studies but with a largely divergent series of conflicts, Fredric Jameson notes that the field of "literary and cultural studies" is "always in crisis, that is to

say, that its object is never given in advance, but must always be constructed, and is always a matter of dispute" (16). The almost casual linkage of literary and cultural studies is a product of Jameson's own construction and that of others for whom "ideological revision" of the field is a naturally recurring process. Critics of cultural studies tried, mostly in vain, to resist this linkage: to keep aesthetic appreciation separate from the sullying influences of contemporary trends and obscurantist theorizing. It is comforting, for those in the midst of professional conflict, to remember that such disputes are simply a healthy part of the discipline.

Jameson's analysis in 1987 anticipates Gayatri Spivak's 2003 manifesto, proclaiming a "new comparative literature" in her book *Death of a Discipline*. Literary studies has died a hundred deaths, and has been reborn just as often. In eighteenth-century studies, this duality was dramatized by the appearance of *The New Eighteenth Century: Theory, Politics, English Literature*, a collection (edited by Felicity Nussbaum and Laura Brown) that has influenced a generation of students and specialists, followed by Brian McCrea's provocative book *Addison and Steele Are Dead: The English Department, Its Canon, and the Professionalization of Literary Criticism*, which deplored recent trends in criticism at the expense of once-beloved works of literature. The new-old split has been a prominent feature in scholarship ever since, and has created a passionate—and easily audible—schism at such events as the conferences of the American Society for Eighteenth-Century Studies.

What conception of literature can be *constructed*, then, in the postlapsarian academy, where *greatness* has been reduced to a nearly invisible and retrograde interdisciplinary program in "Great Books"? Following Jameson's notion of a discipline always in flux, its "core" up for grabs, one might see the rises and falls as necessary adaptations to cultural change. The idea of a fixed literary canon is itself a myth: works and authors have always dropped in and out of style as a reflection of the *weltanschauung* (or general philosophical orientation) of the moment. My father's college textbook for seventeenth-century literature (Coffin and Witherspoon), a standard choice for the late 1940s, begins with an extensive selection from the writing of Nicholas Breton, devotes significant space to Sir Thomas Overbury's "Characters" and John Selden's "Table Talk," and selects extensively from the letters of James Howell. There is literally no mention of women writers of the period until the last two pages, when under the heading of "Miscellaneous Authors," short poems by Katherine Philips and Aphra Behn are reproduced. The same anthology, reedited fifty years later, still ignores women's writing, but responds to the explosion of critical interest in poets such as Donne and Herbert and dares to recognize an American, Edward Taylor, the "New England metaphysical poet." The 2000 *Broadview Anthology of Seventeenth-Century Verse and Prose* (Rudrum, Black, and Nelson) devotes only a couple of pages to Breton and to Overbury and omits any mention of Selden or Howell, but represents more than a dozen women writers, including a place of honor for Aphra Behn, who now rivals Donne and Herbert as critical cottage industries. A generation ago, critics were noting, some with regret, the decline in the reputations of Longfellow, Scott, and Goldsmith—all writers once at the center of the literary curriculum. Now some departments are debating whether a course in Shakespeare should be required of all English majors, many of whom are slipping through innocent of either Dryden or Milton, with perhaps only a brief nod toward Pope or Johnson.

As one terribly fond of both Addison and Steele, individually and collectively, I am nonetheless not at all horrified by the fact that *Things Fall Apart* and *Their Eyes Were Watching God* and "The Yellow Wallpaper" have supplanted them in the curriculum (if, indeed, they have). The experience of teaching the same work repeatedly suggests the importance and vitality of having a curriculum always under construction. If students have the confidence, critical skill, and heightened appetite for investigating the past; if they can touch it by virtue of the talismanic power of old documents and long-forgotten poems; if some can find in the kinetic thrill of literary discovery a sense of vocation—then the fate of *greatness* need not be lamented. The spell of silent worship, passed on from one generation to the next, might well be broken, but a curiosity about the past and a desire to reconstruct its literature must be sustained. If the past, as a foreign country, is prohibitive—its language impenetrable, its concerns unrecognizably remote—then I think literary study, or at least the study of literary history, fails in its mission.

Alvin Kernan, who has done important work on the connection between literature and the development of print technology, argues that literature "realizes in art the condition of consciousness, the epistemological situation implicit in the printed page and the act of reading [. . .]. Humanism's long dream of learning, of arriving at some final truth by enough reading and writing, is breaking up in our time" (134–35). For many literature specialists, even the most skeptical, this romantic assertion of the importance of aesthetics—the fundamental importance of literary study—still resonates with a sense of mission. It is a reminder that literary study has a long history of trying to justify itself to a materialistic culture and to university administrations for which "long dreams" and musing on the nature of consciousness are foreign and "unproductive."

For other specialists in literature, though, the tendency to empathize with the disciplinary struggles of their diverse colleagues is irresistible. Proximity leads to friendships, as well as to tensions, and a dramatically underestimated factor in English studies generally is the consequence of personal friendships, informal collaborations, and efforts to forge interdisciplinary approaches. Specialists are rewarded for adhering to their own terrain and discouraged, subtly or explicitly, from trespassing on other disciplines; on the other hand, the sharing of expertise across these boundaries is transforming and has transformed the academy. The impetus toward interdisciplinarity is embedded deeply within criticism, past as well as present. To read closely with any kind of thoroughness, one must attend to the myriad "contexts" that form and inform texts, and that reading process demands multidisciplinary awareness and study. The field of comparative literature is inherently interdisciplinary, as is its structural alternative in the academy, multicultural literature. A knowledge of different languages, histories, and literary traditions is the minimal price of student admission. The walls of the disciplinary divide, in this case as with most aspects of literary study, are and have always been permeable, drawing on and contributing to the sum of human knowledge.

At this peculiar juncture, interdisciplinary study is expanding at an astonishing rate, even while the old structural discouragements remain: resistance to dedicating hiring lines to interdisciplinary programs; tenuring still largely a function of departmental tradition and disciplinary focus. For those literature specialists coming of age in the 1980s, anger toward the founders of such newly forming doctoral areas as "rhet-comp" was part of the cacophony of shouting between the diehard philologists and evangelical theorists, between feminist and multicultural critics and those who railed against "teaching sociology in the literature classroom." Allan Bloom's pompous screed against "moral relativism" and against the university culture in general seemed oddly to validate the changes that were in the air; if someone like Bloom felt frightened and appalled, if oppositional groups like the National Association of Scholars felt compelled to establish a covert network of academic freedom fighters, then some pretty positive developments must have been in the works. E. D. Hirsch, Jr., capitalizing on those fears, ironically helped provide many with a sense of mission: to complicate this simplistic view of literacy, to push the "long dream of learning" against whatever currents impelled it.

The task ahead for professors of literature is a clear articulation, rather than an unstated presumption, of the purpose of literary study and its function in departments and universities. Kernan observes that "literary criticism is one of those many human activities that flourish like the green bay tree without anyone ever being able precisely to say what they are or what might be their function" (63–64). The work of literary study itself is remarkably diverse, and its advocates need to recognize and communicate the value of the different tasks they undertake. One ongoing task is what Robert D. Hume calls "archaeo-historicism." Archival scholarship, unearthing the texts and contexts that defined past generations, continues to provide a more complete picture of earlier realities and assists in the epiphanic connection between contemporary reader and ancient writer. The discoveries encourage new narratives of authorship, of book production, of past discovery and intellectual musing, all of which can foster a curiosity about the past made vivid for students when they can achieve that powerful emotional connection. The study of multicultural literature encourages the sort of global awareness that should be the sine qua non of a university education—not at the expense of understanding and celebrating the achievements of British and American writers, but in conjunction with that task. Among its many accomplishments, critical theory has forced an institutional self-consciousness without which we stumble along with a kind of blind assurance of our own rectitude. The concepts of *genius* and *greatness* and *timelessness* can no longer be proclaimed uncritically and absorbed by the next generation of students and teachers; the challenge to those terms should heighten the stakes involved in teaching students critical thinking and practicing analytical habits of mind. To pursue an understanding of the multifaceted relationship between reading and writing—surely that is one of the many challenges that transcend disciplinary boundaries.

Institutional efforts to expand the definition of research to be more inclusive, more representative of the totality of academic work, have lagged, in part because they threaten prerogative and in part because of an always-governing institutional inertia. Counting is easy; subjective analysis of all aspects of performance is far more complicated and, above all, time-consuming. Yet some recognition of the totality of our contributions, across disciplinary lines, might again foster the sort of collegial respect that will encourage unity. Let us profess.

Spivak's notion of "reading the world," an activity that brings together varieties of critical thinking, theory, history, and pedagogy, is another potentially unifying construct. Learning how to decipher various cultural codes is surely an interdisciplinary enterprise. Perhaps the role of literary study is to read writers reading different worlds—with an authorial filter contributing to and complicating the student's reading of the world. Another sort of imaginative reading must serve as a precursor, though: students reading their professors, and professors reading "the student" or students. Not much explicit discussion of this process occurs, even though it is invited on the many occasions faculty members or candidates are asked for "statements of teaching philosophy" or students are asked to evaluate their instructors. And yet one of the differentiating assets of English studies is the proximity of students and instructors: relatively small class sizes, subject matter that invites intense introspection and even personal revelation, the lively and productive community that English classes can and should foster.

The conflicts within literary study and within English studies generally are part of the subject and ought to be taught as such. A discipline in conflict is, in many respects, more interesting than one that is static and unified. Part of the subject of the literature seminar, the rhetoric seminar, the seminar in bibliography is the very question of how the pieces of English studies fit together, how the profession might be differently constructed. The graduate course in methods and bibliography, once required of graduate students and still on the books at many universities, can be an arena for exploring points of contact among the various areas of specialization; not just for learning the profession, but for imagining it. If students in all the various areas can listen and argue productively from the beginning, to forge theoretical and practical connections, then the fields of English studies can prosper under one roof.

Works Cited

Arnold, Matthew. "Dover Beach." *The Poems of Matthew Arnold, 1840–1867*. London: Oxford UP, 1930.

———. "The Function of Criticism at the Present Time." 1865. *Critical Theory since Plato*. Ed. Hazard Adams. New York: Harcourt, 1971. 533–95.

Bloom, Allan. *The Closing of the American Mind: How Higher Education Has Failed Democracy and Impoverished the Souls of Today's Students*. New York: Simon, 1987.

Bloom, Harold. *The Book of J*. Trans. David Rosenberg. New York: Vintage, 1991.

Booth, Wayne C. *The Rhetoric of Fiction*. Chicago: U of Chicago P, 1961.

Coffin, Robert P. Tristram, and Alexander M. Witherspoon, eds. *Seventeenth-Century Prose and Poetry*. New York: Harcourt, 1946.

Damrosch, David, gen. ed. *The Longman Anthology of British Literature*. New York: Longman, 1999.

Foster, Don. *Author Unknown: On the Trail of Anonymous*. New York: Holt, 2000.

Graff, Gerald. *Professing Literature: An Institutional History*. Chicago: U of Chicago P, 1987.

Harner, James L. *Literary Research Guide: An Annotated Listing of Reference Sources in English Literary Studies*. 3rd ed. New York: MLA, 1998.

Hirsch, E. D., Jr. *Cultural Literacy: What Every American Needs to Know*. Boston: Houghton, 1987.

Hume, Robert D. *Reconstructing Contexts: The Aims and Principles of Archaeo-Historicism*. New York: Oxford UP, 1990.

Jameson, Fredric. "The State of the Subject." *Critical Quarterly* 29 (1987): 16–25.

Kernan, Alvin. *The Death of Literature*. New Haven: Yale UP, 1990.

Lauter, Paul. *Canons and Contexts*. New York: Oxford UP, 1991.

———, gen. ed. *The Heath Anthology of American Literature*. 2 vols. Lexington, MA: Heath, 1990.

McCrea, Brian. *Addison and Steele Are Dead: The English Department, Its Canon, and the Professionalization of Literary Criticism*. Newark: U of Delaware P, 1990.

McKeon, Michael. *The Origins of the English Novel, 1600–1740*. Baltimore: Johns Hopkins UP, 1987.

———. "Recent Studies in the Restoration and Eighteenth Century." *Studies in English Literature, 1500–1900* 45 (2005): 707–82.

Nussbaum, Felicity, and Laura Brown, eds. *The New Eighteenth Century: Theory, Politics, English Literature*. New York: Methuen, 1987.

Pope, Alexander. "Essay on Criticism." *Poetry and Prose of Alexander Pope*. Ed. Aubrey Williams. Boston: Houghton, 1969. 37–57.

Rudrum, Alan, Joseph Black, and Holly Faith Nelson, eds. *Broadview Anthology of Seventeenth-Century Verse and Prose*. Peterborough, Ont.: Broadview, 2000.

Schweitzer, Albert. *The Quest of the Historical Jesus: A Critical Study of Its Progress from Reimarus to Wrede*. 1901. Trans. W. Montgomery. New York: Macmillan, 1968.

Spivak, Gayatri Chakravorty. *Death of a Discipline*. New York: Columbia UP, 2003.

———. "Reading the World: Literary Studies in the Eighties." *In Other Worlds: Essays in Cultural Politics*. London: Methuen, 1987. 95–102.

Stein, Gertrude. "What Is English Literature." *Look at Me Now and Here I Am: Writings and Lectures, 1909–45*. Ed. Patricia Meyerowitz. Baltimore: Penguin, 1971.

Wimsatt, W. K., and Monroe C. Beardsley. *The Verbal Icon: Studies in the Meaning of Poetry*. Lexington: U of Kentucky P, 1954.

Witherspoon, Alexander M., and Frank J. Warnke, eds. *Seventeenth-Century Prose and Poetry*. Rev. ed. New York: Harcourt, 1982.

CHAPTER FIVE

Critical Theory and Cultural Studies

AMY J. ELIAS
University of Tennessee

C ritical theory is not one discipline. It is an array of ways to analyze texts, and it has a complicated place in English studies. Some people see it as an attack on aesthetic and Anglo-American cultural values and resist incorporating it into English curricula because of its political and philosophical roots outside of literary criticism. Others view "theory" as a necessary and revitalizing component of English studies that is the tie that binds together literary criticism, rhetoric, creative writing, linguistics, and media/culture studies. It is true that only critical theory crosses these branches of English studies, sometimes giving them a common vocabulary or foundation. It is also true that theory redefines the focus and priorities of all of these areas of English studies even as it unites them.

Defining critical theory apart from literary criticism is difficult because literary criticism and critical theory are interdependent and intertwined. As its title suggests, *The Johns Hopkins Guide to Literary Theory and Criticism* (Groden and Kreiswirth), a popular scholarly encyclopedia of theory, in fact does not distinguish between the terms *literary criticism* and *theory*. Further, defining critical theory, and also to some extent cultural studies, is complicated because each kind of critical theory has an origin in a different set of ideas. Louis Montrose has noted at least two factors relevant to the growth of culturally based or ideological theories in the 1970s and after: first, the increasing diversity (in terms of race, gender, class, religion, ethnicity, political allegiance, and sexual orientation) of humanities faculty who add social and dissonant voices due to experiences of exclusion; and second, the reorienting of the profession during these years by critics whose social values were formed in the politically turbulent 1960s (393). Considered globally, what we call "theory" is indebted to these cultural trends and is in fact an interdisciplinary conversation that is almost impossible to trace to a starting point or single initiating moment.

For example, feminist theory is indebted to the reorienting of the profession by female faculty entering the humanities since the 1960s. When imported into English curricula, feminist theory can change the focus and objectives of rhetoric and composition studies, literary criticism, creative writing, English education, and, perhaps, linguistics. Feminist theory is a diverse, global conversation about the relation of women to cultural and literary texts, and it asks questions such as "How do women use language, and is it different from the way men use language?" and "How did Shakespeare think about women in his own time?" and "How can women's writing change our perceptions of the culture in which we live?" and "Do 'First-World' women have the same concerns as 'Third-World' women?" These feminist conversations range through historical periods and nationalities, through different genres of political and personal writings, and through the fields of psychology, political science, history, art history, philosophy, literary criticism, literature and art, religious studies, sexuality studies, cultural studies, sociology, and medicine. There are as many different kinds of "feminist theory" as there are university majors, and then some, and all have a historical and philosophical provenance, and not all of them like one another. And this is just feminism. Complicate this by adding Marxism, psychoanalysis, gender/sexuality theories, critical race theories, and other disciplinary perspectives, and you have a cacophony of voices ranging across disciplines and through historical time. How can we possibly sum up, in one chapter, what all this "theory" really is?

We can generally define this thorny subject, however, because "critical theory" and "cultural studies" are not empty sets or contentless terms, and the difficulty of defining them is in fact one indicator of the fields' vibrancy and scope. For practical purposes, this chapter considers "critical theory" within the Western European tradition only (it will not, for example, consider theories that originate in Eastern or other traditions, such as those of China or of India). In addition, the chapter will follow the separation of literary criticism and critical theory made by this volume's editor: that literary criticism investigates how or why texts *formally* signify or "mean," while critical theory identifies how texts *culturally or ideologically* signify or "mean." This can also be stated as an ontological distinction. As Lois Tyson puts it, "Strictly speaking, when we interpret a literary text, we are doing literary criticism; when we examine the criteria upon which our interpretation rests, we are doing critical theory" (7). If literary criticism analyzes texts, critical theory analyzes literary criticism. Critical theory is the field in which we ask why we interpret texts the way we do. Where do our interpretive strategies come from? What social values do they promote or disguise or transform? Why should we pick one interpretive strategy over another?

At this point in the professional conversation about critical theory, there are many good introductions, handbooks, and readers available that define the history, terms, objectives, and major voices of its different branches, and this brief introduction draws partly from these sources in order to illustrate their range and usefulness.[1] The term *critical theory*, while originating in Marxist social philosophy, has come to be a catchall term for many kinds of twentieth-century ideological criticism. Much more specifically used, the term *cultural studies* refers to the examination of specific cultural trends and artifacts that began as an idea or project within critical theory. This chapter examines each of these areas of theory individually, to make clear their differences as well as their links to one another.

I. Critical Theory

One might date the split between criticism and theory to the classical dichotomy between an Aristotelian view of art, focusing on formal and intrinsic characteristics of a work, that would be the progenitor of literary criticism, and a Platonic view of art, focusing on the extrinsic, social, and utilitarian value of a work, that would be the progenitor of critical theory. Critical theorists would disagree with Plato, however, that poets have no place in the

Republic. For most critical theorists, art is both a revealing mirror of a society's values and power structures and a site where alternatives to oppressive social systems can be formulated. Marxist, feminist, psychoanalytic, and race/ethnicity theories all turn to art as the battlefield where psychological, social, and ideological wars are waged.

Technically, however, the most accurate definition of critical theory is that it was the theory produced by participants in the *Institut für Sozialforschung* (Institute for Social Research), known as the "Frankfurt Institute" because it was located at the University of Frankfurt in Germany. Members of this institute were greatly influenced by Karl Marx and Friedrich Engels and by the work of those after them who attempted to define the relation between "vulgar Marxism" and the arts—writers such as Vladimir Ilyitch Lenin, Leon Trotsky, and the Hungarian-born Georg Lukács. The term *critical theory* was coined by Max Horkheimer and Herbert Marcuse in essays published in 1937 through the school's influential *Journal of Social Research* (*Zeitschrift für Sozialforschung*), itself published from 1932 to 1941. In this context, "critical theory" described the dialectical social criticism created by members of the institute.

The term *critical theory* thus was created by Frankfurt School writers, within the purview of Marxist political theory, and the study of art and literature was privileged by some institute members such as Theodor Adorno, Horkheimer, and Walter Benjamin because art was understood to both reflect and challenge dominant ideologies within cultures. Because their work identified and analyzed ideology in both popular and high culture, as well as in various art forms, the institute's writers are often seen not only as the creators of critical theory but also as the original practitioners of what would much later be developed as "cultural studies." The key idea—and the idea that links together all later theory and cultural studies—was that the world of lived social experience needed to be central to any theoretical project, and that ideology affected all cultural productions, including literature.[2]

The term *critical theory* has now branched out from, but retained the emphasis of, its early Marxist and Frankfurt School roots to include all ideological criticism. We now apply the term *critical theory* to all ideologically based criticism or social criticism that makes ideas originating "outside the text" (in the world of social experience) integral to the interpretive process. Critical theory inhabits the fields of psychology, philosophy, linguistics, aesthetics, and political theory. It is the study of interpretation itself, and it asks what interpretation is and what aesthetic, ideological, and psychological forces constitute its operation.

What Is Critical Theory?

The term *critical theory* was coined by the Frankfurt School writers and was originally associated with Marxist critique, but the term has come to refer more generally to ideological and/or contextual criticism. In this more general sense, critical theory is a cross-disciplinary field that attempts to define and evaluate the effects of social forces that influence critical and creative textual production, interpretation, and literary canonization.

Let's form an example. When in our English class we read Edith Wharton's *The Age of Innocence*, we might focus on its formal characteristics in order to show why it is good literature. We would examine the way that the text is beautifully written—looking at word choice, use of metaphor and literary allusion, characterization, plot complexity, complexity of themes, and felicitous phrasing—and we might compare it to other texts to show its superiority and worthiness of a place in the literary canon. We might also place Wharton's novel within a historical context: students might learn when and where the text was written and learn some information about Wharton's life and the times in which she lived in order to get a "context" for the novel. Finally, we might discuss the text's place in literary history: what genre and subgenre is this? With what literary "movements" or styles is this text associated? (Is this an example of realism or literary naturalism or the novel of manners?) This kind of discussion about *The Age of Innocence* would be seen as a *formalist* approach because as interpreters, we are concentrating on the form of the work and its internal properties as a work of literature. This kind of "close reading" approach certainly serves teachers of English well in high school and college classrooms, where students often need to be taught such methods of textual analysis.

Yet suppose that when you and I read this book, we have very different reactions to it. When you read *The Age of Innocence*, you see yourself reflected in May Welland ("She seems to be going through exactly what I went through last year"), love the language of the book ("This book is beautifully written"), and think its themes are socially significant ("Everyone should read this—it says really important things about our society"). On your recommendation, I read the novel, but unlike you I feel alienated from the text ("Who *are* these people? Their lives are nothing like my life"). Moreover, I don't like the language of the book at all ("This book is boring to read"), and I think its themes are nonexistent or have little social value ("Why would anyone care about this?").

Why did we have such radically different reactions to and evaluations of this book if both of us could understand its sense equally well? The problem was not a matter of interpretation, for both of us understood the book and could perform a close reading of it if we were asked to do so. So if we both understood the book's *content* to the degree that we both could analyze its formal characteristics, why did we arrive at such different evaluations of the book's *merit*?

While literary criticism answers this question through aesthetic appraisal of the novel (e.g., this text is better than another because it is more beautiful or better structured), critical theory answers this question by examining the cultural, psychological, and political contexts of the novel. Critical theory assumes that a text's merit may be evaluated in terms of its intervention in, or reflection of, the politics of culture. In other words, critical theory might posit that perhaps the reason we reacted so differently to Wharton's novel is that you saw the book relating to your life experience and I did not. Critical theory and cultural studies would address this issue and posit that our life experiences are important to our literary values, and even that one's race, gender, class, and nationality may affect what one considers to be good literature and good ideas. Perhaps, however, the reason we disagreed was that the book evoked some memory or positive self-image for you that it did not stir in me; psychoanalytic theory might posit how our personal psychologies affected our evaluations of this text. Or, perhaps, you thought the book (implicitly or explicitly) advocated positive social or cultural values—such as valid standards for fairness, human flourishing, and freedom—while I thought that it did not. In this last case, we disagree on the book's ideological meaning, and critical theory would give us the terms to compare ideological systems with one another.

As this example illustrates, critical theory assumes that there is no unmediated aesthetic experience. First, everything we perceive is potentially a text to be read. "Text" in this sense might be a work of literature, but it also might be a television commercial, a magazine, a film, a public speech. (A "text" in the context of literary theory tends to be defined as anything within a culture that needs interpretation; a short story can be a text, but so can a man, or a living room, or a restaurant menu. This redefinition of the text by structuralist and poststructuralist theories has wide-ranging implications for English studies.) Second, when people read written texts, hear oral texts, or see visual texts, they *always* filter their perceptions through some kind of interpretive (cultural, psychological, and linguistic) "screen." Different theories look at different screens and attempt to define the screen and show how it affects our evaluation of written, oral, or visual texts. Theories that look at similar screens in a similar way are sometimes called "schools" of critical theory, in the way we might talk about "schools of thought." Thus one school of theory (psychoanalytic theory) may emphasize how psychology affects critical judgment, while another school (Marxist theory) may emphasize how readers' class positions in society affect how they read texts.

Like rhetoric, then, critical theory focuses on reader, text, audience, and context. Critical theories privilege one or another of these elements when offering explanations for why and how readers read, hear, or see texts. Feminist theory, for example, might focus on the audience ("How would a woman read *The Age of Innocence*, and was it written for women?"), or it might focus on the text ("Is *The Age of Innocence* an example of women's writing or women's language?"), or it might focus on the author ("How did Wharton's life as a woman in 1920 influence her choice of themes in this novel?"), or it might focus on context ("Was the male-dominated post–World War II literary scene responsible for the neglect of this novel by critics after the war?"). Yet all of these questions within feminist theory assume that something in the social world—in this case, definitions of "woman"—impinge on interpretation and how we read texts.

So critical theory attempts to articulate how ideology and social selves are *constituted* (where both come from and how they shape interpretation) and how ideology and social forces defining selfhood might be *revealed and transformed* through the reading of texts. All critical theories assume that literature and other aesthetic products bear cultural values and that they are thermometers telling us what the ideological temperature of a society, or the psychic temperature of a personal psychology, may be. For critical theorists, written and visual art is revelatory: it can unmask beliefs we didn't know we had. Critical theories thus assert that the visual and literary arts may be vehicles for social change: once beliefs and values are revealed in literature, for example, we may reevaluate them and perhaps offer alternatives to them.

Thus, critical theory understood as ideological theory asks:

♦ What cultural and ideological assumptions underlie and form the questions addressed by literary criticism and aesthetics?

♦ How do language, culture, and ideology construct our identities as producers, interpreters, and/or consumers of visual, oral, and written texts?

♦ Under what social circumstances are the ability and freedom to produce and interpret texts given to or taken from communities and individuals?

♦ How do visual, oral, or written texts create as well as reflect their social and ideological contexts?

Important Debates about Critical Theory

Because of its origins in multiple disciplines and contexts, the debates in critical theory are legion. Certainly, within each of the "schools" of theory, there are important and heated debates. For example, within psychoanalytic theory, there are debates about the focus of interpretation. Should we use psychoanalytic language to analyze the author's psychology, characterization (the "psychology" of the characters in the text), or the reader's psychology? Should we use a Freudian or a Lacanian or a post-Lacanian psychoanalytic model as our interpretive starting point? What assumptions about gender, race, and class may be embedded within the psychoanalytic models we use? Can we interpret texts written hundreds of years ago using a Freudian psychoanalytic model created to describe human development in the early twentieth century? Is there a psychology to social movements (e.g., a fascist psychology) and can we apply this to texts to aid in interpretation? These and other questions are not resolved within psychoanalytic theory, and they show the vitality of the field and the interesting questions such theory can raise. All critical theories— Marxist, feminist, psychoanalytic, poststructuralist, race/ethnicity —have internal, ongoing debates of this kind.

The important questions within English studies concerning critical theory, however, are not these kinds of internal debates but rather more global concerns about the place of critical theory in the English curriculum, the value of theory to students, and critical theory's substitution of a political for a formalist method of interpretation.

Theory has become central to interpretation for many professionals in English studies; when we write books and articles these days, we rarely ignore the insights and debates of critical theory. Yet most of our undergraduate students—and, in fact, many graduate students—never take a class in critical theory and sometimes know little about the kinds of theory available or the complexity of the field(s). This disjunction between professional practice and pedagogy has led many English departments to reconsider and debate the role and place of theory in their curricula. Admittedly, these debates can be heated and divisive for departments whose faculties are divided in their critical commitments between ideological and aesthetic/formalist ways of analyzing texts. But a debate about the role of critical theory in undergraduate and graduate English studies also can result in a more updated curriculum that better integrates what professional critics in specific departments do and what they teach; that better correlates the criticism students read in order to write their term papers with the criticism they write as apprentice textual interpreters; that reasserts the importance of critical thinking and

English studies to the real world and the real lives of students living in a participatory democracy; and that asserts real relationships (rather than oppositions) among different branches of English studies, such as rhetoric, literary criticism, linguistics, and creative writing.

Why are ideological approaches so controversial? Ideological critical theories assert that showing why Wharton's *The Age of Innocence* is beautiful and complex as a work of literature is not as important as examining the approaches to race, class, and gender of the culture in which it was produced. That is, we should not spend our time analyzing abstract, universal ideas seemingly generated by the text (i.e., thematic ideas) or compositional questions (i.e., creative writing techniques), but rather we should analyze the specific culture at the specific time in which Wharton wrote the book in order to see how the novel both supports and subverts the race, class, and gender politics of its time. Thus, while formalist criticism puts context in the service of close reading, critical and cultural theory tends to put literature in the service of context analysis. What is truly important about *The Age of Innocence* is not that it is a novel of manners, or a good novel, or an important addition to English literature, but that it was written in 1920 by a white woman from the American upper class: the context does not explain the novel, but rather the novel helps to explain the context. Reading *The Age of Innocence* reveals to us what Wharton and her society felt about people of color, the hidden or not-so-hidden problem of class in the United States, and women's roles and identities at the turn of the century. As critics, we need to search the text for the revealed and hidden ideological values about race, class, gender, and sexuality in Wharton's society.

As a result of this focus, one of the major criticisms of critical theory is that it puts textual interpretation in the service of cultural politics. Reactions to this methodology often lead to debates about the purpose of criticism itself. What should professional critics and teachers of (literary, public, rhetorical, and creative) texts focus on when they read texts? Literary critics such as Elaine Scarry and Harold Bloom have argued that teaching students that the only important thing about a novel is how it reveals its own society's class conflicts misses the whole point of literature. Literature, they claim, is constructed to do this, but also more than this; because it is both a fabrication *and* a mirror of reality, it can reveal the values of its culture but it can also give pleasure simply as an aesthetic object—and it is probable that art's aesthetic component may have ethical and/or moral value. These critics ask, did we come to love literature because it revealed ideology? Or did we come to love literature because it had a unique appeal as an aesthetic and ethical object and because its original vision, felicitous phrasing, and beautiful imagery made us think about new ideas in new ways? Critical theorists tend to respond that literature did and does all these things, but that critics need to analyze art's place within a larger social context, because the point of any analysis is not mere enjoyment or personal enlightenment but rather the promotion of justice and political freedom in the world.

Those suspicious of critical theory tend to respond that fighting for justice is fine, but that analyzing literature hardly constitutes a revolutionary fight for political freedom; critical theorists have a puffed-up sense of self-importance if they think that reading Wharton's *Age of Innocence* and writing an article about it in an academic journal will free the enslaved and liberate the poor in real life. Yet critical theorists such as Marxist critics, cultural materialists, or new historians do in fact claim that it would; to them, any revelation of crippling ideologies and any promotion of social justice agendas have effects in the society at large. Negotiating these two positions can be delicate work.

Even those sympathetic to the aims and methods of critical theory, however, sometimes argue that looking at a text in this way gives uncommon status to the textual analyst. Because critical theory assumes that texts can support and subvert dominant ideologies of the societies in which they are written and argues that the purpose of analyzing texts is to reveal these circulating ideologies, it tends to portray the critic as an analyst of culture and a promoter of specific moral and social values. The critical theorist reveals a "hidden" ideological content in the text, and the method assumes that the critic is better informed about what the text is doing than are the author and other, less theoretically sophisticated, readers. (To some extent, this perspective has been built into Marxist criticisms since the writings of Lenin, who argued that revolutionary intellectuals would need to stir and organize the complacent or beleaguered proletariat to action against their bourgeois oppressors.) In ideological criticism, the importance of the writer as shaper is thus subsumed by the importance of the critic as analyst, diagnostician, and political freedom fighter. Creative writers and artists understandably resent this, particularly when critics point out the racist, classist, or sexist nature of their creations. But others also accuse ideological critical theory of maintaining a strident, self-congratulatory tone when analyzing texts to reveal dangerous ideologies that until then only the ideological critic was able to discern, while still others point to what they see as the hypocrisy of critics' assuming an anticapitalist, Marxist political agenda at the same time that these critics remain protected by tenure in reasonably well-paying jobs funded by the capitalist state. Ideological critics often answer this charge by redefining "ideological work" itself through a Gramscian model of hegemony and resistance: a political critic might work *through* a system to systematically undermine its power and control, until the day when the system itself falls.

A different debate about putting texts in the service of cultural analysis is generated by historians and anthropologists, who often argue that reading cultural values and ideologies from literary or individual cultural texts (like advertisements) is simply a shoddy way of doing history or sociology. A novel, they claim, is fiction and therefore not a piece of historical documentation in the same way that is a court record; furthermore, no self-respecting historians would look at only one document and think they could reconstruct the values of an entire culture from that one piece of documentation. Yet this is precisely what some critical theorists do when they approach texts: when I read *The Age of Innocence* or "read" a magazine advertisement, I feel empowered to make claims about the race, class, and gender politics of the societies in which both were created. Critical theorists respond to this charge differently depending upon what branch of critical theory they practice. One general response might be that the example is bad: anyone who infers knowledge of a whole society from one of Wharton's novels is doing bad ideological criticism. New historicist critics might address the charge made by practicing historians by countering that they do not look at just the text; in fact, new historicism demands that before making a claim about how literature relates to the larger culture and its underlying ideological values and ideas, the critic must place an art work in relation to sometimes hundreds of other texts of very different kinds (e.g., court records, legal rulings, journal entries, play receipts, published letters, and other fiction and nonfiction texts) all written in the same period.

The "cultural politics" of theoretical interpretation is itself a topic of debate within, and especially outside, the academy. The term *cultural politics* grows out of the utopian orientation of most critical theory, the idea that culture determines (or is largely responsible for determining) individual psyches and social trends. In the old terms of the nature/nurture debates, critical theory is firmly in the "nurture" camp. In particular, ideological criticism focuses on how ideology within culture determines people's attitudes toward race, gender, and class, and how ideology actually *constructs* us as classed, raced, and gendered beings. We are subject to ideology, which itself grows organically out of specific economic systems, so changing economic systems means changing ideology, and this means changing our views of ourselves, our views of others, and the possibilities for justice within society. This materialist perspective not only tends to denigrate capitalism as an economic system; it tends to be highly suspicious of ideologies central to "Western" capitalist nations—ideas such as individualism, self-determination, competition versus cooperation as the path to excellence, and universalist human values (versus cultural difference).

The values promoted by critical theory, with the exception of psychoanalytic theory, tend to be linked to socialist or Marxist politics; ideological critical theories often imply that supporting gay rights, women's rights, and racial equality means supporting socialist or communist economies. Opponents note that the Marxist agenda underlying much critical theory tends to discourage real political debate that would allow ethics-based, politically conservative, religious, or non-Marxist social philosophies equal time or consideration in this kind of cultural analysis. Thus this debate about critical theory hinges on the claim that it is not a way to analyze texts but is rather the promotion of a specific political, moral, and cultural agenda in the (supposedly open and bipartisan) public classroom. In essence, opponents of critical theory argue that it attacks Western values. Those critical theorists who identify themselves as the most radical simply reply, "Yes, we do." Less radical critical theorists might point to the West's own history of intellectual debate and claim that what critical theory offers is multiple additions to this as well as new ways to integrate political discussion, aesthetics, ethics, and cultural analysis in the English studies classroom.

Lastly, a very different kind of debate involves critical theory and pedagogy. This debate centers around a simple question: Is critical theory teachable—i.e., accessible—to undergraduates? Opponents of critical theory as a required part of English studies argue that undergraduates and even graduate students often (1) need instruction in literary history, basic methods of close reading, and the use of critical terminology more than they need instruction in ideological criticism, and (2) enter English classrooms with little or none of the background in literary history, aesthetics, philosophy, economics, psychology, or intellectual history needed to understand or really grapple with critical theory. Instead of teaching our students watered-down Marxism or race theory, these opponents argue, wouldn't our students be better served if we taught them vocabulary, art appreciation, literary and aesthetic history, and literary and rhetorical analysis? Critical theorists counter with the claim that critical theory *is* literary and rhetorical analysis. Furthermore, they argue, what good does it do students to know that *The Age of Innocence* was a novel of manners written by Wharton in 1920 if they can't discuss the cultural significance of that novel? A critical theorist might add: which becomes the education of a citizen in a democracy better, the knowledge of literary history or the ability to discern when, where, and how ideology is created and maintained within cultures?

These debates about critical theory are serious, and they are not easily resolved. The middle-ground approach can be taken by English studies: that is, critical theory as a *component* of English studies—given equal emphasis in the English curriculum with creative writing, literature and literary criticism, rhetoric and composition, linguistics and discourse analysis, and English education—might in fact lead to more cross-disciplinary policing as well as cross-disciplinary interchange. Currently, most college English departments compartmentalize these disciplines, so that students rarely hear them in dialogue with one another. In the English studies model, some of the more outrageous aspects of critical theory might be curbed or rethought if critical theorists were forced into dialogue with creative writers, rhetoricians, and aestheticians and formalist critics—and vice versa. Certainly, however, what critical theory offers is a radical rethinking of what the purpose of criticism should be, and all must acknowledge that its presence has galvanized English studies and made it more dynamic since the 1960s.

Critical Theory Methodologies

There are four main branches of a generally defined critical theory, or ideological criticism, that have flourished since the 1960s: one originating in Marxist political theory, one originating in Freudian psychology, one originating in feminist politics and social history, and one originating in race politics and social history. At a certain point after the 1960s, they began to converge and form hybrid theories while retaining, in some branches, essential differences. All of these branches of critical theory share one overriding belief: that when critics analyze texts to try to discern the texts' meaning and significance, they must take the texts' cultural context into consideration, for the cultural context is a vitally important factor influencing the texts' creation and meaning.

Marxist Theory and New Historicism

Marx, of course, was not a literary critic or a rhetorician. He was a political theorist, and he created a theory of history (known as dialectical materialism) that attempted to explain how and why societies move through different kinds of economic systems. He claimed that social change happened because of changes in a society's economic *base:* how a society produced material goods indicated what kind of economy it had, from agrarian economies (based in agriculture and associated with specific kinds of living and working arrangements) to capitalist societies (based in urban industrial production and associated with different kinds of living and working arrangements). But a society's economic base also determined its *superstructure*—including religion, art, philosophy, and law. Marx's legacy was a theory of history and social systems based in economics and material production; a detailed analysis of how capitalism works; and an analysis and advocacy of what he considered the best and inevitably final state of societies, Communism.

Marx's theory of history and culture had far-reaching influence. By the twentieth century, it had influenced not only real politics (in the Russian Revolution of 1917), but it had also introduced new ideas into history studies, sociology, and even art and literary criticism. Marxist theory's new, important claim for these disciplines was that one could not analyze things produced in society without taking the social context into consideration, for the social context—specifically, the economic system of each society and the class conflict deriving from it—was the *determining* factor in their identity as objects or ideas. One of the most famous lines from Marx's writing comes from the preface to *A Contribution to the Critique of Political Economy:* "It is not the consciousness of men that determines their existence, but their social existence that determines their consciousness" (21). Economics determines character—of societies, of people, of objects, of art—and class conflict is the engine driving history.

This focus on a text's social context continued in Marxist writing during the twentieth century in the writing of Lenin and Trotsky. Lukács adapted formalist techniques of reading to develop his "reflection theory" of art that identified how texts directly reflect a society's class consciousness; in *History and Class Consciousness* he made alienation and Hegelian dialectic the cornerstones of Marxist analysis (Bannet 476–78). Two figures writing in the 1920s, Antonio Gramsci and Mikhail Bakhtin, developed Marxist thought in different directions. Gramsci's notion of hegemony (domination by consent) and Bakhtin's notion of dialogism (multivoicedness) in literature would be influential to Marxist theory and cultural studies in the latter half of the twentieth century (see Bottomore; W. Cohen; and Eagleton).

Many of the Frankfurt School writers in the mid-twentieth century used early Marxism as a social model, though their work diverged widely and members were often at odds with one another. But they soon deviated from traditional Marxist ideas. As Vincent Leitch has noted, the Frankfurt School reexamined the foundations of Marxist thought—redefining, for example, the assumptions of "vulgar Marxism" about the relation between economic base and superstructure—but preserved its focus on the relation between art and life: "the Frankfurt School insisted on the political nature of all art [. . .] because it preserves human yearnings for utopian ways of life. Art not only reflects existing social realities (as all Marxists affirm) but also embodies radical impulses. The Kantian and Arnoldian notion that art is 'disinterested' is erroneous: art protests domination" (*American* 20).

Members of the Frankfurt School did share a project that would come to define their own (and later) critical theory: the critique of ideology in the service of a political agenda of human freedom. Originally under the direction of Horkheimer and established at the University of Frankfurt in Germany in 1922, the Frankfurt Institute was temporarily housed in the United States starting in 1933, upon Hitler's rise to power, and then reestablished in Germany in the 1950s. The institute's members included, in addition to Horkheimer, Adorno, and Marcuse, Otto Kirchheimer, Leo Löwenthal, Franz Leopold Neumann, Friedrich Pollock, Erich Fromm, and Jürgen Habermas as well as, peripherally, Benjamin (see Stirk). Inspired by the Soviet revolution and the Marx-Engels Institute in Moscow, the Frankfurt Institute inaugurated the study of Marxism as a sociological science, and "the original works of the Institute were associated with capitalist accumulation and economic planning, studies of the economy in China, agricultural relations in France, imperialism, and along with this, through close collaboration with the Soviet Union, the establishment of a collection of the unpublished works of Marx and Engels" (Rasmussen 16–17).

Individually, the school's writers provided differing accounts of ideology at work in the world, but collectively they understood the critical process as *critique*, a term taken from Immanuel Kant but reformulated in Marxist social philosophy. To perform ideological critique, the Frankfurt School critical theorists combined Marxist concerns with ideology and art with insights from sociology, philosophy, psychoanalysis, and cultural criticism (see Stirk).

Since the 1960s, Marxist criticism has merged with virtually every other kind of critical theory: there are now Marxist feminisms, Marxist historicisms, Marxist race theories, and Marxist-inflected psychoanalytic theories.[3] Some of these branches or "schools" of theory, such as new historicism or cultural poetics, have become distinct theories in their own right. In the late twentieth century, Marxist writers such as Raymond Williams, Terry Eagleton, and Fredric Jameson have revised much of Marx and Engels' original theory, but they retain a desire to analyze literature and other aspects of culture in relation to capitalism and class conflict. As many scholars have noted, Marxist criticism has thrived since the 1940s not in Communist countries but in Western capitalist ones, and it tends to be less associated with Communist propaganda than with cultural critique. Marxist "theory" became increasingly distanced from the practice of real-world Marxist societies; the theory revised itself in light of revealed deficiencies in Marx and Engels' communist social philosophy.

A different kind of ideological theory emerged in the 1980s that both had close ties with Marxist theory and diverged from Marxism's modes of critique: new historicism. Influenced by the cultural theory of Michel Foucault, and associated with the work of Stephen Greenblatt and Catherine Gallagher, *new historicism* was the term used by Renaissance scholar Greenblatt in a special 1982 issue of *Genre* to describe a new kind of historically based criticism (Childers and Hentzi 208). Like historiography, new historicism asserted that all aspects of a culture—from court records to theater productions to working-class taverns—needed to be studied historically, but, unlike traditional history, new historicism did this in the service of cultural critique, in order to define the character and power of cultural hegemony at a specific historical moment.

According to new historicists, all historical accounts—whether literary or documentary—are "texts," and none has any more historical veracity than any other. History is understood to be as much a fiction—an ideologically constructed tale or story incorporating narrative conventions as well as authorial bias and cultural prejudice—as any Jacobean play. According to this view, literature becomes a significant historical document, providing a snapshot of cultural values and anxieties of specific societies at specific historical moments (see Gallagher and Greenblatt; Brannigan; and Ryan). Moreover, because it is a fully fleshed-out fictional world (unlike a documentary account of the time), literature encodes even more information about culture than would an official treatise or historical account. Thus, a play by Shakespeare may tell us more about Elizabethan England than might any documentary or "true history." New historicists thus reverse the traditional context/work relation: while literary criticism investigates historical context in order to better understand a literary text, new historicists read literary texts in order to better understand historical contexts—or, rather, new historicists assert that the context/work distinction is a false one altogether. The agenda of new historicist criticism is overtly political and leftist in orientation: it reexamines cultures in specific historical time frames in order to expose the dynamics of social power operating at that time, to show what elements of society held control and what elements were oppressed and/or offering resistance to their domination.

The most significant influence on new historicism was the cultural theory of Foucault. Spanning the disciplines of sociology, anthropology, political theory, history, philosophy, and social science, Foucault's work has radically altered all humanistic studies since the early 1960s, and more than twenty years after his death in 1984 his work is still changing the interpretive questions of fields as different as religious studies and film theory. Foucault argued that there is no such thing as "human nature" but rather that what we call human nature is constructed by the "discourses of power" circulating within a culture. His theories attack the notion of the holy spirit as well as the humanistic mind, both sacred and secular traditions of human achievement and possibility: institutions such as churches and universities are not liberators of human beings but rather the sites of their training in subjectification to power. For Foucault, "Nothing—whether selves, desires, or truth—is external to the productive power/ knowledge that creates the categories by which it is known. Thus, the truth to which dissidents appeal is no less a product of interested strategies [. . .] than the truth spoken by the officials whom they oppose" (Leitch, *Norton* 1620). Foucault analyzed topics as diverse as systems of knowledge, punishment of criminals, medical practices and the role of physicians, the role and social function of authors, and human sexuality. His work enacted a new way of doing historical analysis and also provided provocative new conclusions about the specific practices or concepts under consideration.

Generally speaking, today any critical theory in a neo-Marxist or new historicist vein assumes that

- ◆ a text's cultural context, particularly the economic system in which it is produced, is vitally important to interpreting the text's meaning;

- ◆ criticism should aim to identify ideologies informing and resisted by texts;

- ◆ "texts" appropriate for cultural analysis include visual, written, and oral documents—that is, virtually anything animate or inanimate within a culture to which "critique" can be applied;

- ◆ there are no grounds that legitimately distinguish works based on their aesthetic quality—a text's quality is measured not in terms of its "beauty" but in terms of its cultural value, particularly in terms of its ability to reveal ideologies circulating within a culture; and

- ◆ the value of a work is gauged by how effectively it reveals and subverts capitalist ideologies or discourses of power that inhibit human freedom and flourishing.

Psychoanalytic Theory

A second strain of critical theory originates not in Marxist theory but in Freudian psychoanalysis. Like Marxist theory, psychoanalytic theory is a true import: it begins in a specific discipline (psychology and human behavior) and emigrates into English studies as a method for analyzing texts. Psychoanalytic theories share with other branches of critical theory the belief that one must usually go beyond formal analysis and include analysis of the text's cultural context (Ellmann; for readings, see Vice). Unlike other theories discussed above, psychoanalytic theory is not overtly ideological in focus. Its insights, however—particularly in later, poststructuralist versions—have ideological implications, for they challenge dominant cultural definitions of what human beings *are*—how much free agency they have, how much they can control the world around them, how much they might "know themselves" and their own motivations, and, ultimately, what their abilities are to read, write, and interpret texts.

The history of psychoanalytic theory begins with Sigmund Freud. Starting his career as a clinical neurologist, Freud turned to clinical interests in human psychology and opened his famous consulting room in Vienna in 1891. His writings began to appear soon after, ranging from studies of the human psyche to studies about larger cultural forces. From Freud we derive many of our modern ideas about dreams and their interpretation, the structure of the mind, the developmental stages of childhood, and the relation of language to unconscious drives and desires. From Freud's work certain ideas have entered our common vocabulary—e.g., the unconscious; the id, ego, and superego; dream symbolism; Freudian slips; the libido; the pleasure principle; neurosis; the Oedipus complex; the uncanny; repression; fetishism; and transference.

More important for today's critical theory, Freud opened up a new attentiveness to texts and new models for interpretation. Not only did Freud's clinical method stress attentive listening to his patients and assessment of the "texts" they created about themselves; it promoted a "metapsychology" or a seemingly structuralist thesis that in the human mind there was a deep structure (the unconscious mind) beneath a surface structure (the conscious mind) that we assumed was our "self." Analysis demanded a penetration and interpretation of the deep structure, from the latent (versus the manifest) content of dreams to the origins of neurosis in everyday behavior. Careful "reading," interpretation of symbols, and a respect for art forms as records and manifestations of universal fears and desires were staples of Freudian analysis. Freud not only looked to myth and literature to derive some of his own insights about human drives (such as his use of Sophocles' play *Oedipus Rex* to articulate the Oedipus complex); he also gave to textual criticism the idea that a text expresses its author's unconscious desires and fears. Thus, from Freud's work, psychoanalytic theory derives both its method and its terms of analysis. Its method of analyzing the psychology of an author, character, or reader is similar to Freud's method of analyzing patients, and the terms of analysis it uses are Freudian.

However, just as Freud's own pupils revised Freud's theories about the human mind, so too have later psychiatrists revised the terms of psychoanalytic theory. Jacques Lacan is probably the Freudian revisionist whose work has provoked the most response within critical theory. From 1932 through the 1970s, Lacan combined his own insights as a practicing clinician with Freud's clinical insights and ideas drawn from philosophy, literature, and structuralist linguistics, particularly the theories of language developed by Ferdinand de Saussure. *Écrits,* a collection of Lacan's essays and papers, caused a sensation upon its publication in 1966, and it brought to the public a new, highly difficult and allusive style of writing.

For Lacan, human beings only enter selfhood through language, which always forms a scrim between them and the real world (we can only know the world through the language we speak, but this language will always distort the thing it attempts to describe). Lacan rewrites the Freudian id, ego, and superego as the Imaginary, the Symbolic, and the Real "orders" in the psyche, all equally important in the development to adulthood. The Real is always inaccessible to us, since it stands beyond language. We enter the Imaginary Order, associated with the mother, as small children, particularly when we see a mirror image of ourselves for the first time; the Symbolic Order is associated with the father, and we enter it between the ages of three and six, at which point we learn language that constantly posits relationships between things instead of a concrete and truthful reality that could anchor us. These theories about the nature of the psyche pointed to Lacan's major revisionist ideas—that the self was defined not by the identity it accrued but by what it lacked or failed to accrue; that the unconscious was not the chaotic, seething cauldron of drives and desires that it was for Freud but rather was structured, and could be analyzed, as a kind of language; and that the literal male and female body parts on which Freud's theory centered could be understood in a less sexist and more accurate way if redefined as metaphorical symbols of power (Lacan's rewriting of the penis as the phallus, for example).

Other Freudian and Lacanian revisionists—such as Carl Jung, Norman Holland, Melanie Klein, Julia Kristeva, Luce Irigaray, Nancy Chodorow, and Shoshana Felman—have formulated new emphases for psychology that have had lasting importance to critical theory. From the work of Swiss psychiatrist Jung was derived an analytical psychology that posited not only a (Freudian-compatible) personal conscious and unconscious, but also a collective unconscious in the mind where universal archetypes (patterns or images) of human experience were stored. From Jung, critical theory inherits "archetypal criticism" that reads texts to find and interpret archetypes that appear in them (see Sugg). In contrast, in *The Dynamics of Literary Response* and in much later work such as *Holland's Guide to Psychoanalytic Psychology and Literature-and-Psychology*, Holland focuses on how readers' own psychologies interface with the texts that they read. Holland's work is often aligned with reader-response theories because it is concerned with what the reader brings to the text and how the anxieties and desires of interpreters affect the interpretations they produce.

Still another psychoanalytic perspective is offered by the works of Irigaray and Kristeva, associated with French feminist thinking. Irigaray's work in the 1970s, such as *Speculum of the Other Woman*, attacked Freudian and Lacanian analysis for constructing theories of sexuality on an exclusively male model and virtually ignoring the difference of female sexuality. A practicing psychoanalyst, linguist, and political activist, Kristeva rewrote Freudian psychoanalysis through structuralist linguistics to argue that language is always in a dialectic between the "semiotic" (aligned with the mother and representing psychological drives manifested in language through rhythm and tone) and the "symbolic" (aligned with the father and associated with syntax and grammar). She rewrites Lacan's Imaginary as the place of the "chora," characterized by fluidity and rhythm; this can break through the Symbolic Order, disturbing the male-dominated discourse of this order (see Kristeva; Oliver). In a different vein, Klein has investigated child psychology in a way important to later feminist theorists such as Toril Moi and has written of the language of the emotions, such as envy, love, and guilt (see Klein;

Mitchell), while Felman, in *Writing and Madness* and other works, has explored the relation between creativity and madness and the nature of trauma. In addition to these and other revisionist psychoanalytic theories, an "anti-psychiatry movement" arose in the 1950s that also had later importance to critical theory; it "exposed hidden levels of domination in the practices of [. . .] a humane science" and included such later luminaries as R. D. Laing in England and Foucault and Félix Guattari in France (Poster 278). Like Foucault investigating the relationship between psychological and social structures, Gilles Deleuze and Guattari, in *Anti-Oedipus* and other writings, produced cultural analyses that map the "psychology" of contemporary social forms—what they term *schizoanalysis*—and that are centrally important to cultural studies and postmodern theory.

Generally, psychoanalytic theory

♦ engages a "hermeneutics of suspicion" about observable reality, maintaining that actions, beliefs, and identities have deep psychological causes not easily seen or even easily unearthed by analysis;

♦ works to elucidate the hidden, psychological causes of human behavior;

♦ sometimes correlates the workings of human psychology to the workings of social systems, arguing that since human beings create culture, societies will reflect or be structured like human thinking patterns, desires, and drives; and

♦ values art and language as coded systems of signs that might, when analyzed, reveal concealed motivations by artists, general human thinking patterns, or structural beliefs within a culture.

FEMINIST THEORY, GENDER STUDIES, AND SEXUALITY THEORY

A third strain of critical theory originates in feminist social politics and later is subsumed under the general rubric of "cultural theory." Known as feminist theory, gender studies, and sexuality theory, these branches of critical theory share at least one assumption with Marxist theories: namely, that when trying to understand a text's meaning or significance, one must go beyond formal analysis and include analysis of the text's cultural context. "Cultural context" for Marxist critics means the economic and class systems; for feminist theory and gender/sexuality studies, "cultural context" means when and where the text was written and how people felt about and "legislated" the body at that time and place.

The origins of feminist theory are difficult to determine because defining an origin depends upon primary definitions of the term. It is possible, that is, to see feminism beginning with Sappho of Lesbos in Greece and continuing through the "Woman Question" and various women's suffrage movements of the nineteenth and twentieth centuries; certainly, writers such as political theorist Mary Wollstonecraft, who published *A Vindication of the Rights of Woman* in 1792, would be included in a history of feminist writers. The term *feminism* in English, however, originates in the 1890s to refer to movements advocating women's legal and cultural rights, and so it is customary to align feminist *theory* with late-nineteenth-century and twentieth-century writing.

As many introductions to critical theory note, feminist theory is generally separated into three "waves" or movements associated with social feminism. First-wave feminist theory can be dated roughly from the mid-nineteenth century (Margaret Fuller was writing in the 1840s, and Susan B. Anthony helped to start the National Women's Suffrage Association in America in 1869) and ran through the Progressive Era to the early 1960s. It tended to focus on the problem of male sexism, patriarchy (male-centered and male-dominated societies) and female exclusion from public culture. The second wave began in the 1960s and developed through the 1970s women's liberation movements to the present. It is often characterized as an ongoing conversation between three types of feminist analysis: American, British, and French feminist theory. The American scholar Elaine Showalter coined the term *gynocriticism* to describe criticism that analyzes how women are portrayed in texts, how the literary canon is formed and revised, and how women's literary forms and writing techniques are defined. French feminism, in contrast, tends to be aligned with psychoanalytic theory. For example, the French feminist Hélène Cixous defined *l'écriture feminine* as writing by women in a woman's voice, a language, different from men's language, that springs forth from the unique character of a woman's body and biological rhythms (see Marks and Courtivron; Moi). British feminism tends to be Marxist in orientation and focus on how capitalist ideologies construct women's identities and roles. Donna Landry and Gerald MacLean have noted the newer strain of "materialist feminism" that combines neo-Marxist analyses with feminist politics (as in work by Juliet Mitchell, Michèle Barrett, Parveen Adams and Elizabeth Cowie, and Nancy Hartsock) (247–51). All of these second-wave branches of feminist theory examine women's place within the literary, critical, psychological, cultural, and linguistic history of culture.[4] The third wave of feminist theory, commonly referred to as "postfeminism," dates from the 1990s and is characterized by a diminished focus on legal rights of women and an increased focus on women's polymorphous pleasure, sexual power, individualism, and conscious manipulation of social and sexual roles and taboos in capitalist economies. It includes work by sex activists and poststructuralist cultural critics such as Laura Mulvey, Susan Faludi, and Naomi Wolf; new voices in feminism that work for broader, more inclusive definitions of women's desires, lived activities, and identities, such as that of Chandra Talpade Mohanty and Jee Yeun Lee; and new arenas for feminist investigation, such as global feminism and ecofeminism.

What all feminist theories have in common, however, is an assumption, shared with Marxist theories, that one cannot divorce analysis of bodies or (bodies of) texts from ideological context. One of the rallying cries of 1970s feminism was, "The personal is the political." Sex (biology) and gender (the socialized rules of male or female behavior) must be considered when analyzing texts and culture, if only because cultural values associated with sex and gender have been determining factors throughout history for the degree of personal and political freedom allowed to women in patriarchal cultures.

Because feminist theory attempts to theorize women's social roles and cultural productions, it must make broad claims about women's natures, social positions, and language use. Such broad claims are constantly called into question by dynamic feminist theory itself as it comes to terms with the national, religious, geographical, racial, sexual, and class differences between women around the world. In fact, "movement analysis" was challenged as early as the 1970s by women of color, such as Toni Cade (later Toni Cade Bambara), who presented women's lives that differed from the white, middle-class activists' identity paradigm (see also Collins and James and Sharpley-Whiting for discussions of black feminisms; on postcolonial feminisms, see McCann). Feminist theory since 1970 has thus fractured into many hybrid theoretical areas of investigation, such as postcolonial feminism, Marxist feminism, black feminism/womanism, and lesbian studies. Because feminist theory radically raises the question of "difference," it is congenial to these alliances with other critical theories. Feminist theory includes work in psychoanalysis and studies of motherhood, such as Nancy Chodorow's *The Reproduction of Mothering: Psychoanalysis and the Sociology of Gender;* historical investigations of the role of women in history and literary culture, such as the essays in Shari Benstock's *The Private Self: Theory and Practice of Women's Autobiographical Writings* or Sandra M. Gilbert and Susan Gubar's pivotal study of nineteenth-century British fiction, *The Madwoman in the Attic;* investigations of women and the law, such as Drucilla Cornell's *Beyond Accommodation: Ethical Feminism, Deconstruction, and the Law;* studies of women in art forms other than literature, such as cinema studies (e.g., Teresa de Lauretis's *Alice Doesn't: Feminism, Semiotics, Cinema*); and studies of androgyny (e.g., Carolyn Heilbrun's *Toward a Recognition of Androgyny*), often stemming from interest generated in the topic by Virginia Woolf in first-wave feminist writing. Calling herself a socialist feminist, Donna Haraway claimed in "The Cyborg Manifesto" that "cyborgs" provide a new androgynous wedding of machine and human that is postpatriarchal and thus important to feminism. In feminist race theories, writers interrogate received notions of privilege as a nexus of race, class, and gender identities: bell hooks investigates how race blindness causes lacunae in feminist analyses; Gayatri Chakravorty Spivak works to formulate a theory of subaltern speech and postcolonial women's writing; and Hortense Spillers has argued that feminism is often hijacked by feminists unaware of their complicity with Anglocentrism, liberalism, patriarchy, and imperialism. The newer field of masculinity studies may be understood as a direct outgrowth of feminist theory's investigation of the social importance of sex and gender.

Deeply indebted to feminist theory's introduction of the gendered body into theoretical and political discourse, gay and lesbian theories also developed a broad spectrum of questions about sexuality and sexual practice in relation to social structures, freedom, and social power. As with feminism, gay and lesbian activism goes far back in history; but just as feminist *theory* derived from the women's suffrage movements of the nineteenth and twentieth centuries, gay and lesbian *theories* derive from the gay liberation movements of the 1970s and 1980s, in the United States following the Stonewall Riot in New York in 1969. Gay rights activists formed political organizations to protest discrimination and violence against homosexuals (homophobia) and to confront heterosexual oppression (heterosexism) in all aspects of culture. Gay liberation "had two main goals; to resist persecution and discrimination against a sexual minority, and to encourage gay people themselves to develop a pride in their sexual identities" through consciousness raising and "coming out" (Selden, Widdowson, and Brooker 243). Growing out of these separatist movements of the 1970s and 1980s, gay theory and lesbian theory study gay and lesbian identities. The theories go well beyond identifying and arguing for the importance of gay and lesbian characters in novels; the theories ask what role sexual identity plays in the production and reception of texts themselves, and they investigate how same-sex desire forms literary tropes that are revelations of cultural values and of how straight and gay/lesbian identities are defined and determined. Gay and lesbian theories also prompted a new interest in "straight" discourse and straight cultural identity, defined now not as the "normal" (versus the "deviant" homosexual identity) but as one of many possibilities for identity construction and subjectivity and demanding analysis as a cultural construct (see Abelove, Barale, and Halperin; Colebrook; and Lancaster and di Leonardo).

Related to gay and lesbian theories, "queer theory" emerged in the 1980s through the work of political activist groups such as Queer Nation and ActUp; it is the study of "queer" or "border" identities performed by individuals challenging hegemonic sexual or gender classifications (predicated on the binary terms male/

female) within Western societies. Queer theory goes beyond gay/lesbian homosexual liberation theory to investigate bisexual, transgender, transvestite, nongendered, and transsexual identity, but also sadomasochistic, group, and other sex practices and sex-related practices (such as body mutilation) termed "deviant" within the hegemonic culture as well as prosex practices (such as pornography) that first- and second-wave feminist theory typically condemned. It has also come to designate all definitions of identity that elude or stand outside of those accepted by bourgeois heteronormative patriarchy. Queer theory, in fact, challenges the entire notion of *sexual identity*, particularly as that term is understood to mean one of two "natural" sexes, male or female (see Corber and Valocchi; Jagose; and Sullivan).

Like feminist theory, queer theory investigates how power relates to identity and investigates how sex and gender identities are culturally determined. But queer theory avoids the "identity politics" promoted by much feminist theory. Judith Butler, for example, argues against a normative notion of gender and for a performative definition of gender and the self; Eve Sedgwick contends that sexuality is linked to gender construction but must be understood as a continuum of desire and relations between persons of the same (chromosomal) sex. Queer theory thereby focuses on difference and marginality as positive and necessary, and it historicizes sexuality itself. Foucault's *History of Sexuality: An Introduction* illustrates how definitions of sexuality may be constructed over time through discourses within cultures (and are not, therefore, something "natural" with which we are born). Foucault also contends that, after the nineteenth century, sexuality became loaded with enormous cultural weight: "as sex learned an infinity of new paths into discourse, the value of truth itself—in particular the truth of individual identity—came to be lodged in the uncovery [sic] or expression of the truth of sexuality" (Sedgwick, "Gender Criticism" 280). The study of literature is particularly important to queer theory, for it reveals the over-determined nature of sexuality and the fact that how a culture defines "proper" gender/sexuality relations will reveal structures of power and dominance within that culture. Since Foucault's study, Leo Bersani, Michael Warner, and Monique Wittig have illustrated how investigations of identity reveal its essential "queerness" and the continuing need to elucidate the intersection of political power, disciplinary technologies, subjectivity, and desire.

Thus feminist, gay and lesbian, and queer theories—and related studies such as masculinity studies or gender and sexuality studies—all assert in different ways that

- ◆ the personal is the political—even when a theory posits that sex identity is essentialist, it will acknowledge that personal "identity" is formed largely or completely by culture as a *discourse*, and consequently it serves specific political ends;

- ◆ "male," "female," "sex," "gender," "sexuality," and "sexual practice" are culturally loaded terms that need to be examined politically and philosophically because they may encode meanings and promote practices that limit human choices and freedoms; and

- ◆ literature as well as critical theory, rhetoric and composition, and linguistics and discourse analysis can reveal the socially and historically constructed nature of gender relations and offer alternatives to hegemonic norms for gender and sexuality—cultural texts (written, oral, and visual) both support and dismantle essentialist notions of sexual identity, but they can also show how in the twentieth century sexuality becomes the locus where cultural power is marked and negotiated.

THEORIES OF RACE, ETHNICITY, AND NATIONHOOD

A fourth strain of critical theory, like Marxist and feminist theory, concerns political and cultural power—the use of it and resistance to it—and the degrees of freedom accorded to people within cultures. Sometimes grouped together as "cultural theory," these theories—of race, ethnicity, and nationhood—are concerned with the *de facto* and *de jure* rights accorded to people of different racial or ethnic backgrounds and with how people of different races, ethnicities, and/or nations are represented in written, spoken, and visual texts. Like feminist theory, these theories focus on identity politics; and, like feminist and Marxist theories, race/ethnicity theories combine easily with other critical theories. For example, one may find race theory merging with feminist theory to form Latina feminist theory, as in the work of Denise Chavez,

Pat Mora, and Gloria Anzaldúa; one may find ethnicity theory merging with psychoanalytic theory to form Jewish Holocaust trauma theory, as in the work of Marianne Hirsch or Cathy Caruth; or one might find deconstruction and semiotics merging with Native American writing, as in the work of Gerald Vizenor. There are at least two major branches of race/ethnicity theories: multicultural criticism, which can be broken down into many subgroups based on racial categories; and ethnic studies, including postcolonial theory and diasporic studies.

Multicultural criticism is often associated with critical theory in the United States and includes African American, Native American, Latino/Latina, and Asian American textual criticism (see Taylor et al.). Paul Lauter, a leading multiculturalist, has written in *Canons and Contexts* that the literature of the United States should be understood less as a national literature than as comparative literature, for it represents the literary heritages of many racial groups with distinct language origins and cultural histories (48–96). This perspective advocates the study of *differences* between racial groups and how those differences form and uniquely imprint the group's cultural productions, such as literature (see Niro on race). In the 1990s, multiculturalist perspectives such as those of Charles Taylor were hotly debated, for they challenged the traditionally accepted idea of the United States as a "melting-pot society" where immigrant groups eventually assimilated into a unique but uniform "American-ness." Multiculturalists argue that this melting pot is not desirable, and never existed anyway in the extremely race- and class-conscious culture of the United States. In response to this movement, the American Studies Association promotes multicultural approaches to United States history and culture internationally and is linked to the development of American studies departments and programs in universities worldwide. Similarly, multicultural "ethnic studies" programs, such as Africana studies and Latino/Latina studies, are now common at many universities. In 1973, the Modern Language Association formed the Commission on Minority Groups and the Study of Language and Literature (now the Committee on the Literatures of Peoples of Color in the U.S. and Canada), which since 1974 has sponsored conference panels, colloquia, and conferences to promote the study of multicultural literatures. The MLA also published new guides for the study of multicultural literatures (see Ruoff and Ward; Greenblatt and Gunn). The term *multiculturalism* is now out of favor, and the preferred terminology used to describe race/ethnicity theories is *critical race theory*, though this theory has a more globalized, political focus than the earlier *multiculturalism* (see Essed and Goldberg; Appiah and Gates).

Arguably it was African American theory and feminist theory that spawned the multiculturalist movement in the United States. Defined originally by W. E. B. Du Bois to describe the black American's double identity as both a black person of African heritage and an American (*The Souls of Black Folk*), the idea of "double consciousness" characterizes the cultural position of minority groups and women in the United States. Like Marxist, feminist, gay/lesbian, and postcolonial theories, African American theory asserts that textual arts must be studied not only for their aesthetic beauty but also for their ideological import. With their unique history going back to the beginnings of New World development, African American theory and Africana studies strive to recover and define the richness and diversity of past and present aesthetic productions of peoples of African heritage; to reconstruct lost, or revise misguided, history about African American people and cultures; and to develop a canon of African American cultural artifacts (art, literature, music, philosophy). Some of this literary art is found in the *Norton Anthology of African American Literature* (Gates and McKay), a vitally important source for the institutionalizing of African American literature. The development of African American theory and criticism is divided into a number of stages, e.g., late nineteenth- and early-twentieth-century social criticism, the Harlem Renaissance in the 1920s, the Black Arts Movement in the mid- to late 1960s, a formalist movement of the 1970s, and a cultural studies stage from the 1980s onward, and perhaps in the twenty-first century a New Black Aesthetic (see Gates, "African American Criticism"; Leitch, *American* 332–65; Mason; and Ellis). Black feminist criticism—in work by Alice Walker, Barbara Christian, Hazel Carby, hooks, Spillers, Patricia Hill Collins, and others—has also blossomed, focusing the insights of feminist theory on the particular context of African American women's lives.

Some scholars characterize African American theory as part of the more general and diverse field of ethnic studies known as diaspora studies. Diaspora studies analyzes what Homi Bhabha calls "unhomeliness," or how groups exiled or forced to migrate from their indigenous territories through enslavement, through war, or through the search for economic security settle in other territories and struggle to maintain cultural identity in the face of geographic change and the continuing influence of encroaching cultures (see, for example, *The Location of Culture*). These might include groups as different as African Americans initially brought to the Americas through the slave trade; the "Windrush Generation" of black writers in Great Britain; Native American tribes forced to relocate to reservation lands; Asian peoples who migrated to the United States during frontier expansion; Jewish people exiled through pogroms in Europe; and citizens exiled from the Balkan states after the wars of the 1990s (see Robin Cohen; Braziel and Mannur).

Multicultural criticism and diasporic studies are also closely related to postcolonial theory, the study of the power relations between Western nations and the territories they colonize (Tyson 365). Emerging after Indian independence from British rule and the war for freedom in Algeria, as well as other wars against colonizing powers in African, Asian, and Latin American countries, postcolonial theory examines the social mechanisms of imperialism and colonialism, analyzing the relationships between colonizing and colonized cultures as well as new actions and attitudes allowed by independence movements and national independence. The ideas of Edward Said, Spivak, and Bhabha, as well as work by Ngugi wa Thiong'o, Chinua Achebe, and Benita Parry, are usually the starting points for students of this theory.[5] A key idea for Bhabha is "hybridity," an idea that harks back to Du Bois's notion of double consciousness and is linked to the idea that postcolonial identity—and indeed any national culture—is always mixed, always heterogeneous, always in flux. Postcolonial theory arises "in a cultural context informed by the attempt to build a new hybrid culture that transcends the past but still draws on the vestigial echoes of precolonial culture, the remnants of the colonial culture, and the continuing legacy of traditions of anticolonial resistance" (Booker 153). In this sense, postcolonial theory also identifies Eurocentrism and involves study of precolonial and colonial states of postcolonial cultures and art.

Postcolonial theorists' work may combine other critical theories with specific national histories or analysis of Eurocentrism and colonial politics. For example, Aimé Césaire, whose pamphlet *Discours sur le colonialisme* developed a theory of "négritude" important to later African American theory, was a poet; the Martinique-born Frantz Fanon, whose book *The Wretched of the Earth* is a key text in postcolonial studies, was a psychoanalyst. The Palestinian-born Said was a humanist literary critic who, in *Orientalism,* articulated the Occident's four-thousand-year history of constructing stereotypes and literary tropes of the Orient. Spivak describes herself as a "practical deconstructionist feminist Marxist" (qtd. in Leitch, *Norton* 2193). She is largely responsible for the creation of "subaltern studies" within the academy. *Subaltern* is a military term meaning "of lower rank," and it was used by Spivak and the Subaltern Studies group to designate the study of colonized peoples, women, minorities, and the working class (Childers and Hentzi 288; also see Guha). In the 1990s and after, postcolonialist critics analyzed the literary work of authors from India, Australia, the West Indies, Canada, Africa, Southeast Asia, and other postcolonial nations and regions, while others traced the history of postcolonialism itself (Ashcroft, Griffiths, and Tiffin; and Young). More recently, some critics point to political figures in Latin America, Africa, and Asia who are defining their postcolonial identity as real political opposition to global capitalism (see San Juan). Globalization theory analyzes capitalism as a system intent upon global economic and cultural domination; it is linked to the study of "cultural imperialism" (see Jameson and Miyoshi). Global studies programs, often offering cross-disciplinary academic majors, are now common at U.S. universities.

Generally, race and ethnicity theories maintain that

- ◆ race, color, or national origin are culturally constructed categories that serve ideological ends, and they *matter* in the local and global networks that distribute and control power;

- ◆ there are distinct yet, paradoxically, constantly fluctuating relations between dominant races or cultural centers and dominated races or cultural margins, and these relations must be surveyed and revealed if subaltern peoples are to gain recognition and power;

- ◆ art serves the ends of both oppressors and oppressed, for while it can discipline minority peoples and spread dominant ideologies, it can also be a vehicle that exposes oppression by the dominant class, race, or nation and thus be a vehicle for resistance to power by dominated peoples; and

- ◆ the role of the critic is ideological, to work toward the equal distribution of goods and freedoms among all peoples of the world through the analysis of texts and the ideologies they promote or resist: the critic is a "cultural worker."

II. Cultural Studies

All of the critical perspectives described in this chapter might be understood as cultural theories. What is called "cultural studies" shares many characteristics with these: cultural studies is leftist in political orientation, ideological in aim, and cultural in focus. Yet cultural studies as a disciplinary focus tends to attend to specific material aspects of culture—elements of culture as diverse as media studies and theater, food, religion, hip-hop music, sex clubs, maps and cartography, political parties, and motorcycle gangs.

For example, when one goes to a national bookstore chain these days, one is confronted by whole rows of historical romance novels. These are easily identified by their cheap print quality, glossy and semierotic covers, and lurid titles. Clearly, they are not what T. S. Eliot would have defined as "high literature." So why do we buy these books so obsessively? While a formalist critic might answer by discussing the lack of standards permeating the art world today, and a moralist critic might cite our own moral failings (philistines like bad books), a cultural studies critic would try to determine what cultural *work* these novels perform without judging their value or lack of value in aesthetic terms. Janice Radway, for example, has sketched complex relations between readers and their search for pleasure, the publishing industry and its demand for profit, and literature as produced by writers with aesthetic as well as political aims.

But cultural studies is not just the study of popular culture; it also can focus on the elements of "high" culture—such as literature, politics, or even science—to decode what seems like a natural or politically neutral element of culture to reveal how it resists, participates in, or even helps to form ideological structures. It can also analyze how race, class, gender, and sexual politics are contested by different groups within a culture; for instance, the "culture wars" of the late twentieth century are firmly within the purview of cultural studies (see, e.g., Gates's *Loose Canons*). In this sense, cultural studies analyses are loosely predicated on older forms of "cultural semiotics."

Cultural studies also has many overlaps with what has come to be known as postmodern theory, or theories of postmodernism. *Postmodernism* is a term denoting the post-1945 phase of Cold War history in which First World nations fashion postindustrial economies and in which capitalism increasingly becomes global in scope and influence. Key theorists of postmodernism, such as Jameson, Jean-François Lyotard, Jean Baudrillard, Deleuze, and Linda Hutcheon, have inflected this position differently, but generally, sociocultural postmodernism may be defined by an increased standard of living in First World nations, campaigns for global democracy, and escalating medical, military, and communication technologies; it is often also characterized by violence and

> diminished importance of the nation-state and of manufacturing industries; the increased importance of service and entertainment industries, communication technologies, and the military-industrial complex; ever more sophisticated war technologies; an increased disparity between rich and poor within and between nations and a concomitant rise in global exploitation of the poor; greater ethnic "tribalism"; more exploitation of diminishing natural resources; and a fracturing of markets to the advantage of capitalist production and ideology. (Elias xxiii)[6]

Studies of literary postmodernism illustrate its relation to modernist poetics as well as to postwar culture (see McHale; Natoli and Hutcheon; and Woods).

Cultural studies also shares many features with Frankfurt School cultural critique. As noted above, the Frankfurt School writers believed that all aspects of a culture needed to be subject to critique (analysis) in order to reveal the cultural relationships between ideology and aesthetics. Particularly in the work of Adorno and Horkheimer, this focus on the "culture industry" was pronounced. Yet Gramsci is the figure most central to cultural studies. One of the leading figures in the formation of the Communist Party in Italy in the 1920s (activity that led him to be tried and imprisoned for nine years in fascist Italy), Gramsci attempted to revise Marxist theory to account for why workers' revolutions had not occurred in Europe according to Marx's dialectical model of historical process. Observing that the proletariat not only did not rise up against the bourgeoisie that oppressed them but even seemed to support political parties and movements unsympathetic to their interests, Gramsci formulated the concept of *hegemony*. Hegemony offers an alternative to vulgar Marxism's base/superstructure model (see Macey). Like Louis Althusser's policeman, who "hails" the subject/citizen, hegemony operates in popular culture that is generated by the whole of civil society and in which the oppressed willingly participate. A Gramscian model of class relations is dynamic: the governing or ruling class is always striving to win the consent of the governed, essentially by seducing them through cultural productions. We work hard to buy and consume the cultural products (things, ideas) that enslave us. Cultural studies thus "strives to analyze the hegemonic practices by which social groups are bound (institutionally, intellectually, emotionally, and economically) to dominant social forms. And it examines how forces of resistance creatively intervene in those practices. Since hegemony works through and on every social site and practice, cultural studies has deemed anything a potential object of study" (Leitch, *Norton* 1896). Studying all forms of mass culture (comics, health products, television) can reveal how popular culture in civil society is aimed at gaining the assent of the masses to the hegemonic power of the dominant class (Leitch, *Norton* 1135–37). Such study may also reveal how consumers of mass culture might resist hegemony and consider alternatives to the enslaving seductions of consumer capitalism.

Raymond Williams has been a major influence in cultural studies; a committed socialist, he taught at Cambridge University until retiring in 1983. Defining "cultural materialism" as a new combination of Marxist materialism and cultural analysis, Williams examined how "keywords" (culture, art, etc.) operated within the entire cultural terrain of a society. In *The Long Revolution*, Williams identified three approaches to culture that he believed must be integrated (the ideal, the documentary, and the "social") with the purpose of reconstituting a culture's "structure of feeling," or its shared values. "Structure of feeling" is not quite ideology and not quite values; it is the thing that distinguishes cultures from one another—for example (Williams notes) as one generation (e.g., the 1950s generation) will perceive its culture differently than will the generation following it. A "structure of feeling" is not an abstract but a *lived* understanding of culture that seems to come from nowhere, but it in fact grows organically out of experience.

A third figure central to cultural studies is Clifford Geertz. An American who gained prominence for his work in cultural anthropology, Geertz is best known in critical theory and cultural studies for his theory of "thick description," in which social systems are examined as networks of sign systems. For Geertz, influenced by the earlier work of Claude Lévi-Strauss, culture is an accumulated body of sign systems and can be read as a text, a "fabric of meaning." Implicit in Geertz's work are the ideas that there is no "right" way to organize a social system, that all cultures are produced by and produce human action based on human need, and that anthropology and the other human sciences cannot impose interpretive meaning on a society from outside of its own meaning systems but should work from "local knowledge" outward to larger conceptual frameworks.

These approaches animate cultural studies' continual engagement "with the political, economic, erotic, social, and ideological" that "entails the study of all the relations between the elements in a whole way of life" (Nelson, Treichler, and Grossberg 14). Gramsci's neo-Marxist model and the post-1950s work of Williams were taken up and modified in various ways by British scholars Richard Hoggart, Stuart Hall, and E. P. Thompson through the 1970s. After publishing *The Uses of Literacy* in 1957, Hoggart founded the University of Birmingham's Center for Contemporary Cultural Studies (BCCCS), which stressed the importance of literary studies to cultural analysis. In 1968, Hall replaced Hoggart as director of the BCCCS. Hall's involvement in the 1960s New Left movement in Britain had led him to found *The New Left Review*; after an appointment as lecturer in film and mass media studies he moved to the University of Birmingham in 1964. Important cultural studies scholars such as Carby, Dick Hebdige, and Paul Gilroy worked with Hall when he served as director for the BCCCS and shifted the emphases of the center from literature to cultural practices and institutions. Since that time, Hall's is perhaps the name most closely associated with cultural studies. In 1979, Hall stepped down as director of the BCCCS, which, under more recent directors, has focused on subcultures, colonial/postcolonial cultures, and feminism (Leitch, *Norton* 1895–97; Childers and Hentzi 28–29). Today, scholars such as Hebdige, Mulvey, Cary Nelson, Cornel West, Andrew Ross, and Peter Stallybrass practice cultural studies methodologies on both sides of the Atlantic, writing about topics as diverse as sports, heavy metal rock music, television shows, film, Shakespearean texts, revolutionary poster art, widow burning in India, crime fiction, chaos theory, and cultural representations of AIDS. The French poststructuralist writer Roland Barthes famously analyzed striptease as a semiotic practice; Radway has examined the relation between the Book-of-the-Month Club and commodification; Meaghan Morris has analyzed the social function of shopping malls; Laura Kipnis has examined the social significance of pornography; a group of scholars calling themselves the Project on Disney analyzed Disney's worlds of entertainment. The popular, mass culture, the culture of everyday life: these are the subjects of cultural studies analyses (see Hartley).

Cultural studies is now well established, with its own international societies and PhD programs throughout the United States—to the point of generating a backlash of criticism. Conservative critics cite the tendency of cultural studies analyses to focus on the extreme and "taboo" within popular culture (pornography, fetishism, body piercing, civilian militias, etc.) and thus accuse this analysis of pandering to a diminishing market for scholarly work. Sensationalism sells, often when a remarkable, scholarly study of eighteenth-century lyric poetry will not, and so, say these critics, this work can encourage younger scholars to go further and further away from literature and criticism and closer to publishing equivalents of the Jerry Springer Show. Other critics of cultural studies accuse the field of sacrificing scholarly rigor to ideological agendas. These critics note the overwhelmingly Marxist character of cultural studies and the devotion of its practitioners to Marxist ideology. This objection forms a corollary claim for critics such as Alan Sokal: that in fact cultural studies is bad sociology and/or bad science, investigation that has sacrificed scientific inquiry for ideological indoctrination. To some critics, cultural studies methodology seems circular or predicated upon suspect representative samples: critics often discover exactly the capitalist exploitation and consumer "resistance" they set out to find, often basing their assertions on an extremely limited field of inquiry or number of examples.

These objections have been answered repeatedly by cultural critics, and after the initial burst of cultural studies work in the 1970s and 1980s, and in the face of backlash in the 1990s, cultural studies has become increasingly self-aware about its own methodologies and claims. Today, cultural studies programs at major U.S. universities argue that the field is central to new definitions of civic humanism. Critical readers and anthologies by Simon During; Houston Baker, Manthai Diawara, and Ruth Lindeborg; Lawrence Grossberg, Cary Nelson, and Paula Treichler; Andrew Milner; and others attest to the growing popularity and complexity of the field. Supported by academic presses, international societies, and scholarly journals, cultural studies has growing links to digital culture (such the weblogs of Michael Bérubé and John McGowan) and new studies of democracy and ethics (e.g., the work of Amanda Anderson), and it offers a field of inquiry that may vitally link all aspects of English studies.

Where Is Theory Now?

As the twenty-first century begins, critical theory and cultural studies are both defending themselves against detractors and re-organizing themselves in the face of new institutional and political environments. After the collapse of the Soviet Union and East Berlin, Marxist theory—the heart of critical theory—seemed increasingly out of date to many in and outside of the profession. In 1999, Sokal and Jean Bricmont published *Fashionable Nonsense: Postmodern Intellectuals' Abuse of Science,* which purported to reveal the poor research foundations of cultural studies; only a short time passed before David Horowitz and other former leftists attacked academic theory for its political extremism and monologism. The controversial anthology *Theory's Empire* (edited by Daphne Patai and Will Corral) was published in 2005 and reprinted decades of articles that argued that theory had become self-referential, illogical, and/or just plain silly. Facing challenges from a new U.S. economic liberalism allied with capitalism, advancing religious fundamentalism of various stripes, the aftermath of twenty years of poststructuralist theory that challenged the basis of critique, and the decimation of funding for the humanities on university campuses, theory found itself caught by surprise, almost speechless as it faced attacks from both the Left and the Right, within and outside of the academy (see Bérubé and Nelson).

Critical theory and cultural studies are fighting back, however. Studies in digital technologies and digital cultures—supported by the Electronic Literature Organization, *Electronic Book Review,* and commercial outlets such as Eastgate Systems—are thriving as the global community increasingly is defined by access to and control of technology (see, e.g., Trend). The field of disability studies, which gained momentum in the 1990s, is now also thriving as an important vehicle for critiquing old definitions of "normality" and the body, and for introducing new definitions of both, into critical and cultural discourse (see, e.g., Davis). At the 2005 meetings of both the School of Criticism and Theory at Cornell University and of the Modern Language Association in Washington, DC, many famous intellectuals expressed an overwhelming need for theory to regroup and redefine itself in the post-9/11 period. Critical theory either will participate in the polarization of discourses common to twentieth-century political environments, preaching to the choir and retreating even further into the academy, or it will find new ways to critique paradigmatic aesthetic and cultural structures and learn to engage actively with its detractors—thereby creating a new, vibrant debate and dialogue about values and ethics and art in the twenty-first century.

Notes

1. See "Selected Bibliography of Theory and Criticism" in Leitch, *Norton Anthology* 2525–52, and Additional Resources, below.

2. See Bottomore; Wiggershaus; Feenberg; and the introductions in Arato and Gebhardt for discussions of critical theory and the Frankfurt School.

3. See, e.g., Hennessy and Ingraham; Robinson.

4. See Messer-Davidow; Leitch, *American* (307); Selden, Widdowson, and Brooker (124–32); Bressler, Chapter 8; and Additional Resources, below.

5. At this point in the critical conversation, there are many, many good critical readers and studies of postcolonialism and global studies. See Additional Resources, below.

6. For additional introductions to postmodernism, see Best and Kellner; Jameson; and Chen.

Works Cited

Abelove, Henry, Michèle Aina Barale, and David M. Halperin, eds. *The Lesbian and Gay Studies Reader*. New York: Routledge, 1993.

Appiah, Kwame Anthony, and Henry Louis Gates, Jr., eds. *The Dictionary of Global Culture*. New York: Knopf, 1996.

Arato, Andrew, and Eike Gebhardt, eds. *The Essential Frankfurt School Reader*. New York: Continuum, 1997.

Ashcroft, Bill, Gareth Griffiths, and Helen Tiffin. *The Empire Writes Back: Theory and Practice in Post-Colonial Literatures*. London: Routledge, 1989.

Baker, Houston A., Manthai Diawara, and Ruth H. Lindeborg, eds. *Black British Cultural Studies: A Reader*. Chicago: U of Chicago P, 1996.

Bannet, Eve Tavor. "Lukács, Georg." Groden and Kreiswirth 475–78.

Benstock, Shari. *The Private Self: Theory and Practice of Women's Autobiographical Writings*. Chapel Hill: U of North Carolina P, 1988.

Bérubé, Michael, and Cary Nelson, eds. *Higher Education under Fire: Politics, Economics, and the Crisis of the Humanities*. New York: Routledge, 1994.

Best, Steven, and Douglas Kellner. *Postmodern Theory: Critical Interrogations*. New York: Guilford, 1991.

Bhabha, Homi K. *The Location of Culture*. New York: Routledge, 1994.

Booker, M. Keith. *A Practical Introduction to Literary Theory and Criticism*. White Plains, NY: Longman, 1996.

Bottomore, Tom. *The Frankfurt School and Its Critics*. New York: Routledge, 2002.

Bottomore, Tom, et al., eds. *A Dictionary of Marxist Thought*. Oxford: Blackwell, 1983.

Brannigan, John. *New Historicism and Cultural Materialism*. Basingstoke, Eng.: Palgrave, 1998.

Braziel, Jana Evans, and Anita Mannur, eds. *Theorizing Diaspora: A Reader*. Malden, MA: Blackwell, 2003.

Bressler, Charles E. *Literary Criticism: An Introduction to Theory and Practice*. 3rd ed. Upper Saddle River, NJ: Prentice, 2002.

Cade, Toni, ed. *The Black Woman: An Anthology*. New York: NAL, 1970.

Césaire, Aimé. *Discours sur le Colonialisme*. 1955. *Discourse on Colonialism*. Trans. Joan Pinkham. New York: Monthly Review P, 1972.

Chen, Kuan-Hsing. "Post-Marxism: Between/beyond Critical Postmodernism." *Stuart Hall: Critical Dialogues in Cultural Studies*. Ed. David Morley and Kuan-Hsing Chen. London: Routledge, 1996. 309–25.

Childers, Joseph, and Gary Hentzi, eds. *The Columbia Dictionary of Modern Literary and Cultural Criticism*. New York: Columbia UP, 1995.

Chodorow, Nancy. *The Reproduction of Mothering: Psychoanalysis and the Sociology of Gender*. Berkeley: U of California P, 1999.

Cixous, Hélène. "The Laugh of the Medusa." Trans. Keith Cohen and Paula Cohen. *The Signs Reader: Women, Gender, and Scholarship.* Ed. Elizabeth Abel and Emily K. Abel. Chicago: U of Chicago P, 1993. 279–99.

Cohen, Robin. *Global Diasporas: An Introduction.* Seattle: U of Washington P, 1997.

Cohen, Walter. "Marxist Criticism." Greenblatt and Gunn 320–48.

Colebrook, Claire. *Gender.* New York: Palgrave, 2004.

Corber, Robert J., and Stephen Valocchi, eds. *Queer Studies: An Interdisciplinary Reader.* Malden, MA: Blackwell, 2003.

Cornell, Drucilla. *Beyond Accommodation: Ethical Feminism, Deconstruction, and the Law.* Lanham, MD: Rowan, 1999.

Davis, Lennard J. *The Disability Studies Reader.* New York: Routledge, 1997.

de Lauretis, Teresa. *Alice Doesn't: Feminism, Semiotics, Cinema.* Bloomington: Indiana UP, 1984.

Du Bois, W. E. B. *The Souls of Black Folk: Authoritative Text, Contexts, Criticism.* Ed. Henry Louis Gates, Jr., and Terri Hume Oliver. New York: Norton, 1999.

During, Simon, ed. *The Cultural Studies Reader.* New York: Routledge, 1993.

Eagleton, Terry. *Ideology: An Introduction.* London: Verso, 1991.

Eagleton, Terry, and Drew Milne, eds. *Marxist Literary Theory.* Oxford: Blackwell, 1996.

Elias, Amy J. *Sublime Desire: History and Post-1960s Fiction.* Baltimore: Johns Hopkins UP, 2001.

Ellis, Trey. "The New Black Aesthetic." *Callaloo* 38 (1989): 233–43.

Ellmann, Maud, ed. *Psychoanalytic Literary Criticism.* New York: Longman, 1994.

Essed, Philomena, and David Theo Goldberg, eds. *Race Critical Theories: Text and Context.* Malden, MA: Blackwell, 2002.

Fanon, Frantz. *The Wretched of the Earth.* Trans. Constance Farrington. New York: Grove, 1965.

Feenberg, Andrew. *Lukács, Marx, and the Sources of Critical Theory.* Oxford: Robertson, 1981.

Felman, Shoshana. *Writing and Madness: Literature/Philosophy/Psychoanalysis.* Trans. Martha Noel Evans. Palo Alto: Stanford UP, 2003.

Foucault, Michel. *The Foucault Reader.* Ed. Paul Rabinow. New York: Pantheon, 1984.

———. *The History of Sexuality: An Introduction.* 1978. Trans. Robert Hurley. New York: Vintage, 1990.

Freud, Sigmund. *The Interpretation of Dreams.* 1900. Trans. Joyce Crick. New York: Oxford UP, 1999.

Gallagher, Catherine, and Stephen Greenblatt. *Practicing New Historicism.* Chicago: U of Chicago P, 2001.

Gates, Henry Louis, Jr. "African American Criticism." Greenblatt and Gunn 303–19.

———. *Loose Canons: Notes on the Culture Wars.* New York: Oxford UP, 1992.

Gates, Henry Louis, Jr., and Nellie Y. McKay, gen. eds. *The Norton Anthology of African American Literature.* New York: Norton, 1997.

Geertz, Clifford. *The Interpretation of Cultures: Selected Essays.* New York: Basic, 1973.

Gilbert, Sandra M., and Susan Gubar. *The Madwoman in the Attic: The Woman Writer and the Nineteenth-Century Literary Imagination.* New Haven: Yale UP, 1984.

Gramsci, Antonio. *An Antonio Gramsci Reader: Selected Writings, 1916–1935.* Ed. David Forgas. New York: Schocken, 1988.

Greenblatt, Stephen, and Giles Gunn, eds. *Redrawing the Boundaries: The Transformation of English and American Literary Studies.* New York: MLA, 1992.

Groden, Michael, and Martin Kreiswirth, eds. *The Johns Hopkins Guide to Literary Theory and Criticism.* Baltimore: Johns Hopkins UP, 1994.

Grossberg, Lawrence, Cary Nelson, and Paula A. Treichler, eds. *Cultural Studies.* New York: Routledge, 1992.

Guha, Ranajit, ed. *A Subaltern Studies Reader, 1986–1995*. Minneapolis: U of Minnesota P, 1997.

Haraway, Donna J. "A Cyborg Manifesto: Science, Technology, and Socialist-Feminism in the Late Twentieth Century." *Simians, Cyborgs, and Women: The Reinvention of Nature*. New York: Routledge, 1991. 149–81.

Hartley, John. *A Short History of Cultural Studies*. Thousand Oaks, CA: Sage, 2003.

Heilbrun, Carolyn G. *Toward a Recognition of Androgyny*. New York: Knopf, 1973.

Hennessy, Rosemary, and Chrys Ingraham, eds. *Materialist Feminism: A Reader in Class, Difference, and Women's Lives*. New York: Routledge, 1997.

Hoggart, Richard. *The Uses of Literacy: Aspects of Working-Class Life, with Special Reference to Publications and Entertainments*. 1958. New York: Oxford UP, 1970.

Holland, Norman N. *The Dynamics of Literary Response*. New York: Oxford UP, 1968.

———. *Holland's Guide to Psychoanalytic Psychology and Literature-and-Psychology*. New York: Oxford UP, 1990.

hooks, bell. *Ain't I a Woman: Black Women and Feminism*. Boston: South End, 1981.

Hutcheon, Linda. *A Poetics of Postmodernism: History, Theory, Fiction*. New York: Routledge, 1988.

Irigaray, Luce. *Speculum of the Other Woman*. Trans. Gillian C. Gill. Ithaca: Cornell UP, 1985.

Jagose, Annamarie. *Queer Theory: An Introduction*. New York: New York UP, 1996.

James, Joy, and T. Denean Sharpley-Whiting, eds. *The Black Feminist Reader*. Malden, MA: Blackwell, 2000.

Jameson, Fredric. *Postmodernism, or, the Cultural Logic of Late Capitalism*. Durham: Duke UP, 1991.

Jameson, Fredric, and Masao Miyoshi, eds. *The Cultures of Globalization*. Durham: Duke UP, 1998.

Jung, Carl G. *The Portable Jung*. Trans. R. F. C. Hull. Ed. Joseph Campbell. New York: Viking, 1976.

Kipnis, Laura. *Bound and Gagged: Pornography and the Politics of Fantasy in America*. Durham, NC: Duke UP, 1999.

Klein, Melanie. *Love, Guilt and Reparation and Other Works, 1921–1945*. New York: Dell, 1977.

Kristeva, Julia. *The Kristeva Reader*. Ed. Toril Moi. New York: Columbia UP, 1986.

Lacan, Jacques. *Écrits: A Selection*. Trans. Bruce Fink. New York: Norton, 2002.

Lancaster, Roger N., and Micaela di Leonardo, eds. *The Gender/Sexuality Reader: Culture, History, Political Economy*. New York: Routledge, 1997.

Landry, Donna, and Gerald MacLean. "Materialist Feminisms." Groden and Kreiswirth 247–51.

Lauter, Paul. *Canons and Contexts*. New York: Oxford UP, 1991.

Leitch, Vincent B. *American Literary Criticism from the Thirties to the Eighties*. New York: Columbia UP, 1988.

———, gen. ed. *The Norton Anthology of Theory and Criticism*. New York: Norton, 2001.

Lukács, Georg. *History and Class Consciousness: Studies in Marxist Dialectics*. 1923. Trans. Rodney Livingstone. Cambridge: MIT P, 1971.

Macey, David. *The Penguin Dictionary of Critical Theory*. New York: Penguin, 2000.

Marks, Elaine, and Isabelle de Courtivron, eds. *New French Feminisms: An Anthology*. Amherst: U of Massachusetts P, 1980.

Marx, Karl. *A Contribution to the Critique of Political Economy*. 1859. Trans. S. W. Ryazanskaya. Ed. Maurice Dobb. London: Lawrence, 1971.

Mason, Theodore O., Jr. "African American Theory and Criticism." Groden and Kreiswirth 9–20.

McCann, Carole R., and Seung-Kyung Kim, eds. *Feminist Theory Reader: Local and Global Perspectives*. London: Routledge, 2003.

McHale, Brian. *Postmodernist Fiction*. New York, Routledge, 1987.

Messer-Davidow, Ellen. "Feminist Theory and Criticism." Groden and Kreiswirth 231–37.

Milner, Andrew. *Contemporary Cultural Theory: An Introduction*. Sydney: Allen, 1991.

Mitchell, Juliet, ed. *The Selected Melanie Klein*. New York: Free, 1987.

Moi, Toril, ed. *French Feminist Thought: A Reader*. Oxford: Blackwell, 1987.

Montrose, Louis. "New Historicisms." Greenblatt and Gunn 392–418.

Morris, Meaghan. "Things to Do with Shopping Centres." *Grafts: Feminist Cultural Criticism*. Ed. Susan Sheridan. London: Verso, 1988. 193–225.

Natoli, Joseph, and Linda Hutcheon, eds. *A Postmodern Reader*. Albany: SUNY P, 1993.

Nelson, Cary, Paula A. Treichler, and Lawrence Grossberg. "Cultural Studies: An Introduction." Grossberg, Nelson, and Treichler 1–22.

Niro, Brian. *Race*. New York: Palgrave, 2003.

Oliver, Kelly, ed. *The Portable Kristeva*. New York: Columbia UP, 2002.

Patai, Daphne, and Will H. Corral. *Theory's Empire: An Anthology of Dissent*. New York: Columbia UP, 2005.

Poster, Mark. "Foucault, Michel." Groden and Kreiswirth 277–79.

The Project on Disney. *Inside the Mouse: Work and Play at Disney World*. Durham, NC: Duke UP, 1995.

Radway, Janice A. *Reading the Romance: Women, Patriarchy, and Popular Literature*. Chapel Hill: U of North Carolina P, 1991.

Rasmussen, David M. "Critical Theory and Philosophy." *The Handbook of Critical Theory*. Ed. Rasmussen. Oxford: Blackwell, 1996. 11–38.

Robinson, Cedric J. *Black Marxism: The Making of the Black Radical Tradition*. London: Zed, 1983.

Ruoff, A. Lavonne Brown, and Jerry W. Ward, Jr. *Redefining American Literary History*. New York: MLA, 1990.

Ryan, Kiernan, ed. *New Historicism and Cultural Materialism: A Reader.* London: Arnold, 1996.

Said, Edward W. *Orientalism.* New York: Vintage, 1979.

San Juan, E., Jr. *Beyond Postcolonial Theory.* New York: St. Martin's, 1998.

Sedgwick, Eve Kosofsky. *Between Men: English Literature and Male Homosocial Desire.* New York: Columbia UP, 1985.

———. "Gender Criticism." Greenblatt and Gunn 271–302.

Selden, Raman, Peter Widdowson, and Peter Brooker. *A Reader's Guide to Contemporary Literary Theory.* 4th ed. London: Prentice, 1997.

Showalter, Elaine. "Toward a Feminist Poetics." *The New Feminist Criticism: Essays on Women, Literature, and Theory.* Ed. Showalter. New York: Pantheon, 1985. 125–43.

Sokal, Alan D., and Jean Bricmont. *Fashionable Nonsense: Postmodern Intellectuals' Abuse of Science.* New York: Picador, 1999.

Spillers, Hortense J. *Black, White, and in Color: Essays on American Literature and Culture.* Chicago: U of Chicago P, 2003.

Spivak, Gayatri Chakravorty. *In Other Worlds: Essays in Cultural Politics.* New York: Routledge, 1988.

Stirk, Peter M. R. *Critical Theory, Politics and Society: An Introduction.* London: Pinter, 2000.

Storey, John. *An Introductory Guide to Cultural Theory and Popular Culture.* Athens: U of Georgia P, 1993.

Sugg, Richard P., ed. *Jungian Literary Criticism.* Evanston, IL: Northwestern UP, 1992.

Sullivan, Nikki. *A Critical Introduction to Queer Theory.* New York: New York UP, 2003.

Taylor, Charles. *Multiculturalism and "The Politics of Recognition": An Essay.* Princeton, NJ: Princeton UP, 1992.

Taylor, Charles, et al. *Multiculturalism: Examining the Politics of Recognition.* Ed. Amy Gutmann. Princeton, NJ: Princeton UP, 1994.

Trend, David, ed. *Reading Digital Culture.* Malden, MA: Blackwell, 2001.

Tyson, Lois. *Critical Theory Today: A User-Friendly Guide*. New York: Garland, 1999.

Vice, Sue, ed. *Psychoanalytic Criticism: A Reader*. Cambridge: Polity, 1996.

Wharton, Edith. *The Age of Innocence*. 1920. New York: Modern Lib., 1999.

Wiggershaus, Rolf. *The Frankfurt School: Its History, Theories, and Political Significance*. Trans. Michael Robertson. Cambridge: Polity, 1994.

Williams, Raymond. *The Long Revolution*. 1961. Harmondsworth, Eng.: Penguin, 1965.

Wollstonecraft, Mary. *A Vindication of the Rights of Woman: An Authoritative Text, Backgrounds, Criticism*. Ed. Carol H. Poston. New York: Norton, 1975.

Woods, Tim. *Beginning Postmodernism*. Manchester: Manchester UP, 1999.

Young, Robert J. C. *Postcolonialism: An Historical Introduction*. Oxford: Blackwell, 2001.

Additional Resources

Anthologies of Primary Works in Critical Theory and Cultural Studies

Davis, Robert Con, and Ronald Schleifer. *Contemporary Literary Criticism: Literary and Cultural Studies*. 4th ed. New York : Longman, 1998.

Easthope, Antony, and Kate McGowan. *A Critical and Cultural Theory Reader*. Sydney: Allen, 1992.

Kaplan, Charles, and William Anderson. *Criticism: Major Statements*. Boston: Bedford, 2000.

Newton, K. M. *Twentieth-Century Literary Theory: A Reader*. New York: St. Martin's, 1998.

Rice, Philip, and Patricia Waugh. *Modern Literary Theory: A Reader*. 2nd ed. New York: Arnold, 1992.

Richter, David H. *Falling into Theory: Conflicting Views on Reading Literature*. Boston: Bedford, 1999.

Rivkin, Julie, and Michael Ryan. *Literary Theory: An Anthology.* Malden, MA: Blackwell, 1998.

Glossaries, Dictionaries, and Encyclopedias

Cuddon, J. A., and C. E. Preston. *The Penguin Dictionary of Literary Terms and Literary Theory.* 4th ed. London: Penguin, 1999.

Hawthorn, Jeremy. *A Concise Glossary of Contemporary Literary Theory.* 3d ed. London: Arnold, 1998.

Makaryk, Irene R. *Encyclopedia of Contemporary Literary Theory: Approaches, Scholars, Terms.* Toronto: U of Toronto P, 1993.

Marshall, Donald G. *Contemporary Critical Theory: A Selective Bibliography.* New York: MLA, 1993.

Murfin, Ross C., and Supryia M. Ray, *The Bedford Glossary of Critical and Literary Terms.* 2d ed. Boston: Bedford, 2003.

Wolfreys, Julian. *Critical Keywords in Literary and Cultural Theory.* Houndsmill, Basingstoke, Hamps.: Palgrave, 2004.

General Introductions

Barry, Peter. *Beginning Theory: An Introduction to Literary and Cultural Theory.* Manchester: Manchester UP, 1995.

Bertens, Hans. *Literary Theory: The Basics.* London: Routledge, 2001.

Carpenter, Scott. *Reading Lessons: An Introduction to Theory.* Upper Saddle River, NJ: Prentice, 2000.

Clayton, Jay. *The Pleasures of Babel: Contemporary American Literature and Theory.* New York: Oxford UP, 1993.

Collier, Peter, and Helga Geyer-Ryan. *Literary Theory Today.* Ithaca: Cornell UP, 1990.

Culler, Jonathan. *Literary Theory: A Very Short Introduction.* Oxford: Oxford UP, 1997.

Eagleton, Terry. *Literary Theory: An Introduction.* Minneapolis: U of Minnesota P, 1983.

Guerin, Wilfred L., et al. *A Handbook of Critical Approaches to Literature.* 5th ed. New York: Oxford UP, 2005.

Ryan, Michael. *Literary Theory: A Practical Introduction*. Malden, MA: Blackwell, 1999.

Resources for Teaching Feminist Theory

Eagleton, Mary. *Feminist Literary Theory: A Reader*. 2nd ed. Oxford: Blackwell, 1996.

Jackson, Stevi, and Jones, Jackie, eds. *Contemporary Feminist Theories*. New York: New York UP, 1998.

Kemp, Sandra, and Judith Squires, eds. *Feminisms*. Oxford: Oxford UP, 1997.

Warhol, Robyn R., and Diane Price Herndl. *Feminisms: An Anthology of Literary Theory and Criticism*. Rev. ed. New Brunswick, NJ: Rutgers UP, 1997.

Resources for Postcolonial Studies

Ashcroft, Bill, Gareth Griffiths, and Helen Tiffin, eds. *Key Concepts in Post-Colonial Studies*. London: Routledge, 1998.

———, eds. *The Post-Colonial Studies Reader*. London: Routledge, 1995.

Benson, Eugene, and L. W. Conolly, eds. *Encyclopedia of Post-Colonial Literatures in English*. 2 vols. 2d ed. Routledge, 2005.

Childs, Peter, and R. J. Patrick Williams, eds. *An Introduction to Post-Colonial Theory*. London: Prentice, 1997.

Chrisman, Laura, and Benita Parry, eds. *Postcolonial Theory and Criticism*. Cambridge: Brewer, 2000.

Gandhi, Leela. *Postcolonial Theory: A Critical Introduction*. New York: Columbia UP, 1998.

Mongia, Padmini, ed. *Contemporary Postcolonial Theory: A Reader*. London: Arnold, 1996.

Thieme, John, ed. *The Arnold Anthology of Post-Colonial Literatures in English*. London: Arnold, 1996.

Williams, Patrick, and Laura Chrisman, eds. *Colonial Discourse and Postcolonial Theory: A Reader*. New York: Columbia UP, 1994.

CHAPTER SIX

English Education

ROBERT P. YAGELSKI

State University of New York, Albany

When I teach methods courses for students seeking to become secondary school English teachers, my first assignment is always the same: I ask my students to collaborate with a small group of classmates on a statement of purpose for the study of English at the secondary level. I define the assignment as the kind of mission statement they might be asked to write for a department or school. In effect, they are to address the question of why students should be required to study English. The texts my students have produced for this assignment over the years have been predictable. Most of their statements extol the importance of reading and writing and the centrality of literacy in the curriculum; the value of clear and effective communication in "the real world," especially when it comes to applying for jobs; the joys of reading for pleasure and personal enrichment; and the advantages of being familiar with cultural knowledge embodied in great literary works. Once in a while, I receive a statement that mentions the importance of literacy in a democratic society, but such statements are rare. For the most part, my students never address the larger question of purpose: To what end do we help students learn to write and read so that they can succeed in school, find jobs, enjoy reading, or acquire cultural knowledge? What, ultimately, are we educating our students *for?* What do we want students to be and do with the literate knowledge and abilities we hope they develop? Is our purpose exclusively to help students acquire literacy skills so that they can earn good grades and good salaries? When I push the matter in this direction, many of my students resist. Successful in school themselves, few have thought about the purposes of education beyond the vague but widely accepted idea that success in school provides opportunities for students to succeed in life. The specific definitions of "success" are often left unarticulated and unexamined. In these discussions, it is usually taken for granted that school is not only important but also a *good;* furthermore, most of my students would never think to question the proposition that English is a vitally important subject in school and therefore also a *good.*

Admittedly, when I question students in this way, I am asking them to engage in an uncomfortable kind of inquiry that calls into question their deepest beliefs about the value of what they seek to do: to teach English. As a young graduate student, flush with the sense of possibility that seemed to characterize my chosen field—a sense of possibility that emerged from the lesson of my own upbringing that education is advancement—I too wholeheartedly embraced the view that English, as an academic subject, is a *good,* and I also resisted critiques of the field that called that view into question. Yet I propose that we *do* question the proposition that the study of English, as we currently understand it, is a *good.* I make such a proposal by way of pursuing the main purpose of this chapter, which is to examine English education as a subdiscipline of English studies. Such an examination is, in my view, pointless without asking the larger question of the purpose of English studies itself. My answer to that question points to a need for a reexamination of English studies as both a practice and a body of knowledge.

I argue in this chapter not only that English education is a crucial component of a vision for a redefined English studies, but also that it is uniquely situated among the other subdisciplines of English studies to take up that challenge, despite its apparently low status as an academic field. At the center of this argument is my sense that English education, with its inevitable focus on the *practice* of teaching, is inherently dialectical in a way that other areas of English studies are not—a characteristic that fits in well with the call for English studies to address matters of broader social importance in its curricula and scholarship. This dialectical character is partly a legacy of the history of public education in the United States and of the evolution of education as an academic profession, which has always been directly concerned with the "training" of classroom teachers; it is also partly a function of the history of English as an academic discipline in the modern university, which has placed increasing emphasis on research and theory. Perhaps more important, however, the dialectical character of English education arises from the concrete sense of purpose that informs the work of English educators, which tends to be defined in terms of the students who populate English classrooms in schools throughout the country. In other words, the work of English educators is always somehow connected to the lives of those students. My preservice teachers may have difficulty articulating a larger sense of purpose for the teaching of English, but they enter the profession with a strong sense that teaching English matters in concrete ways in the lives of their own students.

As a field grounded in practice, English education can serve a unique and vital function within English studies as a site where theory and practice inevitably converge and where the various subdisciplines of English studies can come together in the service of a project that transcends these separate disciplines. In this regard, English education is not so much a subdiscipline of English studies as a kind of composite of the other subdisciplines, an ongoing project of language practice and professional training that is informed by the other subdisciplines as it addresses various versions of the theory-practice problematic. But my interest here does not lie in defining English education as a discipline.[1] Instead, I am interested in articulating a larger project for English education that is at heart an argument for redefining English studies—and secondary and postsecondary education more generally. I propose that English education should become more proactive in promoting a progressive activist vision for literacy education at the secondary and postsecondary levels. Such a proposition coincides with Bruce McComiskey's proposed definition of English studies as "the analysis, critique, and production of discourse in social context." But in my view, this "analysis, critique, and production of discourse in social context" cannot of itself be the goal of English studies; rather, the analysis, critique, and production of discourse must be pursued in the service of some larger social vision; it should be part of a "design for a future social subject" and "a design for a future society," as Gunther Kress puts it (16). Moreover, the effort to define that "future social subject" and society should be the framework for English studies as a discipline. In other words, while the subject of English studies might be the analysis, critique, and production of discourse in social context, the purpose of that work should be the larger Utopian project of defining, examining, and fostering that "future social subject" who can contribute to the building of just and sustainable communities.

In short, like Kress and other scholars (e.g. James Berlin), I understand English education—and English studies more generally—as primarily subject-forming enterprises that should be structured around a vision of a certain kind of literate subject. The primary task of English educators should be to work out what that literate subject is and how a redefined "English" might foster that subject.

Why It Matters

As I write this essay, more than fifty-three million students in grades K–12 attend American schools (U.S. Dept. of Ed.).[2] That figure represents more than 96 percent of the total school-age population (ages five to seventeen) in the United States. With very few exceptions, all of them are required to take English. That means that professionals in English education directly or indirectly participate in the formal education of virtually *every* child in the United States. That fact alone carries with it an enormous responsibility to understand the implications of the research, teaching, and related work that constitute the field. I wish to promote a vision for English education defined by that responsibility.

As I will show momentarily, it is widely accepted among scholars that formal schooling is an ongoing process of indoctrination by which certain beliefs, values, attitudes, knowledge, and social and intellectual practices are encouraged and others discouraged. For all its platitudes about individual responsibility and individual empowerment, the institution of formal education does not foster individuality so much as conformity.[3] And although the purposes and practices of formal education have always been—and will continue to be—the focus of intense debate and conflict, there is little question but that schooling fosters certain kinds of individuals who conform to a few narrowly defined categories and who share fundamental beliefs and attitudes about such important matters as self, community, knowledge, the physical world, and the relationships among these. In other words, schooling profoundly shapes how we understand ourselves as *beings-in-the-world*. Although this fact is widely acknowledged by theorists, educators—including academics at the postsecondary level—often function as if they are separate from this process. The first step to redefining English studies, then, is to acknowledge the central role that all educators play in the shaping of students as beings-in-the-world.[4]

Once we take that step, we can begin to examine the role of educators in this process and set about changing it in ways that are consistent with the kind of society we hope to create. What that society might be is, of course, an open question, a site of ideological and social struggle (as schools themselves have always been), a social problem to be worked out through the structures and processes of a democratic society. The central problem with English studies—indeed, with education in general—is that it does not understand its function as encompassing the knowledge, skills, and beliefs needed for communities to take up that struggle in a way that might result in a more just and sustainable future. English—and education—are not about any kind of Utopian vision for a better future, or even a *different future*; rather, they are about maintaining a status quo that rests on specious assumptions about the nature of social and individual progress.

The primary reason for this problem lies in the epistemological foundations of modern education. The modern curriculum at all levels of education continues to rest on a positivist understanding of knowledge and reality, with its associated Cartesian self as autonomous and fundamentally intellectual.[5] The resulting fragmentation of knowledge into separate subjects organized hierarchically (with science at the top) has given rise to the familiar academic disciplines and the conventional school curriculum. Formal education thus becomes a matter of disseminating certain kinds of knowledge that are "discovered" through these disciplines. An educated person is someone who possesses the knowledge associated with these disciplines. And a professional academic is an expert in one of those disciplines. This allegiance to a subject matter shifts the focus of postsecondary academic work away from education as a social project and thus enables professionals in the academic disciplines to sidestep or ignore the central role they play in producing that educated person and in reproducing the status quo—or reshaping it.

In teaching the modern curriculum, then, we are not only delivering bodies of knowledge but also reinforcing this Cartesian self. And in fostering this sense of self, we are reinforcing a fundamental binary between mind and body, between human *being* and everything else. I have argued elsewhere that this Western self is at the root of the serious social and environmental problems we face early in the new millennium (Yagelski, "Computers"). To address these problems, therefore, requires us to reexamine how we understand ourselves as beings-in-the-world and to adjust our educational practices accordingly. Education should be about "the development of the whole person," one who has "the capacity for clear thought and compassion in the recognition of the interrelatedness of life," as David Orr has argued (100). To that end, academic disciplines should not be about knowledge but about *knowing*.

As James Berlin famously asserted, "a way of teaching is never innocent" ("Rhetoric and Ideology" 492). English studies has essentially ignored its role as a subject-forming activity as it emerged as an academic discipline in the modern university. To a great extent, English education from its beginnings has been focused on this matter of the literate subject, though I believe in a way that has been more conservative than progressive and not always acknowledged as such. But its dialectical legacy as a discipline directly concerned with the practice of teaching gives it the potential to help redefine English studies in the way that I am advocating here.

Some History

The emergence of English as a recognized academic discipline coincided with broader social and economic changes in the latter nineteenth and early twentieth centuries (see Berlin; Eagleton;

Ohmann). In the United States, these changes included patterns of immigration that contributed to the emergence of public schooling as a vehicle for assimilation and the creation of an Americanized workforce for the emerging modern capitalist society. The rise of industrial capitalism in turn helped shape the professionalization of English as an academic discipline in the early twentieth century. In this section, I trace some of these developments to show how they contributed to the emergence of the field of English education and helped shape its relationship to English studies in general.

This brief historical overview is not intended to be comprehensive, for it traverses complex but familiar ground that has been well-worn by historians of education and English (e.g., Arthur Applebee, Berlin, and James Squire). I wish to focus instead on two historical strands as a way to help make sense of the field of English education as we know it today: (1) the emergence of English as a modern academic discipline, and (2) the rise of public schooling in the United States. These two strands are closely related, but they are also distinct in several respects, including the focus of the first on postsecondary education and the focus of the second on K–12 education. The evolution of English education has been profoundly influenced by both—in ways that differ from the other subdisciplines of English studies that are identified in this book.

The Emergence of English as an Academic Discipline

Scholars tend to agree that the modern English department emerged in the latter part of the nineteenth century in the midst of profound changes in higher education that were related to immigration patterns and industrialization (Berlin; Ohmann; Connors). These changes coincided with the adoption of the German model of higher education by American institutions, a model that organized knowledge into the main academic disciplines with which we are familiar today, established the scientific model as the standard for scholarly inquiry, and shifted the primary role of postsecondary faculty from teaching to research. Amidst these changes, the modern English department evolved, with its focus on literary study. Ironically, however, it was writing instruction, not literature, that enabled the modern English department to emerge from the traditional fields of rhetoric and grammar. As Berlin puts it, the initial purpose of the new English department that emerged in the last quarter of the nineteenth century, "was to provide instruction in writing [. . .]. Charles William Eliot, Harvard's president from 1869 to 1909, had in fact considered writing so central to the new elective curriculum he was shaping that in 1874 the Freshman English course at Harvard was established, by 1894 was the only requirement except for modern language, and by 1897 was the only required course in the curriculum" (*Rhetoric and Reality* 20). As Berlin goes on to show, the establishment of the first-year English composition course at Harvard in 1874, along with a written entrance exam, was a watershed moment in the history of modern English studies. Eventually, other institutions followed Harvard's lead, and first-year composition courses became commonplace. These courses were usually required of all students, which gave English departments a central role in the college curriculum. Robert Connors sees these developments at Harvard also as the beginning of what he terms the modern field of "composition-rhetoric," the consolidation of which

> came with startling rapidity after 1885, with the advent of written exams at Harvard in 1874 and the general adoption of such exams at most established colleges. The consolidation of composition-rhetoric did not take place because true theory or practice drove out false, but because pressing social problems demanded solutions. (11)

From its beginnings as a recognized academic discipline, then, English was intimately tied to larger societal matters.

But although English departments had responsibility for first-year composition courses, English as a new scholarly discipline almost immediately began to distance itself from the teaching of writing. Many English professors did not want their professional identities to be defined by what was widely considered a skills-based course whose purpose was to enable students to write well enough to do the "real" work of college study. As a result, according to Berlin, "in order to distinguish the new English professor from the old rhetoric teacher or the new composition teacher, a new discipline had to be formulated, a discipline based on English as the language of learning and literature as the specialized province of study" (*Rhetoric and Reality* 22). Berlin cites the founding of Johns Hopkins University in 1876 as an important moment in this process. Johns Hopkins was based on the German model, which included the formal study of literature in the vernacular language, heretofore not an established part of the American college curriculum. When Johns Hopkins attempted to hire Francis James Child, the Boylston Professor of Rhetoric and Oratory at Harvard, Harvard retained Child by releasing him from teaching first-year composition, which enabled him to focus on literary study. With this move "Harvard had its first specialist in literature who was without responsibility for teaching freshmen [. . . T]he precedent had been established and literature was on its way to becoming the dominant concern for the new English department" (*Rhetoric and Reality* 23).

These largely academic developments might not have made much difference in the long run if the new English department did not serve other important functions within the modern university and the emerging industrial society. As the German model reshaped American higher education and as science became established as the standard of knowledge making, the English department could claim legitimacy not only as the site of new knowledge in the form of rigorous literary scholarship but also as the gatekeeper of the English language, which was both the language of science and the language of industry. Berlin writes that as universities became "committed to the new ideal of scientific research and to the transferal of scientific knowledge in the service of corporate capitalism, English studies was at the center of the new curriculum in both secondary and higher education" (*Rhetorics, Poetics* 22–23). At the secondary level, the spread of compulsory schooling in the nineteenth and twentieth centuries meant that the large numbers of immigrants entering the country learned English as a school language and at the same time could be assimilated into American culture. At the college level, the teaching of writing as a skill fit the needs of industrial capitalism, which required literate, disciplined managers to help run efficient factories (Berlin; Ohmann). Because they were responsible for writing instruction, then, English departments served an important social role in the new university.

But it was literary study that gave English its legitimacy as an academic discipline. Even as composition became a standard part of the college curriculum, literary study began to develop its own "objective" methodology to fit into the positivist paradigm that increasingly defined knowledge making in higher education. As Terry Eagleton points out, the New Criticism emerged from more traditional ways of reading literary texts in the early twentieth century, a time "when literary criticism in North America was struggling to become 'professionalized,' acceptable as a respectable academic discipline. Its battery of critical instruments was a way of competing with the hard sciences on their own terms, in a society where such science was the dominant criterion of knowledge" (49). This professionalizing of English studies increased the distance between the teaching of English at the secondary level and the study of English at the postsecondary level. For the latter, English increasingly became the study of the literary canon. The work of the college English professional was to define and refine this canon and to promote increasingly specialized ways of analyzing it. By contrast, although literature was part of the English curriculum in high schools (see Applebee, *Tradition* Chapter 2), the study of literary texts there was not the specialized kind of analysis that came to characterize English literary scholarship under the influence of New Criticism; rather, literary study in high schools focused on passing on the cultural heritage and supporting basic literacy instruction—as well as communicating certain values and habits of mind. As English faculty at universities became literary specialists, then, high school English teachers remained guardians of the language, keepers of convention, and guides to the Western cultural tradition in literature.

Applebee points out that by the beginning of the twentieth century, the study of literature in high schools had come to be seen as consistent with the value of *all* education, which "lay in mental discipline":

> thus any proposal for the study of English literature had disciplinary value as part of its justification. Another was that the unique value of literary studies was their guarantee of a continu-

ing cultural tradition, an extra-historical perspective encompassing and preserving the values of Western civilization. Third, there
was the conviction that all of the varied studies of language, literature, and composition which had previously had to fend for
separate places within the curriculum were really only different
aspects of the same central study. And finally there was the belief
that this study was the one subject within the school curriculum
to which all students needed a steady exposure. (*Tradition* 38)

Applebee's summary of the consolidation of English as a subject
by the early twentieth century underscores the differences in the
sense of purpose that informed English at the high school level
and postsecondary English studies—differences that obtain today. Yet the influence of college English on secondary school
English was profound, as seen in the impact of Harvard's entrance exam. As they developed within the new American university, college English departments continued to pronounce on
what the study of high school English should be. For example, as
Berlin notes, Harvard's "establishing the entrance test in composition suggested that the ability to write was something the college student ought to bring with him from his preparatory school,
a place which was more and more likely to be one of the new
public high schools that were now appearing everywhere" (*Rhetoric and Reality* 23). In addition to these expectations for writing
ability, colleges also set expectations for the reading that students should do before entering college. Harvard's entrance exam
stipulated that literature would be the subject about which applicants would write, which led to questions about what literary
texts students in high schools should study. For its 1874 entrance
exam, Harvard listed the following texts: *The Tempest, Julius
Caesar*, and *The Merchant of Venice* by Shakespeare; Goldsmith's
Vicar of Wakefield; and *Ivanhoe* and *The Lay of the Last Min-
strel* by Scott. According to Applebee, "This requirement institutionalized the study of standard authors and set in motion a
process which eventually forced English to consolidate its position within schools" (*Tradition* 30). As other colleges followed
Harvard's lead, high schools complained about the lack of agree-
ment among the college reading lists. Those complaints led to
efforts to standardize the reading lists, culminating in 1894 in
the National Conference on Uniform Entrance Requirements in

English. In effect, colleges were determining what high school students were required to read, despite the fact that only about four percent of students from eighteen to twenty-four years old actually attended college at the time (Berlin, *Rhetoric and Reality* 33). One implication of this dynamic was that college English faculty could ascribe to secondary schools the tasks of introducing students to standard literary texts and providing basic writing instruction, leaving college faculty to focus on the increasingly specialized study of literature. Thus, the distinction between English at the secondary level and how it was coming to be practiced at the postsecondary level became institutionalized.

English education did not exist as an academic discipline at the turn of the twentieth century, but these developments help explain how it eventually emerged as such, for it was in part the continuing disputes about the relationship between high school and college English and about the place of writing instruction in college English departments that led to another watershed event, the founding of the National Council of Teachers of English in 1911, which can justifiably be seen as the birth of English education. Berlin writes that "the National Council of Teachers of English was founded in protest against college domination of the high school English curriculum exercised through the agency of the Uniform Reading Lists" (*Rhetoric and Reality* 33). The lists had become extremely controversial in the years after the National Conference on Uniform Entrance Requirements, and the founders of NCTE, who were almost exclusively high school teachers, used the growing opposition to the lists to assert their conception of English in secondary schools as something more than preparation for college. As a professional organization, NCTE "was from the start an agency for improving the teaching of English at all educational levels, even if its main focus initially was secondary school instruction" (35). But the founding of NCTE underscored the growing rift between literature and composition within English departments; it also reflected the distance between high school English, with its concerns for basic literacy instruction, and college English, with its focus on specialized literary study. English education as an academic discipline concerned with the teaching of English emerged amidst these tensions.

English Education and the Rise of Public Schooling

If the founding of NCTE might be seen as the birth of English education, the rise of public schooling in the United States in the twentieth century might be seen as what nurtured the nascent field. Without this fertile ground in which to take root, English education might not have had what eventually came to be its central project: understanding, delivering, and (ostensibly) improving the teaching of English, largely through its role in preparing secondary teachers. As much as English education has been shaped by English studies at the postsecondary level, it is in many ways more closely connected to the ideologies and practices of public schooling. In this regard, the development of English education is inextricably linked to the rise of public schooling in the United States, which exacerbates the tensions between it and English studies.

As I have already suggested, public schooling was shaped by a number of social and economic factors in the latter nineteenth and early twentieth centuries, and it evolved into an important vehicle for the assimilation of immigrants, as well as already established social groups within American society, into the American mainstream. That mainstream can be characterized at that time as reflecting Protestant values and a civic vision based loosely on liberal ideals and cultural values (see Macedo, Chapters 2 and 3). According to Stephen Macedo,

> The public schools were thought to be an appropriate public instrument for promoting the reasonableness and cooperation among citizens that a healthy liberal political order depends upon [. . .]. Even if the religious content of the public school curriculum was low—and even if it had been *nonexistent*—its mission with respect to religion and other "private" normative domains was crucial: to promote tolerant and "charitable" forms of religious and ethical belief. (85; emphasis in original)

In addition, public schooling seems to have evolved in close concert with the needs of the industrial state. The curriculum and social practices of schooling imparted values and emphasized certain kinds of knowledge and skills that coincided with the values, knowledge, and skills needed for an industrialized labor force. In this regard, public schools were not only producing (or trying to produce) the kind of citizen that Macedo refers to as necessary for a democratic society, but they were also preparing a certain kind of worker for the modern industrial state. Berlin sees these developments "as part of a reformation of class relations. The new credentialing process created a meritocracy, with the professional middle class at its apex" (*Rhetorics, Poetics* 20). In this new meritocracy, "high schools provided the training for lower-level skilled labor, while colleges provided the expertise needed to succeed in the upper levels of the meritocracy" (21). To put it in slightly different terms, secondary schooling was about the management of "human capital" in the emerging industrial state; it was engaged in a certain kind of subject-formation consistent with the needs of modern American society.

But these dual projects—producing citizens for a democratic state and producing workers for an industrialized society—were not necessarily compatible. Linda McNeil argues that industrialization in effect turned the Jeffersonian ideal of educating all citizens for participation in democracy "on its head as industrialists around the turn of the century looked to schools to supply them with labor for their expanding factories"; the industrialists' "desire to control schooling went beyond wanting to socialize students into a particular set of values. These industrialists of the late nineteenth and early twentieth centuries wanted to help control the labor supply" (4). According to McNeil, controlling the labor supply meant dealing with growing enrollments in public schools as well as increasing numbers of immigrants to the United States (which of course contributed to the rising school enrollments). In this sense, the industrialists' concerns about immigrant labor coincided with reformers' desires to address various social problems. McNeil concludes that "during this period, industrialists and social reformers alike turned to the school as the only universal institution, as the best organization for breaking down the home culture and replacing it with American values. In addition, the schools could train, sort, select and certify able and willing workers" (5).

In short, as the United States evolved into a modern industrial state, public schools came to serve a variety of social and economic purposes in a vast norming and sorting of the population. Proponents of the early common school recognized that "convergence on liberal democratic civic norms does not come about automatically, that in fact the health of our regime depends on its ability to turn people's deepest convictions—including their religious beliefs—in directions that are congruent with the ways of a liberal republic" (Macedo 42–43). In McNeil's less sanguine view, these social and cultural values are inextricably linked to economic production (12): "Our present high schools were organized, and their reward structures set, at a time when schools were being overtly and deliberately used as agents of economic and social control" (15).

Whether characterized as essential and proper for a healthy democracy or as a form of indoctrination serving the corporate state (or both), schools teach, reinforce, and perpetuate values, beliefs, and habits of mind to an extent that other institutions, even religious ones, cannot. To take one example that is sometimes cited in critiques of schools, the valorizing of individualism that characterizes American culture is woven into the fabric of formal schooling, not only in the form of institutional practices (such as grading, which is inherently competitive and which rests on a set of assumptions about individuals as autonomous configurations of abilities and characteristics), but also in terms of curricular content, such as the study of "great" historical figures and literary works by certain "great" authors. In addition, extracurricular activities such as competitive sports or debating can reinforce ideas about individual ability and merit. These ideas pervade all aspects of the school culture. In this way, schools become powerful institutional vehicles for producing and reproducing American culture—an idea that is by now familiar through the work of Pierre Bourdieu and Jean-Claude Passeron, Henry Giroux, and others. As C. A. Bowers puts it, "It is at the level of public school education that the most basic schemata of the culture are presented and reinforced" (*Educating* 8).

It should not be surprising, then, that since their beginning public schools have been the focus of ambitious reform efforts intended to address a variety of social problems or to further various social agendas. The marquee example of such movements is the Progressive Movement of the 1920s and 1930s, driven largely by the ideas of John Dewey and his adherents. If the schools

could foster conformity, the thinking went, they could also promote positive social change, addressing society's ills in ways that
government programs or private philanthropy could not. In addition, for Dewey and those influenced by his ideas, the central
task of education was the preparation of thinking, productive
citizens who were ethically and politically aware. In other words,
the schools were the places where democracy was nourished, for
they could foster in students the civic ideals necessary for effective citizenship; to produce such citizens was ultimately to improve society.[6] Applebee has identified the idea of a social mission
for education as one distinction between the secondary and
postsecondary levels, arguing that through the initiatives of progressive reformers like Jane Addams "the public elementary and
secondary schools were gradually enlisted as agents of progressive social change. It was a major step in the separation of school
and college functions" (*Tradition* 47). This separation still exists
today in various guises, perhaps most importantly because schooling is compulsory until about the age of sixteen in most states,
whereas postsecondary schooling is not. However, whatever the
progressive impulses of social activists and school reformers in
the early twentieth century (and later), public education at the
elementary and secondary levels has increasingly served the same
conservative function that many scholars have associated with
higher education (e.g., Berlin, Eagleton, and Ohmann). For the
most part, reform efforts have left schools fundamentally unchanged. Perhaps the most revealing evidence of this lack of
change is the fact that the organizational structure of schools,
the conventional curriculum, and basic teaching practices have
remained essentially intact since the rise of public schooling at
the turn of the twentieth century. Classrooms today are, except
for relatively minor details, fundamentally the same as the classrooms our forebears might have entered 100 or 120 years ago.

English as a school subject claimed a central role in both the
reformist and the normative projects of public education in the
United States. No other subject has been so widely required in
modern secondary schools. Today, in most states, students must
take English for all four years of high school and for the three
years of middle school; language arts is a central component of
the elementary school curriculum as well. In effect, all secondary

school students are exposed to and potentially shaped by the English language arts curriculum. As a result, its content and practices constitute an extremely powerful site for the inculcation of values and the shaping of young minds. The oft-heard platitude that teachers have the power to touch young lives becomes a description of the potentially profound importance of—and perhaps a cause for deep concern about—the work of individual English teachers when that work is placed in the context of this vast collective project of teaching English to virtually all American school-age children.

The focus of English on reading and writing has given it special importance as a set of fundamental skills that all students must acquire. Standardized and mandated tests almost always include reading, and increasingly in recent years they are including writing as well. Indeed, the original standardized test in the United States, the Harvard entrance exam discussed earlier, was a writing exam. If standardized testing has been a political battleground in the United States for the past 130-plus years, English has been in the middle of that battle. But it has also evolved in a way that coincides with and even reinforces the growing tendency toward standardized testing. That is, English as a school subject, in terms of its pedagogy and curriculum in secondary schools, has adapted to testing and in some cases has even focused its attention on "testable" skills (such as spelling or correctness in form). One response of English educators to the inevitable public education "crises," such as the one sparked by the publication of the famous *Newsweek* article "Why Johnny Can't Read" in 1974, has been to develop pedagogies that ostensibly address the perceived crisis. The "back-to-basics" movement that grew out of the publication of *A Nation at Risk* (U.S. Natl. Comm.) in the 1980s included a rejection of Whole Language and other "progressive" language arts pedagogies and a return to phonics-based reading instruction in the early grades and skills-based approaches to teaching writing at the secondary level. While such efforts have been resisted by many professionals in English education (often with great vigor), the conventional English curriculum in schools—over which English educators themselves usually have little control and to which they must adjust—always seems to adapt to the latest reform efforts, which is to say that, as studies like Applebee's *Literature in the Secondary School* indicate, it remains largely unchanged. In this regard, English as a school subject has been a crucial component of the norming project of schools.

Reading various histories of English and composition studies (e.g., Connors, Berlin, Applebee), one easily comes away with a sense of how widespread certain beliefs and practices have been. As Applebee has shown, for example, the selection of works of literature that tend to be taught in high schools has been remarkably stable over the years (*Literature*), with the implication that students in schools across the country are exposed to more or less the same literary works. Applebee's study of writing in high schools in the early 1980s revealed a similar dynamic: most students were asked to do the same kinds of writing with similar frequencies, and pedagogies were strikingly similar from one school to another (*Writing*). No study on the scale of Applebee's has been conducted in recent years, but the research we do have suggests that while some students may be writing more often and that more "progressive" writing process pedagogies have become standard in many classrooms, for the majority of students writing instruction still tends to be characterized by the same practices and attitudes as when Applebee conducted his study more than twenty years ago.[7] Moreover, in many states mandated standardized writing exams have encouraged teachers to focus on specific kinds of writing tasks in order to prepare students for these exams. Whatever one thinks of these exams, the implication of this trend is that students in schools are exposed to more or less the same basic (and narrowly defined) kinds of writing instruction and thus emerge from their secondary education with similar attitudes about writing. The same can be said of reading and literary study.

We in English expend a great deal of energy discussing what should and should not be taught and why, and a review of scholarship in the field over the past half-century reveals how dramatic a change we have seen in the kinds of issues that we consider most important in our work. (To take just one example, consider the ways in which we discuss "difference" in literacy instruction today, as seen in the work of scholars like Lisa Delpit and Keith Gilyard.) But the disconnection between so much of our scholarship with its focus on theory and what actually happens in English classrooms seems as large as ever. A close look at how English is taught in schools indicates that despite the apparent impact of movements like Whole Language, the National Writing Project, and the writing process movement, which have certainly influenced how many teachers approached their work, the teaching of English has remained fundamentally unchanged since it became a mainstay of the curriculum of the modern public school. My own sense is that the size and inflexibility of the education bureaucracy that has been constructed around formal schooling is the central reason for that lack of change. It is no coincidence that major reform efforts in the past fifty years or so have all been prompted or driven by government initiatives: the National Defense Education Act of 1958 (which was amended in 1962 to include English as one of the essential subjects to be supported); the back-to-basics reforms that grew out of the report of the U.S. National Commission on Excellence in Education, *A Nation at Risk,* in 1983; and the recent move toward "accountability" in the George W. Bush administration's No Child Left Behind program, which intensifies the already strong push toward a focus on skills measured by standardized tests. All of these efforts have the effect of solidifying the normative role that the teaching of English plays in formal education.[8]

Berlin has asserted, "Every pedagogy is imbricated in ideology, in a set of tacit assumptions about what is real, what is good, what is possible, and how power ought to be distributed" ("Rhetoric and Ideology" 492). If literacy is a way of making sense of the world, of "reading the world," in Paulo Freire's memorable phrase, then English as a school subject has been the most potent of the normative forces in the school curriculum. It is no wonder, then, that English has been the focus of much controversy as well as the vehicle for many reform efforts over the years.

English Education and Academe Today

I have traced the way that English education as an academic discipline has emerged along with English as a school subject and along with formal schooling, which accounts in large measure for its dual and contradictory legacy of being both a normative and a reformist project. But English education has always occupied an uncomfortable position with respect to the schools. For one thing, it has sought to understand the teaching and learning of English (of writing, reading, grammar, and literature) that for the most part happens in schools. Not surprisingly, then, the focus of much of its attention has always been on conventional English instruction in conventional school settings. For another thing, it has come to be charged with the training of secondary school English teachers. Programs such as the one I teach in at SUNY Albany are authorized by states to prepare teachers for certification to teach in public schools. In this sense, English educators (like other teacher educators) act as an arm of the state when it comes to institutionalized education. That role carries with it a responsibility to serve the needs of schools, such as they are. Those of us in English education routinely share the frustration of hearing teachers or administrators in secondary schools complain that our university programs don't adequately prepare teachers-in-training for the real and very pressing "practical" challenges of teaching English in those secondary schools. The widespread expectation is that English educators (and indeed *all* teacher educators) will prepare student teachers to function effectively in those schools as they are currently structured and operated; the expectation is generally *not* that student teachers will be trained as "change agents" or reformers except to the extent that they can help improve schools according to conventional criteria for "improvement" (e.g., higher standardized test scores, higher rates of graduation or college attendance, and so on). The job of English educators is thus not usually considered to be to foster social change but rather to help to maintain the institutional status quo.

At the same time, as university or college faculty, English educators are expected to contribute to knowledge making as it is defined in institutions of higher education; they are expected to be researchers and to "do theory." They are expected to be scholars who do not simply prepare teachers for the classroom but who also study current practices. Thus, they face many of the same pressures as scholars in other disciplines, and they have struggled for legitimacy in the modern university, like their counterparts in disciplines such as rhetoric and composition. Unlike those counterparts, however, English educators are often directly affected by the vagaries of public funding for research and struggle to claim legitimacy as researchers outside the walls of academe as well. A good example of this struggle is the aforementioned No Child Left Behind initiative, which includes rigid requirements governing the kinds of education research that will be funded and used in education reform initiatives. As Nancy Mellin McCracken has recently pointed out, No Child Left Behind amounts to a systematic attempt to exclude colleges of education from full participation in federally funded education research and reform projects. The Department of Education's demand that research be "scientific" (which means studies using randomized experimental designs or similar methodologies) and that curriculum reform efforts be based on such research can be seen as the latest (and an especially virulent) challenge to the legitimacy of scholars in education. McCracken quotes the strategic plan of the Department of Education to highlight the low status assigned to education as compared to other disciplines:

> Unlike medicine, agriculture and industrial production, the field of education operates largely on the basis of ideology and professional consensus. As such, it is subject to fads and is incapable of the cumulative progress that follows from the application of the scientific method and from the systematic collection and use of objective information in policy making. (Dept. of Education 48; qtd. in McCracken 111)

Leaving aside the specious assumption, which is implicit in this statement, that fields such as medicine or agriculture are immune to ideology and do not operate on the basis of "professional consensus," this passage underscores some of the pressures facing English educators in the public arena, where they struggle to claim a professional identity as researchers and scholars in much the same way that they do in academe. But English educators must function in the public arena in a way that, for example, literary scholars do not. If a particular kind of theoretical movement in literary scholarship is dismissed (or, more likely, ignored) by practitioners in K–12 schools, there is no significant impact on scholars advocating such theory. (In this way, the disconnection between theory and practice at the postsecondary level actually insulates scholars from the kinds of pressures that English educators face.) By contrast, if a theory and its associated pedagogies advocated by English education scholars are dismissed, resisted, or even actively opposed by teachers, administrators, or bureaucrats (as in the case of Whole Language Theory, for example), the consequences for English educators can be significant. They can be excluded from funding, their work can be excluded from school reform efforts, and their participation in teacher training can be compromised. Such pressures complicate the role of English educators as academics and as professionals involved in the preparation of secondary school teachers, and they help give rise to the tensions that characterize the field today.

The struggle of English educators for legitimacy in the public arena mirrors their struggle for legitimacy in academe. The very effort to define the field can highlight that struggle. Consider, for example, McCracken's recent definition of the field: "The work of English educators in the twenty-first century is to conduct and provide ready access to research that can provide knowledge and insight to those who choose to devote their lives to teaching the diverse students who populate the United States and its schools" (110). Such a definition, which would likely be acceptable to most professionals in the field, underscores the close ties that English education has to the schools in terms of both its work and its identity as a field; at the same time, it reminds us that English education is also a university discipline that claims a specific area of scholarly inquiry. In other words, as a university discipline, English education is about a certain kind of research and inquiry—not about preparing teachers. To have legitimacy in the university, English education must emphasize its research and scholarly inquiry and in effect downplay its role in preparing teachers; in most research institutions (and I daresay in other kinds of postsecondary institutions as well), a faculty member is not likely to earn tenure on the basis of his or her work in preparing teachers alone. Yet English educators can never completely deny or discard that role, since it is that preparation and its implications—that is, the way English teachers teach English in schools—that provide the field's research focus and its economic viability in the modern university.

This tension between the need to produce scholarship and the responsibility for training public school English teachers also characterizes the field's relationship to English studies. Although many university and college English departments participate in the education of secondary school English teachers, the field of English studies has no formal scholarly concern with that project. For the most part, the role of English studies in the preparation of English teachers is limited to program requirements stipulating that students must complete so many credits in English or hold an undergraduate degree in English. Such requirements help populate university English courses and can bring university funding to English department coffers; they also can help increase enrollments in other English department programs. In this way, like first-year composition, English education programs can be fiscally beneficial to English departments and help fund more esoteric but fiscally less viable areas of study within the English curriculum. Nevertheless, as a scholarly field, English studies has no real interest in either the secondary school English curriculum or the preparation of those who will teach that curriculum. Articles about reflective practice in the teaching of literature, for example, or the application of feminist theory to the literate development of young adults do not appear in the pages of *PMLA* or even in *College English*. To put it somewhat differently, English studies as an academic discipline is not about *teaching* English in any substantive way.

These circumstances can make it difficult for professionals in English education to amass the requisite scholarly credentials for tenure in colleges and universities while they also establish themselves as legitimate colleagues and effective mentors for preservice and inservice teachers in secondary schools. All of us can tell stories about the difficulties that an acquaintance or colleague (or we ourselves) had in making a case for tenure that convinced review committees that our work was indeed legitimate scholarly inquiry. I have no interest in complaining about this state of affairs. Rather, I wish to describe what I see as the status quo of English studies today. The rather vexed position of English education within the field of English studies and within the university can indeed be frustrating for those of us in the field. But despite its seemingly undesirable status within English studies, the dialectical nature of English education, with its inevitable focus on practice, is paradoxically much better positioned than other disciplines within English studies (perhaps with the exception of rhetoric and composition) not only to remain a viable part of higher education as the new modern university emerges in the early decades of the twenty-first century but also to be at the forefront of a much larger effort to redefine education more generally and claim an important role for English within it.

English Education as Praxis

I have suggested that English education has become something of a conservative discipline in the sense that much of its work tends to reflect and reinforce the status quo of institutionalized K–12 education, which serves a broad norming function within American society. But I have also suggested that English education, because of that same close relationship to K–12 education, possesses the potential for playing a central role in shaping American culture that goes well beyond other subdisciplines in English studies and the other academic disciplines represented in current secondary and postsecondary curricula. To understand this potential and the seemingly paradoxical normative-transformative character of English education requires a closer look at how the field currently understands itself and engages in its primary work of (to paraphrase McCracken's definition) conducting and providing ready access to research that offers knowledge and insight to those who teach English in American schools. My analysis here relies on Freire's notion of *praxis* as "reflection and action upon the world in order to transform it" (*Pedagogy of the Oppressed* 51). Freire offers an epistemological framework for understanding what I have been calling the dialectical nature of English education. Furthermore, Freire sees education in overtly teleological terms, something that I think is essential if English is to be a viable part of the shaping of a just and sustainable future.

Freire explains in *Pedagogy of the Oppressed* that praxis rests on an understanding of dialectical thought in which "world and action are intimately interdependent" (53). Dialectic is thus at the heart of Freire's ideas in two respects: (1) it is fundamental to knowledge making—that is, knowledge is a function of a dialectical interaction between humans and the world; and (2) it characterizes his "dialogic" pedagogy, which involves dialectical interchange between teacher and student. For Freire, "knowledge emerges only through invention and re-invention, through the restless, impatient, continuing, hopeful inquiry human beings pursue in the world, with the world, and with each other" (72).⁹ This is an active process in which the world is made and remade and which therefore holds out the possibility of transformation. But Freire's interest here is not just epistemological; it is also ontological, for he is concerned with how persons are conceived—and how they conceive themselves—as beings-in-the-world. In his formulation, knowing and being are fundamentally interrelated; knowledge as a function of dialectical engagement with the world is at the center of what it means to be human: "For apart from inquiry, apart from praxis, individuals cannot be truly human" (72). Conventional education works against this process of becoming "truly human" by defining knowledge as objective and external to the knower and by describing reality as static. Freire's "problem-posing" pedagogy rejects those definitions of knowers and instead defines teachers and students as "critical co-investigators in dialogue" with each other in the service of a "critical intervention in reality" (81). This amounts to a reconceptualizing of the student-as-subject (really, of *all* people):

> Education as the practice of freedom—as opposed to education as the practice of domination—denies that man is abstract, isolated, independent, and unattached to the world; it also denies that the world exists as a reality apart from people. Authentic reflection considers neither abstract man nor the world without people, but people in their relations with the world. In these relations, consciousness and world are simultaneous: consciousness neither precedes the world nor follows it. (81)

This passage dramatically summarizes Freire's ontological and epistemological assumptions. It also implicitly rejects the positivist epistemology that still serves as the foundation for modern schooling as well as for the academic disciplines. In short, Freire offers a critical pedagogy based on a radically different epistemology from that which informs modern education.¹⁰

As I have already noted, English studies implicitly embraced a positivist epistemology and developed knowledge making practices consistent with it as it evolved into a modern discipline. The New Criticism, for example, which became the main theoretical paradigm within English in the mid-twentieth century, essentially applied principles of objectivity to the study of literary texts. More recent theoretical trends in English studies are, I would argue, consistent with this epistemology, appearances to the contrary. This is so because the central project of English studies has been to define and preserve a certain kind of knowledge within academe (though what that knowledge should be has been a matter of intense debate in the field); that project is only incidentally concerned with ontology—that is, with the formation of a certain kind of student subject. And despite the apparent existence of leftists and other radicals in university English departments, a charge heard so often in the corporate media, English studies as an academic discipline is not concerned in any direct way with the transformation of the world, in Freirean terms; rather, its practices are consistent with what Freire has famously called "the banking concept of education, in which the scope of action allowed to students extends only as far as receiving, filing, and storing the deposits" of knowledge as defined by the teacher (or the discipline) (*Pedagogy of the Oppressed* 72).[11] In this sense, English studies has itself become a conservative force that contributes to the maintenance of the institutional status quo, a point to which I will return momentarily.

Such a statement may seem fantastic given the concerns of scholars in English studies today, many of whom promote theoretical views that diverge radically from positivism and who often write about issues of social injustice, racial inequality, the marginalized status of various "nonmainstream" groups, and the silencing of members of those groups, among other genuinely important concerns. But scholarship and teaching in English studies remain decidedly conventional and disciplinary (in both senses of that term); in that sense, scholarship and teaching in English studies are about *English studies,* not about any significant kind of social or individual transformation through the study of English, notwithstanding the work of provocative scholars, such as bell hooks, whose voices have reached beyond academe. Signifi-

English Education

cantly, the broader impact of these scholars outside academe seems to be a function of the extent to which they transcend their academic disciplines and become "public intellectuals." The majority of scholars in English studies have no such impact. Instead, we maintain the discipline and its place within the university, which itself is concerned with maintaining its status within the society at large. (As many observers have noted, the "corporatization" of the university in the past few decades can be seen as an effort to adjust to a new world economic order and thus maintain a role for higher education in that new order. See Noble; White and Hauck.)

English education, by contrast, is directly concerned with something other than its disciplinary identity and status, or, to put it conversely, its professional identity is a function of something outside academe: it is concerned with the practice of teaching English and, inevitably, with the purpose(s) of that practice. In other words, the question of the role of the teaching of English within the society at large is always implicit in the issues that English educators address, whether those issues are various writing pedagogies, assessments, the literary training of English teachers, teacher-research, or any number of related concerns. All these concerns are shaped—indeed, to a great extent defined—by the fact that English is a required school subject for virtually all American school-age children. Thus, English educators are always but a step away from questions of purpose: To what end do English educators help prepare secondary school English teachers? To what end do English educators develop and encourage specific literacy pedagogies? To what end do English educators engage in specific kinds of research? In other words, English education is not only an epistemological enterprise, one involved in producing certain kinds of knowledge; it is not only an ontological enterprise, involved in fostering a certain kind of literate student subject. It is also a *teleological* enterprise, involved in pursuing some larger goal, explicitly defined or not. And that goal is intimately connected to the stated and unstated purposes of public education within an ostensibly democratic and capitalist society.

Given its nature as a teleological enterprise, English education, with its dialectical knowledge-making practices, has a unique capacity for transformation in Freirean terms. Because it is directly concerned with the teaching of English, English education is always engaged in a kind of knowledge making that is characterized by an engagement with the world, in Freirean terms; its knowledge making is situated within the "reality" of classroom practice. And because of its concern with literacy, English education has claim to something that lies at the center of Freire's conception of the dialectical process of knowledge making: language, which is "the essence of dialogue itself" (*Pedagogy of the Oppressed* 87). For Freire,

> the word is more than just an instrument which makes dialogue possible; accordingly, we must seek its constitutive elements. Within the word we find two dimensions, reflection and action, in such radical interaction that if one is sacrificed—even in part— the other immediately suffers. There is no true word that is not at the same time a praxis. Thus, to speak a true word is to transform the world. (87)

Freire goes on to explain the importance of *naming:* "To exist, humanly, is to *name* the world, to transform it"; humans are "not built in silence, but in word, in work, in action-reflection" (88; emphasis in original). From this perspective, the very subject of English education, which can be described as educating literacy teachers, gives it unique transformative possibilities.

The problem, of course, is that English education is so centrally defined by its relationship to formal education that it can be a powerful tool for reinforcing conventional practices and ideologies, as I have already suggested. To realize its transformative potential, in Freirean terms, English education as a professional field must confront its complicated relationship with formal schooling and fully embrace its inherently dialectical character. The difficulty of this task is not trivial, nor is the task itself straightforward.

For one thing, formal schooling, such as it is, has become so deeply entrenched in American culture that it is seen as a normal part of growing up. Despite never-ending controversies about funding, testing, curriculum, and related aspects of formal education, most Americans seem to accept and support the central role that schools play in the upbringing and indeed in the socialization of their children. In general, Americans do not seem much concerned about the extent to which conventional schooling is tantamount to a long-term project of indoctrination into certain ways of thinking about knowledge, the world, the self, and matters of central importance to American political and economic life, including the production and consumption of goods, work, individual rights, and the value of private property. Indeed, polls show that while Americans have concerns about public education in general, they believe the schools that their own children attend are generally doing a good job; these polls suggest a public that is very comfortable with conventional education.[12] And for better or worse, most Americans seem to accept the central role of English in that process; not surprisingly, they tend to hold the utilitarian conception of literacy as a basic skill that characterizes English instruction in schools (see Yagelski, *Literacy* 28–43). To tinker with the teaching of English, then, is to challenge deeply held beliefs about writing, reading, and schooling.

The influence of recent theoretical developments—especially postmodern theory—on higher education has further complicated these challenges facing English educators. Perhaps more than most disciplines in the social sciences and humanities, English education has had difficulty distancing itself from the great modernist project that has been called into question by postmodernism, whereas English studies embraced postmodern thinking and began to redefine itself as a scholarly field in opposition to modernism. Like many other academic disciplines that have been influenced by postmodern thought, English studies seems to have found it easy to jettison the modernist scientific and objectivist principles that informed the New Criticism and shift its focus to the language play and epistemological relativism of postmodernism. In doing so, it has concerned itself with such projects as recovering previously marginalized or ignored literatures, promoting certain kinds of cultural critique, and challenging the literary canon. The stakes for English studies in these developments were relatively low: to preserve its status within the academy. I do not mean to diminish the potential effects of theoretical movements like postmodernism on individual programs and lives in the field; for example, as new areas of inquiry within English studies have gained currency, "old" ones have diminished in importance, resulting in the elimination of some programs and faculty positions in those areas. But as a whole, English studies has maintained its place within the modern university in large measure by maintaining its institutional practices, even though its scholarly concerns have diverged from the ostensibly objective methodology of New Criticism. In other words, while the content of its scholarship has changed to adjust to the rise of postmodern thought, its institutional practices have not changed. English studies thus remains a viable part of the modern university, which, paradoxically, continues to be defined by modernist ideas about knowledge.

English education, by contrast, has faced a more complicated challenge with the rise of postmodern thinking. Defined as it is in relation to formal schooling, English education could not so easily embrace postmodern ideas about language, knowledge, and discourse, because the schools are structured around modernist assumptions about the autonomous self and the Enlightenment ideals of social and material "progress." The focus of postmodern theory on the contingency of knowledge making, the instability of the subject, and the connections between power and discourse has in a sense forced English educators to confront their complicity in the process by which schools, as social institutions, can contribute to injustice and marginalization. Unlike scholars in other subdisciplines of English studies, then, English education scholars cannot simply adjust the focus of their scholarship while maintaining conventional institutional practices. To put it rather more concretely, how could English educators educate teachers-in-training about the functions of power through discourse and the specific ways in which schools manage behavior and maintain institutional power through certain discourse practices, and at the same time prepare those same teachers-in-training to effectively engage in and reinforce those same discourse practices? How could they teach English teachers that common language practices in schools, such as the emphasis on "standard English," can be oppressive and then train them to participate in that same oppression? If postmodern thought helped English educators understand the complex dynamics of language, knowledge, discourse, and power, it also helped reveal their vexed role in the normative process that is formal schooling.

Karen Smith and Patricia Lambert Stock have recently argued that in the past decade or so English educators have embraced the postmodern skepticism of the Enlightenment project and adopted a "praxis-oriented" approach to their work, concerning themselves "with what counts as knowledge, with how that knowledge is produced, with who produces it, and with how it does and doesn't benefit students and the larger society in which we live" (116). They cite the increasingly complex research methodologies and studies that "draw attention to the situation-specific nature of teaching and learning and to multiple views of what counts as effective teaching and learning," and they discuss "the problematics of representation" (116) as related to the work of English educators, describing some of the "poly-vocal inquiries that incorporate multiple perspectives to address the problem" (119) that researchers in English education have devised. Smith and Stock's take on English educators' embrace of postmodernism is no doubt a valid description of trends in the field. But although English education researchers might design studies reflecting the multiple and shifting subjectivities of participants in ways that are consistent with postmodern theory, the secondary English teachers and students with whom they work function in a modernist institutional context that has resisted postmodern ideas and some of the pedagogies and curricular reform efforts that have been informed by postmodernism. In other words, as scholars in the field draw on postmodern theory to understand better what they do, many of their school-based colleagues often remain mired in modernist understandings of language, teaching, and learning. This situation underscores the difficulties that English education professionals face in occupying a professional space that is at once part of the schools and of the intellectual landscape of academe.

Yet this ostensibly tricky position is also ripe with possibilities for a Freirean *praxis* that is genuinely grounded in the concrete realities of language use and social interaction. Acknowledging "the tension between university-initiated inquiries into teaching and learning and the realities of school-life" (121), Smith and Stock quote Ruth Ray to point to the teacher-researcher movement as evidence that English education might be characterized as "postdisciplinary": "Free of the constraints of disciplinary practices and ideologies which make university researchers blind to alternative explanations for phenomena, teacher-researchers are 'postdisciplinary' in their ability to admit contradictions and deal with 'overdetermined' situations in which complex phenomena are typically reduced to a single, cause-effect relationship" (71; qtd. in Smith and Stock 121). Teacher-research is one manifestation of what Smith and Stock call a "praxis-oriented" discipline. It is one visible way in which English education engages in a Freirean praxis: knowledge emerges from a dialectical inquiry by teachers and students. As Berlin pointed out a number of years ago, teacher research is "revolutionary" in the way it challenges existing hierarchies and knowledge-making practices: as researchers, "teachers are engaged in challenging the hierarchical power structures of the schools, as they make their own decisions about instruction and use their own expertise to analyze their own situations" ("Teacher" 10).

But English education can do more than involve practitioners in knowledge making. If scholars like Ray, Smith, and Stock foster genuine inquiry among their school-based colleagues only for the purpose of enhancing teachers' understanding of literacy teaching and learning in the context of formal schooling, they have certainly served an important function. But if English educators go no further than that, they leave the status quo effectively unchanged because they focus only on the interaction between teachers and learners within the context of the classroom as it currently exists. Berlin raised this very concern about the teacher-research movement, worrying that it was "not emphasizing and problematizing its own political agenda" and was not confronting "the inescapably value-laden quality of all schooling" ("Teacher" 10). In this sense, to deepen our understanding of practice within schools, even for the purpose of improving that practice, without acknowledging and confronting the political and ideological nature of schooling, paradoxically reinforces the institutional status quo and thus allows that status quo to continue the process of indoctrination that formal schooling is; it allows schools to continue to shape students as modernist subjects.[13]

Given its dialectical character, English education has the potential to challenge that process. But it can realize that potential only if English educators see themselves as directly engaged in a much larger social project. We should fully embrace our central role in the shaping of student subjects as beings-in-the-world, acknowledging that this process of subject formation can be oppressive or transformative and emancipatory. We must, I believe, see ourselves as part of a Utopian project. And in doing so, we can help define a new English studies.

English as a Utopian Project

In Chapter 3 of *Pedagogy of the Oppressed,* Freire describes his dialogic "problem-posing" pedagogy, which begins in "the present, existential, concrete situation" (95). It is a teleological pedagogy whose purpose, literally, is to change the world by fostering in students a sense of agency founded on the epistemological connection between "the word" and "the world": "The object of the investigation is not persons (as if they were anatomical fragments), but rather the thought-language with which men and women refer to reality, the levels at which they perceive that reality, and their view of the world" (97). To put it simply, Freire proposes to teach in a way that encourages students to see themselves and the world differently, and the vehicle for such a project is language.

As many critics have pointed out in the nearly four decades since the publication of *Pedagogy of the Oppressed,* the concrete, existential situations of Freire's students were dramatically different from those of most students today in the United States. Freire was teaching nonliterate, disenfranchised, rural peasants in a military dictatorship and in a specific South American cultural context. The "limit-situations" he encouraged those peasants to explore—that is, the concrete circumstances in which they existed that set "limits" to their freedom (99)—might seem almost exotic to most American students (notwithstanding that some of those students live in similar material conditions today): they inhabited tiny shacks, were essentially living in economic servitude, had limited or no access to formal education, and were subject to overt abuse by landowners and government bureaucrats. Critics are right to point out the differences between such

situations and the circumstances within which educators in the
United States work and within which their students learn. But
the concept of a "limit-situation" can be applied across cultural
contexts, and it can help us understand—and potentially change—
what we do. More important, it reveals that what Freire was
doing and what we do are essentially the same thing: fostering a
certain kind of subjectivity and encouraging a certain kind of
being-in-the-world. What we have to decide is what that subjectivity and being-in-the-world should be.

It is obvious from the foregoing that I advocate an understanding of English education as a broad, progressive social
project, one that ultimately contributes to the creation of just
and sustainable communities. I have suggested above that English education is uniquely positioned to define itself in such terms,
and I have elsewhere begun to articulate what this understanding
of the field might mean in terms of the work of English educators
(Yagelski, "Stasis"). I want to propose that English studies should
do the same: it should pursue a Utopian vision in which the content of the discipline is subordinate to that larger social project
of contributing to the formation of such communities. The task
of English studies, then, is to inquire into the nature of that project
and define its scholarship and related activities accordingly. This
is an inherently social project that cannot be conceived in terms
of *individual* betterment and the "progress" of society, which is
at heart a justification for education based on a modernist view
of the world. Rather, the Utopian project I advocate is one that
challenges the Cartesian self and explores the possibilities for
fostering a different sense of self as inextricably *of* the world.

I accept the label of idealist in making such a proposal. But I
see no viable alternative. There seems to be little question that
we are witnessing in the early years of the twenty-first century
the evolution of a new kind of global culture, emerging as a result of what we have come to call "globalization," which David
Harvey has defined as "a process of uneven temporal and geographical production" (60) that "implies widespread [. . .] acceptance of certain bourgeois notions of law, of rights, of freedoms,
and even of moral claims about goodness and virtue" (85) aris-
ing from modernist ideals. English studies as an academic discipline has the opportunity to confront that process and to

participate directly in the reshaping of American society in the context of the emerging global culture. If it rejects that opportunity, it will remain little more than a minor (and perhaps unwilling or even unwitting) part of the process of globalization and an integral, if lesser, component of the new status quo.

I would argue that the "limit-situations" facing American students today are much more complex, challenging, and potentially dire than even those facing Freire's peasant students, because the extent to which American students participate in the maintenance of their own limit-situations is largely driven by a global, technologically sophisticated, and pervasive culture whose power makes Orwell's Big Brother seem almost amateurish by comparison. I do not apologize for hyperbole here because I don't think such an assertion is hyperbolic. The reach and influence of Western consumer culture and its associated capitalistic economic practices and structures are dramatically illustrated by the no longer startling sight of a New York Yankees T-shirt on a youngster in the remote Himalayan region of India called Ladakh (Norberg-Hodge) or by the privatization by multinational corporations of traditionally communal wells in rural Indian villages a few hundred miles to the south (Shiva). The power of this consumer culture lies in its capacity to construct a reality that is taken to be as "natural" by Americans as the landowning practices and policies in Brazil were taken to be by Freire's peasant students in the 1960s. How else might one explain the fact that freedom of choice is extolled in the almost obscene number of models of cars and SUVs available to American buyers, while the fuel efficiency of automobiles on American roads has actually decreased in recent years even as warnings about disappearing fossil fuels proliferate and a scientific consensus about global climate change emerges?[14] How else might one explain the fact that standard practices of American banks can make approval of a mortgage for the construction of a solar-heated home difficult or impossible even as the environmental and economic costs of conventional methods of heating homes (such as oil) mount? How else does one explain the expanding U.S. prison population and the eagerness of many small communities to build prisons for their "economic benefit"?[15] There is nothing natural about the attitudes and desires that inform such practices or about the institutional structures that maintain them. And the fact that they seem so natural to so many people is testimony to the power of mainstream culture to shape reality (without the need for clerks like Orwell's Winston Smith to rewrite history books). Schools—and institutionalized education generally—help create and maintain that culture; they have the capacity to change it as well.

English as a discipline is ultimately about language, which is the vehicle by which we understand ourselves and act in the world. As professionals in English, we share a history in which we have both embraced and rejected the power that attaches to the work we do. We have argued for course requirements on the basis of the notion that language and literacy can empower individual lives and combat social problems. At the same time, we ignore that same power as it reinforces a status quo that many of us believe is in desperate need of change, a status quo that gives rise to many of those same social problems. I don't think we can have it both ways. We should not ignore the power we do possess—either to maintain a status quo or to imagine and realize a different future. If we acknowledge that power, we can then begin to explore its possibilities for reshaping the reality we have helped to create. But to do so requires that we *can* imagine alternatives. As Harvey has written, "Without a vision of Utopia there is no way to define that port to which we might want to sail" (189). A central part of the task of redefining English studies is to begin to articulate that vision.

I must admit to some ambivalence about the Utopian call I am making because I have long felt that those of us in English studies (whatever our specific scholarly focus) spend far too much time engaged in the very kind of analysis and argumentation in which I am now engaged. We produce a great deal of scholarship focused on defining our field; we argue about whether we are a discipline or something else. Meanwhile, the powerful institutions we work within remain fundamentally unchanged. My cynical side attributes this to understandable self-interest: scholarship focused on defining our discipline "counts" within the small community of academics in English studies, and indeed it can make a career. I don't fault scholars for producing it, since they (like me at the moment) are doing what they are in effect required to do to keep their jobs. And understanding who we are is an important part of defining what we want to be. But it does seem an enormous waste of talent and energy, especially given the great challenges facing us today. If English studies is to be anything more than an academic discipline, if it is to participate in the remaking of society, if it is to embrace a Utopian project, however that project might be defined, we in the field should spend less time talking about ourselves and focus more energy on talking to everyone else. If we do so, we may find that we share a hope for a different future with others, and that we can bring our substantial expertise in language and literacy to bear on a collective effort to realize such a future.

Notes

1. It is worth noting here that the very conception and structure of this book implicitly define English education as a subdiscipline of English studies; however, many English educators would resist this definition. In May, 2005, leaders in the field of English education convened in Atlanta for a Leadership Summit, whose theme was "Reconstructing English Education for the Twenty-first Century." Sponsored by the Conference on English Education, the summit was intended to begin to identify a direction for the future of the field. (For a description of the summit, see http://www.ncte.org/groups/cee/featuredinfo/122844.htm.) Summit participants addressed several key questions, including "What is English education?" The participants' answer to that question, which is available at http://www.ncte.org/groups/cee/positions/122898.htm, challenges the view of English education as a subdiscipline of English studies. Instead, English education is understood as a field of interdisciplinary inquiry intimately related to but separate from English studies; the summit statement asserts that in their work, which focuses on the teaching and learning of English, the preparation of English teachers, and the study of teaching and learning, "English educators conduct interdisciplinary inquiry by drawing on English studies, education, the scientific study of human behavior, and related fields." In this formulation, English studies is understood to be a part of English education, rather than the other way around. Whichever formulation scholars espouse, it is clear that the two fields overlap significantly.

2. According to the U.S. National Center for Education Statistics, about 11 percent of these students attend private or parochial schools; the rest attend public schools.

3. In making this assertion, I am relying on the analyses of schooling and culture by such scholars as Bourdieu and Passeron, Basil Bernstein, and Samuel Bowles and Herbert Gintis; I am also drawing on empirical studies such as that of Jean Anyon. See Chapter 2 in Patrick Finn's *Literacy with an Attitude* for a brief overview of this literature.

4. This "shaping" is neither deterministic nor monolithic; rather, it is dialectical, as pointed out by many theorists (e.g., Paul Smith) and as argued by Paulo Freire, whose ideas I will discuss later in this essay. The question of agency is paramount here, but it is too complex to explain in detail. Suffice it to say that schooling does not determine the kind of subject students become, but its role in shaping that subject is extremely powerful, as Giroux, Bourdieu and Passeron, and others have shown.

5. The questions of the nature of the self as knower and of the nature of *being* are, of course, as old as philosophy itself and have been examined exhaustively by such influential twentieth-century theorists as Jacques Derrida, Edmund Husserl, and Maurice Merleau-Ponty. I have elsewhere explained my idea that the Western sense of self gives rise to a way of knowing and being that ultimately contributes to social and environmental degradation (see Yagelski, "Computers"). One of the best-known critiques of the positivist foundation of formal schooling is the first chapter of Giroux's *Ideology, Culture, and the Process of Schooling*. For a related critique, see Chapters 1 and 2 of C. A. Bowers's *Educating for an Ecologically Sustainable Culture* as well as Chapters 2 and 3 of Bowers's *The Culture of Denial*. For an alternative to the Western philosophical view of the self, see David Loy.

6. It should also be noted that Dewey's theories were in many ways consistent with the rise of science and the modernist ideal of social progress. In this regard, despite his progressive notions about experiential learning, which challenged the passivity of learners encouraged by conventional pedagogies, his theories could also reinforce the fundamental Cartesian dualisms I mentioned earlier.

7. In 2000, Applebee summed up trends in writing instruction since the publication of his large-scale study in 1981:

> Although no more-recent comprehensive survey is available, the responses to background items that have been included as part of the periodic writing assessments given by the National Assessment of Educational Progress (NAEP) suggest that there have been some changes in recent years. In particular, the NAEP results at grades 4, 8, and 12 indicate that teachers are spending more time on writing instruction than they have in the past, with perhaps somewhat more attention to a wider variety of genres. On the 1992 assessment

(Applebee et al., 1994), for example, twelfth grade students reported some regular (at least monthly) attention to persuasive writing, analysis or interpretation, report or summary writing, and story or narrative writing. Grade 4 students were asked fewer questions in the assessment, but reported regular journal writing and story or report writing. ("Alternative" par. 5)

Applebee goes on to say that by 1992, about half of teachers reported using process-oriented approaches to writing instruction, which represents an increase from what he found in his 1981 study. Although these figures do represent some changes in the way writing is taught, the most fundamental beliefs about writing and practices related to writing instruction remain in place in schools, including the focus on form and the importance of learning the conventions of "standard" English.

8. It is some indication of the power of institutionalized education to resist reform and serve this normative function that some of the most influential scholars in English education have consistently advocated various progressive reforms in literacy education over the years with seemingly little significant impact on the actual practice of teaching English in K–12 schools. John Mayher's *Uncommon Sense*, an influential work published in 1990, articulates a vision for English that builds on the perspectives of many important scholars in the field in the past four decades, including James Britton, James Squire, Janet Emig, and John Dixon; despite differences among these scholars, all shared a general sense of a need for change in the way English is taught in schools and a belief that English instruction should be tied to a broader social purpose. That progressive vision continues to be promoted in more recent scholarship, including work by such figures as Cathy Fleischer and Todd DeStigter. However, the teaching of English in schools has remained largely unaffected by this tradition as well as by more conservative reform efforts such as E. D. Hirsch, Jr.'s "Core Knowledge" movement.

9. I am quoting from the revised thirtieth anniversary edition of *Pedagogy of the Oppressed*, which eliminates the sexist language in the original text (or, more accurately, the language of the original translation). In subsequent writing, Freire has acknowledged this sexism and repudiated it (see *Pedagogy of Hope* 65–68).

10. Freire's epistemology is consistent in many respects with other more recent alternative theories of knowing. See, for example, Barbara Couture's *Toward a Phenomenological Rhetoric* and Loy's *Nonduality*. It is also consistent with recent calls for education reform that include challenges to the epistemological foundations of modern education: see especially Bowers's *Educating for an Ecologically Sustainable Culture* and *Culture of Denial* and Orr's *Ecological Literacy*.

11. My evidence for this claim comes from three main sources: (1) the major journals in the field, whose contents tend to reflect the field's concerns and preoccupations; (2) published testimonials and critiques of the profession by English scholars; and (3) my own experiences as a teacher in four universities along with the experiences of colleagues at other institutions. One need make only a cursory review of the field's major journals over the past decade or two to conclude that while the questions that preoccupy scholars in English studies may have changed, the nature of scholarship in the field has not. In other words, scholars in the field continue primarily to publish analyses of texts and arguments about how to interpret texts, and they disseminate those analyses and arguments more or less as they have always done. Thus, a New Critical analysis of, say, a Wordsworth poem has the same fundamental status as knowledge as a feminist critique of contemporary poetry or a cultural analysis of hip-hop: all are concerned with interpreting texts that have been deemed worth interpreting. As Michael Bérubé has put it, "English has become an intellectual locus where people can study the text of *Sir Gawain and the Green Knight* from a Christian perspective, the text of the O. J. trial from a Foucauldian perspective, and the text of the Treaty of Versailles from a Marxist perspective" (qtd. in Delbanco). The point is that the focus of the field remains on the interpretation of sanctioned texts. Many scholars have examined the discipline, including James Sosnoski, Gerald Graff, and Robert Scholes, while others, such as James Phelan, have shared their own experiences of the field. None of these examinations suggests that English as an academic discipline has had anything like a transformative mission within the modern university. As Sosnoski puts it in describing what he calls the "compulsion to be orthodox" in literary studies, "orthodoxy is built into the university system as a self-regulating mechanism" (95), of which the academic field of English is a part. My own experience and those that colleagues have shared with me reinforce the sense that despite some obvious changes in the postsecondary English curriculum in the past two decades (mostly reflecting the rise of "theory"), English as an academic subject remains a decidedly conventional enterprise that is not overtly concerned with redefining either the institution of higher education or the larger society.

12. For example, see Lowell C. Rose and Alec Gallup, "The Thirty-fifth Annual Phi Delta Kappa/Gallup Poll of the Public's Attitudes toward the Public Schools." Rose and Gallup report that 48 percent of Americans polled assigned the public schools a grade of A or B; only 21 percent give the schools a D or F. The same poll showed that 68 percent of parents give an A or B to the school attended by their oldest child. Seventy-three percent of those polled believe that any education reform should happen through existing public schools; only 25 percent believed that alternatives to public schooling should be found.

13. I would argue that the ideological power of the institutional status quo of schooling is the primary reason that reform movements like Whole Language and the writing process movement have either failed or, more commonly, have been co-opted by schools. For a further discussion of the ways in which the revolutionary potential of the "process" approach to writing instruction has been co-opted by schools, see Yagelski, "'Radical.'"

14. The standard for measuring the fuel efficiency of automobiles is the Corporate Average Fuel Efficiency (CAFE), which was set in 1985 at 27.5 miles per gallon (mpg). Since 1996, the CAFE for all passenger cars and light trucks on American roads has been about 20.7 mpg. (See "Automotive Fuel Economy Program Twenty-third Annual Report to Congress Calendar Year 2000" at http://www.nhtsa.dot.gov/cars/problems/studies/fuelecon/index.html.) However, the best-selling automobiles in the last few years have been SUVs, which are much less fuel-efficient than passenger cars and which have slightly reduced overall fuel efficiency. The sustained increases in oil prices since the hurricanes in 2005 will likely slow the demand for gas-guzzling SUVs, but it is telling that in the recent debates about energy policy, increased fuel efficiency and alternative fuels are often extolled while developing new modes of mass transit or restructuring towns are rarely offered as serious proposals.

15. See King, Mauer, and Huling.

Works Cited

Anyon, Jean. "Social Class and the Hidden Curriculum of Work." *Journal of Education* 162 (1980): 67–92.

Applebee, Arthur N. "Alternative Models of Writing Development." Albany, NY: Center on English Learning and Achievement, 2000. 10 Feb. 2004 http://cela.albany.edu/publication/article/writing.htm.

———. *Literature in the Secondary School: Studies of Curriculum and Instruction in the United States.* NCTE Research Report 25. Urbana, IL: NCTE, 1993.

———. *Tradition and Reform in the Teaching of English: A History.* Urbana, IL: NCTE, 1974.

———. *Writing in the Secondary School: English and the Content Areas.* NCTE Research Report 21. Urbana, IL: NCTE, 1981.

Berlin, James [A]. "Rhetoric and Ideology in the Writing Class." *College English* 50 (1988): 477–94.

———. *Rhetoric and Reality: Writing Instruction in American Colleges, 1900–1985*. Studies in Writing and Rhetoric. Carbondale: Southern Illinois UP; Urbana, IL: CCCC/NCTE, 1987.

———. *Rhetorics, Poetics, and Cultures: Refiguring College English Studies*. Refiguring English Studies. Urbana, IL: NCTE, 1996.

———. "The Teacher as Researcher: Democracy, Dialogue, and Power." *The Writing Teacher as Researcher: Essays in the Theory and Practice of Class-Based Research*. Ed. Donald A. Daiker and Max Morenberg. Portsmouth, NH: Boynton, 1990. 3–14.

Bernstein, Basil. *Towards a Theory of Educational Transmissions*. London: Routledge, 1973.

Bérubé, Michael. *The Employment of English: Theory, Jobs, and the Future of Literary Studies*. New York: New York UP, 1998.

Bourdieu, Pierre, and Jean-Claude Passeron. *Reproduction in Education, Society, and Culture*. 1977. 2nd ed. Trans. Richard Nice. London: Sage, 1990.

Bowers, C. A. *The Culture of Denial: Why the Environmental Movement Needs a Strategy for Reforming Universities and Public Schools*. Albany: SUNY P, 1997.

———. *Educating for an Ecologically Sustainable Culture: Rethinking Moral Education, Creativity, Intelligence, and Other Modern Orthodoxies*. Albany: SUNY P, 1995.

Bowles, Samuel, and Herbert Gintis. *Schooling in Capitalist America: Educational Reform and the Contradictions of Economic Life*. New York: Basic, 1976.

———. "*Schooling in Capitalist America* Revisited." *Sociology of Education* 75 (2002): 1–18.

Connors, Robert J. *Composition-Rhetoric: Backgrounds, Theory, and Pedagogy*. Pittsburgh: U of Pittsburgh P, 1997.

Couture, Barbara. *Toward a Phenomenological Rhetoric: Writing, Profession, and Altruism*. Carbondale: Southern Illinois UP, 1998.

Delbanco, Andrew. "The Decline and Fall of Literature." *New York Review of Books* 4 Nov. 1999. 14 May 2006 http://www.nybooks.com/articles/318.

Delpit, Lisa. *Other People's Children: Cultural Conflict in the Classroom*. New York: New P, 1995.

DeStigter, Todd. *Reflections of a Citizen Teacher: Literacy, Democracy, and the Forgotten Students of Addison High*. Urbana, IL: NCTE, 2001.

Eagleton, Terry. *Literary Theory: An Introduction*. Minneapolis: U of Minnesota P, 1983.

Finn, Patrick J. *Literacy with an Attitude: Educating Working-Class Children in Their Own Self-Interest*. Albany: SUNY P, 1999.

Fleischer, Cathy. *Teachers Organizing for Change: Making Literacy Learning Everyone's Business*. Urbana, IL: NCTE, 2000.

Freire, Paulo. *Pedagogy of Hope: Reliving Pedagogy of the Oppressed*. Trans. Robert R. Barr. New York: Continuum, 1994.

———. *Pedagogy of the Oppressed*. 30th anniversary ed. Trans. Myra Bergman Ramos. New York: Continuum, 2000.

Gilyard, Keith. *Voices of the Self: A Study of Language Competence*. Detroit: Wayne State UP, 1991.

Giroux, Henry A. *Ideology, Culture, and the Process of Schooling*. Philadelphia: Temple UP, 1981.

Graff, Gerald. *Professing Literature: An Institutional History*. Chicago: U of Chicago P, 1987.

Harvey, David. *Spaces of Hope*. Berkeley: U of California P, 2000.

King, Ryan S., Marc Mauer, and Tracy Huling. *Big Prisons, Small Towns: Prison Economics in Rural America*. Washington, DC: Sentencing Project, 2003. 12 Feb. 2004 http://www.soros.org/initiatives/justice/articles_publications/publications/bigprisons_20030201/bigprisons.pdf.

Kress, Gunther. "Representational Resources and the Production of Subjectivity: Questions for the Theoretical Development of Critical Discourse Analysis in a Multicultural Society." *Texts and Practices: Readings in Critical Discourse Analysis*. Ed. Carmen Rosa Caldas-Coulthard and Malcolm Coulthard. New York: Routledge, 1996. 15–31.

Loy, David. *Nonduality: A Study in Comparative Philosophy*. Amherst, NY: Humanity, 1998.

Macedo, Stephen. *Diversity and Distrust: Civic Education in a Multicultural Democracy*. Cambridge, MA: Harvard UP, 2000.

Mayher, John S. *Uncommon Sense: Theoretical Practice in Language Education.* Portsmouth, NH: Boynton, 1990.

McCracken, Nancy Mellin. "Surviving Shock and Awe: NCLB vs. Colleges of Education." *English Education* 36 (2004): 104–18.

McNeil, Linda M. *Contradictions of Control: School Structure and School Knowledge.* New York: Routledge, 1986.

Noble, David F. *Digital Diploma Mills: The Automation of Higher Education.* New York: Monthly Review P, 2002.

Norberg-Hodge, Helena. "The March of the Monoculture." *Ecologist* 29 (1999): 194–97.

Ohmann, Richard. *English in America: A Radical View of the Profession.* New York: Oxford UP, 1976.

Orr, David W. *Ecological Literacy: Education and the Transition to a Postmodern World.* Albany: SUNY P, 1992.

Phelan, James. *Beyond the Tenure Track: Fifteen Months in the Life of an English Professor.* Columbus: Ohio State UP, 1991.

Ray, Ruth E. *The Practice of Theory: Teacher Research in Composition.* Urbana, IL: NCTE, 1993.

Rose, Lowell C., and Alec M. Gallup. "The 35th Annual Phi Delta Kappa/Gallup Poll of the Public's Attitudes toward the Public Schools." *Phi Delta Kappan* 85 (2003): 41–56. 20 Feb. 2004 http://www.pdkintl.org/kappan/k0309pol.pdf.

Scholes, Robert. *The Rise and Fall of English: Reconstructing English as a Discipline.* New Haven: Yale UP, 1998.

Shiva, Vandana. "Captive Water: Privatising Water Will Lead to War." *Resurgence* 219 (2003). 8 Jan. 2004 http://resurgence.gn.apc.org/issues/shiva219.htm.

Smith, Karen, and Patricia Lambert Stock. "Trends and Issues in Research in the Teaching of the English Language Arts." *Handbook of Research on Teaching the English Language Arts.* 2nd ed. Ed. James Flood, Diane Lapp, James R. Squire, and Julie M. Jensen. Mahwah, NJ: Erlbaum, 2003. 114–30.

Smith, Paul. *Discerning the Subject.* Minneapolis: U of Minnesota P, 1988.

Sosnoski, James J. *Token Professionals and Master Critics: A Critique of Orthodoxy in Literary Studies*. Albany: SUNY P, 1994.

Squire, James R. "The History of the Profession." *Handbook of Research on Teaching the English Language Arts*. 2nd ed. Ed. James Flood, Diane Lapp, James R. Squire, and Julie M. Jensen. Mahwah, NJ: Erlbaum, 2003. 3–17.

U.S. Dept. of Education. Natl. Center for Education Statistics. *Digest of Education Statistics, 2002*. Washington, DC: GPO, 2002. 20 Feb. 2004 http://nces.ed.gov/programs/digest/d02/index.asp.

U.S. National Commission on Excellence in Education. *A Nation at Risk: The Imperative for Educational Reform; A Report to the Nation and the Secretary of Education, United States Department of Education*. Washington, DC: GPO, 1983. 11 May 2006 http:// www.ed. gov/pubs/NatAtRisk/index.html.

White, Geoffry D., and Flannery C. Hauck, eds. *Campus, Inc.: Corporate Power in the Ivory Tower*. Amherst, NY: Prometheus, 2000.

Yagelski, Robert P. "Computers, Literacy, and Being: Teaching with Technology for a Sustainable Future." *Kairos* 6.2 (Fall 2001). 14 May 2006 http://english.ttu.edu/kairos/6.2/features/yagelski.

———. *Literacy Matters: Writing and Reading the Social Self*. New York: Teachers College P, 2000.

———. "'Radical to Many in the Educational Establishment': The Writing Process Movement after the Hurricanes." *College English* 68 (2006): 531–44.

———. "Stasis and Change: English Education and the Crisis of Sustainability." *English Education* 37 (2005): 262–71.

INDEX

EDITOR

 **Bruce McComiskey** is associate professor of English at the University of Alabama at Birmingham. Throughout his career, McComiskey has taught courses in rhetoric and composition, literature, discourse analysis, critical theory, and English education, and he currently directs the Red Mountain Writing Project. McComiskey's most recent publications include *Teaching Composition as a Social Process* (2000), *Gorgias and the New Sophistic Rhetoric* (2002), and *City Comp: Identities, Spaces, Practices* (2003), a coedited collection on teaching writing in urban spaces. In addition to his academic writing, McComiskey has also published a number of poems in literary anthologies and magazines.

CONTRIBUTORS

Ellen Barton is professor of linguistics and English at Wayne State University in Detroit, Michigan. Barton has taught courses in linguistics (syntax, pragmatics, discourse analysis, language and medicine, and linguistics and education) and composition-rhetoric (research methods, composition theory and research, rhetoric of disciplinarity). In the field of syntax, she is coeditor of *The Syntax of Nonessentials: Multidisciplinary Perspectives* (2007) and is author of *Nonsentential Constituents: A Theory of Grammatical Structure and Pragmatic Interpretation* (1990). Her work on the discourse analysis of the language of medical encounters has appeared in journals and collections including *TEXT, Discourse Studies, Discourse and Society,* and *Communication and Medicine.* In composition-rhetoric, she has published in the *Journal of Advanced Composition, College English, College Composition and Communication,* and the *Journal of Business and Technical Communication.* She is co-editor of the collection *Discourse Studies in Composition* (2002) and the guest editor of a special issue on the discourse(s) of medicine for the *Journal of Business and Technical Communication* (July 2005).

Amy J. Elias is associate professor in the English Department at the University of Tennessee, where she teaches contemporary literatures and critical theory. She has taught composition, business and technical writing, and cultural studies courses, as well as literature, at various U.S. colleges and universities. Her first book, *Sublime Desire: History and Post-1960s Fiction* (2002), concerns interdisciplinary connections between historical fiction, historiography, and postmodern theory; her second book, in progress, concerns the ethics of narrative fiction within democratic societies. She currently chairs the Contemporary Arts and Society Working Group at UT.

Katharine Haake's most recent books are a novel, *That Water, Those Rocks* (2003), and a collection of short stories, *The Height and Depth of Everything* (2001). Her first book of stories, *No Reason on Earth,* was published in 1986. New stories have recently appeared in the *Iowa Review, Witness, One Story,* and the *Santa*

Monica Review, and were featured in the online magazine, *Segue,* as well as in the New Short Fiction Series, Los Angeles's only "live literary magazine." She is currently at work on a novel. A recent recipient of an Individual Artist's Grant from the Cultural Affairs Department of the City of Los Angeles, she was also recognized as the 1998/99 Jerome Richfield Memorial Scholar at California State University, Northridge. Her other books are *What Our Speech Disrupts: Feminism and Creative Writing Studies* (NCTE, 2000) and, with Hans Ostrom and the late Wendy Bishop, the textbook *Metro: Journeys in Writing Creatively* (2001). She currently chairs the Creative Writing program at CSU Northridge, where, since 1986, she has taught and developed a wide range of courses in narrative, writing, and theory.

Janice M. Lauer is professor of English emerita at Purdue University. She has been Reece McGee Distinguished Professor of English at Purdue University, where she founded and directed a doctoral program in rhetoric and composition. In 1998, she received the Conference on College Composition and Communication's Exemplar Award. She has served on the executive committees of CCCC, the National Council of Teachers of English, the Rhetoric Society of America, and the Division on the History and Theory of Rhetoric and Composition of the Modern Language Association, and has coordinated the Consortium of Doctoral Programs in Rhetoric and Composition. For thirteen summers she directed a two-week international rhetoric seminar. Her publications include *Four Worlds of Writing: Inquiry and Action in Context; Composition Research: Empirical Designs; New Perspectives on Rhetorical Invention;* and *Rhetorical Invention in Rhetoric and Composition,* as well as essays on invention, disciplinarity, writing as inquiry, composition pedagogy, historical rhetoric, and empirical research.

Richard C. Taylor is associate professor of English at East Carolina University, where he has served as director of first-year writing and is currently director of undergraduate studies in English. He is the author of *Goldsmith as Journalist* (1993) and articles on eighteenth-century culture, theater history, pedagogy, and women's studies.

Robert P. Yagelski is associate professor of English education in the Department of Educational Theory and Practice at the State University of New York at Albany, where he teaches courses in composition theory and pedagogy, rhetoric, and qualitative research methods and helps prepare secondary school teachers. He is also director of the Capital District Writing Project in Albany. Previously, he directed the Writing Center at SUNY Albany, co-directed the English education program at Purdue University, and chaired the English Department at Vermont Academy, an independent high school, where he taught writing, literature, and journalism. He is the author of *Literacy Matters: Writing and Reading the Social Self* (2000) and coeditor (with Scott Leonard) of *The Relevance of English: Teaching That Matters in Students' Lives* (2002). His articles and essays have appeared in *College Composition and Communication, Research in the Teaching of English, English Education, Journal of Teaching Writing,* and *Radical Teacher,* among others. A former freelance writer, he has also written articles for numerous magazines and newspapers and is author of *The Day the Lifting Bridge Stuck* (1992), a children's book.

*This book was typeset in Sabon by Electronic Imaging.
Typefaces used on the cover were Frutiger 65 Bold
and Bureau Agency Bold.
The book was printed on 50-lb. Williamsburg Offset paper
by Versa Press, Inc.*